The Delay of the Heart

The Delay of the Heart

David Appelbaum

State University of New York Press

Volume 3 of *The Intervening Subject*
Volume 1: *The Stop*
Volume 2: *Disruption*
cover: *Orpheus and Eurydice,* Frederico Cervelli (1625–1700). Galleria Querini, Stampalia, Venice, Italy. Courtesy Scala/Art Resource, NY.
frontispiece: Relief of falcon-headed god Horus or Haroeris writing and wearing the sun disk on his head. From Temple of Sobek and Horus. Egyptian, Ptolemaic period, 2nd c. B.C. Kom Ombo, Egypt. Erich Lessing/Art Resource, NY.

Published by
State University of New York Press, Albany

Printed in the United States of America

For information, address State University of New York Press,
90 State Street, Suite 700, Albany, NY 12207

Production by Dana Foote
Marketing by Anne Valentine

Library of Congress Cataloging-in-Publication Data

Appelbaum, David.
The delay of the heart / David Appelbaum.
p. cm.
Includes bibliographical references and index.
ISBN 0-7914-4767-7 (alk. paper)
ISBN 0-7914-4768-5 (pbk. : alk. paper)
1. Subjectivity. I. Title.
B945.A633 D45 2000
126—dc21
00–044627

10 9 8 7 6 5 4 3 2 1

Thou hast visited me in the night; thou hast tried me.
—Psalm 17:3

To my teacher

Contents

Preface / xi

Chapter One
The Heart's Delay / 1

Chapter Two
Memory / 15

Chapter Three
Embodiment / 27

Chapter Four
Initiation / 41

Chapter Five
Discrepancy / 53

Chapter Six
Search / 65

Chapter Seven
Schools / 77

Chapter Eight
The Guide / 91

Chapter Nine
Resurrection of the Flesh / 101

Chapter Ten
Conscience / 113

Contents

Chapter Eleven
Hope / 125

Chapter Twelve
Atonement / 137

Notes / 149

Bibliography / 155

Index / 157

Preface

There is an act of intervention that the subject—you or I—is commanded to undertake. That in which one intervenes is one's immediate and specific process, *this* one currently unfolding. That for the sake of which one intervenes is that to which one is responsible, though the claimant is as yet without claim to name or existence. That the subject is commanded by an unknown voice to intervene *now* in what specifically and immediately is taking place in oneself is enigmatic. This is, therefore, the case despite the fact that a commandment of intervention is far from external to the subject—is intimacy itself—though the source of command is the other. In the syllogism, I give a formula for initiation into subjectivity, which formula transmits a responsibility to the initiate even before that one is born into the world.

The intervening act has a reality all its own, but one which the subject, as it finds itself, must first embody, then struggle to substantiate its dictate. Like any act of overwhelming force and subtlety, intervention—literally, *a movement between*—must be exercised in order to be accomplished. Exercise implies a work against a resistance and has many phases prior to a result, if indeed there is one. Engagement and fructification are stages of practice before accomplishment. This implies that the subject's exercise of the act may not reach the point of intervention but is nonetheless a right practice. From the standpoint of exercise, initiative is what is up to us. The outcome is not. Needless to say, continued practice extends facility in and control of intervention, but it is never correct to assume success.

When one adopts the standpoint of exercise and walks the path that early Hellenistic philosophy uncovered (later to be adopted and co-opted by early Church philosophy), the writing of philosophy undergoes a shift. Its aim is less to produce an essay, exposition, or exemplary discourse and more to utilize *the act of writing* to practice the intervening act, *now* with regard to *this* specific process. Since there can be no recipe for intervention (its parries with the causal order preclude as much), its practice is one of poise, equilibrium, deftness, and aptness. I have tried the approach in what follows, though often lacking in skillful means. In form, my prose corresponds to the *hypomnemata* of the Stoic writers, though because I am far removed from their source, I have been mindful also of historical developments in philosophical thought. Because the *hypomnemata* serve as reminders of the intervening act for the subject who is writing, they have an intimate, confessional, petitional quality. Their communication is essentially to bring thought back into alignment with an obligation that is obscure, enigmatic, and unconditional.

Specifically, what is the dynamism of intervention? I tried, in *The Stop,* volume one of *The Intervening Subject,* to locate the act historically and textually, citing Descartes's work in *The Dioptrics* as data on the position of the intervening subject. The rediscovery of linear perspective represents an essential act of remembrance which embraces both novelty and return. *The Stop* describes means by which consciousness is summoned back to the somatic fold to receive an impression of an act whose obligation is unconditional. By contrast, *Disruption,* volume two of *The Intervening Subject,* gives a philosophical analysis of intervention. In the context of contemporary philosophical discourse, it locates the ground in a particular weakness of thought, namely, its obsession with reproducing the conditions that produce it. *Disruption* examines several themes illustrative of the constriction and limitation resulting from thought's obsessive concern with thinking. It concludes with the possibility of the subject's aligning itself with that which surpasses thought in compass and scope and thereby grasping hold of subjectivity per se.

The present work, *The Delay of the Heart,* volume three of *The Intervening Subject,* concludes an examination of the specific act through a methodology of praxis. That which is in need of an interventionary arrest is the continuous running-on of cognition, the *cogito*'s automatism, by which the world appears and is disclosed moment after moment. The arresting force is a summoning up (an *energeia*) of a potential (a *dynamis*) that returns the subject to sensitivity. The source of both forces is an enigmatic plague from the very first on the smooth functioning of thought, a pebble in the shoe of reason as it takes systematic steps to make sense of things. To cultivate a respect for its intercession, strangely, is to develop an ear for speech that rises from the heart of oneself. The ear, attuned for interior speaking, must take into account an ineluctable delay in audibility. In the account, between pronunciation and articulation and unto audition lies a perilous interval, attendance on which is the crux of the exercise that I undertake. For, what is needed is a passivity more passive than patience in order to submit thought to whose interior speaking commands thought to obey.

The deep connection (etymologically attested) between audition and obedience provides the axis to my approach. Although an interior listening is obscured by an audible shadow of thought's preoccupations, breaking through to the slower tempo of sensibility immediately evokes a concern for the ethical. How does one desist from an irresponsible obsession? What means are there for encouraging practice of a responsibility hitherto unknown? How does one pay off one's indebtedness to the other? Each question surpasses its predecessor in scale. The very sense of surpassing sensitizes a subject to the primordial task that I seek to delineate. To be able to endure suffering the fact of its impossibility opens a subject to an "organ" through which interior speech issues. Attendance to the utterance relates both that which speaks and that spoken to.

No work exists in isolation. All work is related to other work. For the present work, I owe many special debts of gratitude. In particular, I acknowledge that of right companionship provided by Carl Lehmann-Haupt and Roger Lipsey. I am indebted to the intellectual inspiration of Jacob Needleman and Thomas Mether. For the courage of persisting inquiry (the *thymus* of Plato), I have been reliant on the generosity of Margaret Flinsch. And for the magnanimous support during the long research of the extended project, I owe much to Katy Bray.

Chapter One
The Heart's Delay

As the brethren of Mont-Dieu introduce to our Western darkness and French cold the light of the East and that ancient fervor of Egypt for religious observance—the pattern of solitary life and the model of heavenly conduct—run to meet them, O my soul, and run with them in the joy of the Holy Spirit and with a smiling heart, welcome them devoutly and with every attention a dedicated will can show.

—William of St. Thierry[1]

There were three gods in the beginning that were one: Ptah, Horus, and Thoth. They together divided the cosmos and all that was contained therein into three realms, and each assumed the role of lord of one. Ptah was the Supreme Person, the intelligence, the one who becomes heart and tongue. Horus was the heart, and Thoth, the divine instrument, the word. Each brought wisdom to his rule and embued every creature—great and small—with a sense of its place in the ever-diversifying whole. When it came to human beings, they felt the need for a moment's deliberations. "This creature is made in our image," Ptah said, "yet will be bound to honor one of us at the expense of the others. Let us safeguard its impartiality." The others agreed. Then Ptah continued, "Against the impulse from itself alone to speak through unconscious, ill-reasoned things, let thought not think itself supreme. Therefore, let speech issue not directly forth from the mind in order to seek expression on the lips." To this end, he gave the functions of humans their particular arrangement. From that time, thought, born in the heart, rose to the mind and was detained therein for the duration of an interval. This interval he pronounced sacred. In accordance with the delay, human speech was forever nourished by the heart's intelligence and the words spoken were imbued with the divine substance proper to them.

The Underlying Tempo of Thought

Delay is an event that commands several standpoints. From the standpoint of the one lagging behind, there is no delay. There is only the other, up ahead, having proceeded at a pace that caused the gap—the differential in distance and tempo—

or having begun at an earlier time and so having the advantage of a head start. Or if the laggard possesses a sense of delay, it is derivative. Either it comes from the other's looking back, wanting to be together with the one, uncomfortable with the lead, or it results from believing the one should be up ahead also. But otherwise coinciding with itself, there is no delay for the one behind, only a discrepancy in place between it and the other. From this point of view, a mere recognition of difference surpasses the impulse that things should be different, and a passivity results. That is how the laggard takes in its position: as patient as passivity or more so. Then there is how the other, up ahead, grasps the delay. From that standpoint, the question is why the delay persists, how it came about, if it need be so, and what can be done to change the situation. Delay is an irrefrangible fact. It is there, an irritant to be accepted, denied, or ignored. The one ahead wants the other up in tandem or to be differently situated. Delay is cause for restlessness in mind—or its symptom. The restive condition is expressed as desire, in a nervous, retrospective glance over the shoulder. There is, however, a third viewpoint. From the standpoint of a neutral observer who watches the proceedings, delay is neither factual nor nonexistent. Its existence is a contingency that arises in the relation between the parties involved. It is a contingency asking to be annihilated, whose annihilation is an inevitability that results in more delay. This is the view from the heart. The heart views the specificity of things and knows the habit of thought well enough not to cross it. But habit is not necessity, rather the dress put on to conceal the necessary. What is necessary is a need for transformation, for thinking to be made fertile again through a connection with the whole. This is the heart's primary concern, and by keeping it primary, the heart knows the "sidewise" approach that releases the habit of thought from itself. Above all else, the lateral approach is what I consider.

The heart is in delay because thought is always in advance of itself. I am speaking from the point of view of thinking, where one must begin. Why is the state of advance so? In its function, thought takes the conditions "from before" (*ab ante*) and places them ahead of itself, thereby reproducing itself in a staccato rhythm. The movement of retrieving conditions from a past and reinstalling them in a future is the basic and fundamental movement of thought. It is the ordinary mind's "functional beat." It is the movement that predates any specific content that happens to occupy thinking, this, the "muscular" grasp of retention. It is important to get the feel of the movement of reaching back and throwing ahead. It is well known that thinking is a way of grasping again what was once present, of retaining. Two hundred years ago, Locke showed us that thought takes its form from retentive memory.[2] "To know" really means "to have held on to as known." Or more accurately, there is, cognitively speaking, no present tense. Present conditions are imported prior conditions or perhaps re-presented posterior ones. Since all such conditions exist only anterior to themselves, what is called thought is grasped like a fruit from the tree of past consciousness. Thought, at least as we ordinarily recognize it, thereby records what is retained and is in fact a record of retention. Its extraordinary usefulness has to do with its skill in the storeroom of the past. Everything accomplished or to be accomplished resides in the storeroom. In all such thought, we find the yoke of accomplishment.

Being in advance of itself, thought is also pregnant with . . . thought. The movement of retrieving what came before and projecting it onto an afterwards is one of reproduction. Thought forever leads itself forward out of itself, which is to say, its past. The conditions that it retrieves are those of thinking. The conditions that it projects are the same. This is another way of saying that thought, as we know it, is concerned primarily with reproducing the conditions of its own production. Being pregnant with itself, thought gives birth to more of the same. The invention of the concept is often attributed to Socrates. In the concept, the habit of thought, explicitly expressed, is that of *concipere,* to grasp onto itself. Mythologically, thought is parthenogenetic. It repeatedly splits off from its parent to be born a separate and full-fledged identity like Athene from Zeus's skull. For thought, a virginal birth follows an immaculate conception, the enigma of its auto-con-ception. Like a primitive life form, an amoeba, thought attains to a kind of immortality. The feat that it never completely dies is achieved by its successive breaking off from itself, its fission, its self-division, its duplication and duplicity. Immortality comes with a stigma. Lacking proper insemination, thought almost completely lacks genetic material through which it might trace an origin beyond itself. The absence leaves thought an isolated but deafened power. It cannot hear the word of Thoth. Beneath itself, thought—the thinking always thinking about thinking, an endless self-reflection—is poised restlessly over the well of an un-thinkable utterance. To the sound of depth, there is great attraction, a proclivity for a great obedience, and an irresolution. Thought's dysfunctional ambivalence.

The functional beat of thinking makes for a constant theme common to all thinking, a kind of underground drone. Thought thinks about being ahead of itself (and therefore lagging behind) or about being behind itself (and therefore catching up). A common way the theme of being-in-advance-of-itself is taken is in terms of self-advancement. The origin of self-interest may be found here. Self-advancement is the fundamental form of achievement. Planning and preplanning, prioritizing and strategizing, goal seeking and deliberating, choosing and selecting are ways in which thought, in advance of itself, exercises specific powers of achievement. Each means promotes thought, makes thought and its product—results—indispensable to the subject's enterprise of life. What also grows more and more indispensable is the unbroken chain of achievement since it gives the outward manifestation of thought an appealing form. Awareness, taken by accomplishment, neglects to include the inner cognitive rhythm of thinking. In the place of neglect, an avoidance arises, precisely the shape of the double movement. As avoidance, the interior rhythm lends itself to the form of objects, the phenomenal world as an aura of obscurity. This is the self-obscurity of thinking: its basic tempo remains unperceived and imperceptible. It is to this point that Kant's discussion of time as the form of inner sense is directed.[3]

In delay, the heart lacks synchrony with thought. The lack functions as a weight upon the noetic mind. It is how someone left behind, Lot's wife or Eurydice, weighs on thought. Repeatedly, thought is drawn back from its forward motion in a gesture of recouping. No reconstituting of a past is involved but only a nagging thought of escaping the underworld. Like Orpheus who has left that world behind but remains its subject, the mind never leaves what trails it in the rear. Is Eurydice there still? Eventually, *that* thought will overpower the will, even the will steeled against a backward glance. The weight is all too powerful. I do not see such weight wholly as ill-fortune. Like the pendulum that works a clock, the weight of the heart's asynchrony animates thought and keeps it from stagnating aimlessly in the cold desert of logic. Self-advancement is thereby precluded from being the sole impulse of thought's function. I can imagine a world in which thought would not be so impeded. There, many daring edifices would rise from the desert floor, each thought-product imaged in Lot's wife turned to a pillar of salt. Each would be an unlivable habitat for the whole human being. None would serve to make the whole human being inhabitable. Although great devotion is necessary in their construction (and concomitant dismissal of the heart's impulse), dismissal is not the cause of delay. The heart's asynchronous relation returns thought to itself with an ever-repeated dissatisfaction. Though often masked, dissatisfaction provides reason with reason to search beyond an impulse that wagers accomplishment. In search, hope for acknowledging the self-obsessed condition of mind arises.

Delay speaks in the voice of insufficiency. From the standpoint of the laggard, the one in front has shown insufficient consideration for the other's tardiness. That one has failed to inquire into reasons for the other's being in the rear, reasons that would disclose a conflict between the heart's intelligence and thought's autoeroticism. Cognitive velocity is a measure of the ignorance. I have said that maintaining the velocity of producing the conditions of its own reproduction absolves thought from examining its final end. That no stop occurs is proof of thought's inherent insensitivity. From the standpoint of the leader, the situation is different. In the leader's view, the other is insufficiently motivated, equipped, or free to keep up. The restless mood of thought's functional beat sees events through the eyes of impatience. Impatience contains a privative vision; it sees the heart through what it cognitively lacks. Yet because thought cannot understand why the other remains behind, the conditions of the heart's retardation call to it. In this way, the heart's lack echoes an absence within thought, and so, from an attribution of insufficiency, the mind hears its own emptiness. Regardless of whether it is audible to cognition, even in the fit of deprivation, there is a summons and the summons is issued.

Originally, a summons was a secret reminder delivered by a messenger and intended to be understood by no one but its recipient. Its inherent specificity, "for your ears alone," made it an encryption that addressed one regarding a critical matter that involved sacrifice, forbearance, or commemoration. By design, a summons disturbs the automatic order of things. It meets the necessity of order (which is subjective) with another necessity (which is objective) that requires an obedience. Thus the summons is an ordeal, a dangerous test the outcome of which indicates a higher judgment. Delay breaks into the realm of the habitual in the form of a secret message. In the momentary cessation, thought is imperiled and its project (of self-replication) is at risk. The ordeal needs emphasis even though the moment may pass almost unnoticed—as unnoticed as thought's refusal of the summons. With the summons is necessarily associated the judgment. To summon and to judge. It is fair to say that delay has the effect of weighing a situation. Scale and pans is the ancient symbol for judgment. In the scale at a mortal's death, the heart is set against a featherweight. In the scale at life, the mind's substance is set against the breath. If we were to watch the weighing from the point of view of a neutral witness, we would say that delay is the time it takes for the pans to come to rest.

It follows that judgment—a weighing in which the substance of mind is found deficient—belongs to another order of temporality. That time is of patience, time according to the long-suffering one who is in delay. Such time is not the lurching gait of projection, the reaching back and throwing ahead, but rather the halting step of decisiveness that never leaves the ground it covers. Time of judgment then does not belong to the "spatiotemporal continuum" (as Husserl puts it) since that time is always on the verge of running out, wearing thin, decaying, or falling into ruin.[4] Since it predates thought's functional beat, time of judgment still bears the mark of origin through which each thing appears as itself and no more. The mark connects judgment with the silence of things for in the time of silence no thing occludes any other thing. Each stands forth in clarity from the background. Thus, judgment issues from a time that allows thought itself to take its proper place and to cease to occupy the place of the other.

An account of judgment and the summons that brings thought to a stop differs markedly from a view that speaks of the proposition as vehicle of judgment. The nominalist seeks to replace the action of judging with the words said of the act, and places the proposition congruous to judgment. The congruence was worked out by scholastic logicians who substituted for the real work of judging—a determination of the significance or "weight" of particular contents of mind—the mechanical determination of what meanings a given thought assigns. Since the determination of assignation had a form, the form of judgment could be assayed by logic ("the laws of thought") for validity. The result was advantageous to efficiency. Judgment ceased to concern itself with substance and instead substituted syntax for a measure of its correctness—and syntax holds itself together as a set of rules for substitution. There was a further benefit that the scholastic nominalist found in his work. Where a judgment contains what is said (and not the assessment of the saying), it provides a semantic record of the mind's reproduction of itself. The pro-position operates in a manner similar to the pulse of thought inasmuch as it announces in advance what thought's stance will be. The proposition, like thought, is ahead of itself and trails meaning behind. In the history of thinking, propositional syntax begins to represent the project of thought, its self-determination and autoconception. Thought *becomes* pro-position, a positing in favor of thinking. The time is ripe for logic's conquest of thought that leaves the heart a muffled prisoner in the cavity of the chest.

What becomes of Thoth's word, the expression of a primordial responsibility, a subjectivity? Reducing judgment to grammatical form is a consequence of nominalism that unmoors language from its transcendent origin in the intelligence. Instead of relating directly to a source of meaning, nominalism gives language two new roles. First, through language we "raise a dust and then complain we cannot see" (Berkeley) and thus remain blind to the double movement of intellect. Self-obscurity is served. Second, language is given the assignment to serve the conditions of thought and thereby restricted to the assignation of meaning. Since it helps reproduce the conditions of thought's own production, language could be thought to be maieutic, but only with the birth of a homunculus. Language grows oblivious to its original and only task, of rendering the word of the heart audible to the ear of the world. No longer does it grow halting at the summons of delay but rushes headlong into propositional discourse.

When judgment degenerates to syntax, it serves thought rather than the converse—thought serving an articulation of Ptah, the Supreme Person's reality. Lacking weight, judgment lacks conviction, and the mind's own operation remains imperceptible. Opaque to the mechanism of its own reproduction, the Same continuously confronts the mind—the same world, the same things, the same mood toward those things, the same attitude toward itself. Taken over time, the Same yields continuity. The function of the *cogito* is secretly obscured in each moment and the next. In secret, it is continually erased, stated and erased, stated and erased, until statement and erasure both evaporate into thin air. The force of oblivion (which is different from Nietzsche's "active force of oblivion") conceals the fundamental anxiety of thought's position.[5] Should continuity of concealment be broken at any point, the terror of the situation would swamp the mood of indifference. Discontinuity is the alien horror, Attila's Huns on the steppes. The least intimation and thought's self-identity is threatened. Even a temporary fit of transparency loosens the stranglehold of cognitive dogmatism and softens the mind's stance against its relation to the heart.

Delay also is retardation. Relative to thought's tempo, the heart's appears burdened with extraneous sufferings, trappings of concern, and the wraps of expiation. Its labor is with expression which when uttered takes place at some remove from the onset of the event, like a confession trailing an elaborate defense. Its quieter voice comes after the machinations settle down, when the consequences no longer take priority. Such is the visible effect of gravity from an invisible body: it disturbs the planet in its orbit. In a similar vein, a lagging heart pulls at thought's autoeroticism. Eroticism brings a hyperventilation that makes time accelerate. Hypertemporalization, the sped-up passage of things, expresses itself in time's vacuity (boredom), time's shrinkage ("too much to do"), and high-velocity time ("is it already over?"). Fear clouds acceleration. The theme of time as death gains perception as does that of time dying away. Before long, time is subsumed as a category of morality. This is corruption in which delay expresses itself willy-nilly as the worm coiled in the heart of hearts. Delay consumes a subject like a dread preoccupation, an inevitability evidence for which is continually lost, a sentence whose irrevocable terms are forgotten.

"Through suffering is suffering cured." A hindrance of delay hinders the pursuit of inattention the way a thorn works its way into the skin. Gradually or all at once, the heart's languish calls thought from its obsession with perishing and reawakens composure. This is the fact of disruption. That there is disruption follows from another fact, that the pans of judgment must come to rest *in their own time.* When thought obeys a judgment it remains subject to, it practices an obedience to the holy word, the word of healing and of wholeness. That is the practice of delay. It is that practice of which I speak.

Detained by the retardation of the heart, I experience a slackening of psychic tensions. My continuous flight from discontinuity—that state of perpetual extension—ceases. Advance planning, worry over detail, protection against possible lapses, promotion of priorities, and the stress on means all extend the psyche beyond its bounds. I am a factory on a wartime timetable, when deadlines demand an excessive readiness. To delay, in its root meaning, is *lexare,* to relax or decontract. What is relaxed? The focus of thought, which is the *cogito's* finest achievement. When a command to slacken disrupts my schedule, the heart loosens the concentration of thought. Restrained by a less rigid focus, data of immediacy enter into mind. The focal point of habit is a product of mediation and serves the selfsame end as all mediation: to obscure the subject itself. The heart's communication is abrupt, unexpected, paralytic, and destabilizing. It is the sabot thrown into the gears of the machine or the pull cord causing sudden decompression. That the delay brings a slackening, therefore, does not mean that the heart lacks force or that it is reticent. Quite the contrary. The heart does not voice a tender invocation or a poetic paean to wakefulness. The sharp arrest of thought—through tender means—brings disarray. Severed from its impulse to self-reproduction, thought is momentarily related to the other. In the moment, the mind sees beyond itself to that which it is meant to serve. Animated by that which authorizes its proper function, thought is suddenly new and new as only it can be in the face of the sudden.

Autonomy of Tempo

Thought is out of synchrony with the heart because it presumes its own autonomy. Yet the asynchronous movement does not arise from thought's essence nor from that of its relation to the heart. It is thought's profession of autonomy—of being a law unto itself—that desynchronizes its timing. Its obsession with recreating the conditions of its own "immortality" leads it to disregard the organic tempo that envelops its functional beat. That tempo is signature of human wholeness (and holiness). When heeded, the organic tempo brings thought to think *from* its proper place and to function *in* its proper place. Thinking in essence explores origin and expresses the sign of origin: pure energy (*dynamis*). Nonconclusive, inconsequential, without result, no exit—thinking in such a mode assists in animating consciousness and in joining itself to that selfsame animation. The organic tempo, measure of an inner sense of the body, aligns thought's functional beat with other tempos of the whole without impeding thought's individuality of function. One part of the function is to support a circulating attention—an ambient sensation that pervades the interior body. When I am involved in the study, I encounter an articulation of the supernal role of thought even beyond maintenance of the circulation by which the subject remains a whole and in contact with the greater whole.

When disjoined from the inner tempo, thought grows cognitive and puts on the dress of the *cogito*. Any costume sets a new boundary between self and other. The act limits awareness in such a way as to constitute a denial of what encompasses mind. Thought becomes wrapped in itself, a law unto itself. Time is ripe for autonomy. Yet autonomous time is not so much a condition of thought as its product. If Kant is speaking of time as a condition of thought insofar as it is the inner sense, he is misleading.[6] Inner sense is a somatic phenomenon. Passage of a fine attention—a particular *phantasm*—around and throughout the somatic mass takes place in a definite tempo. The rhythmic qualities of movement (which are proper to any movement of life) indicate basic conditions of harmony to which thought may relate. The timing of thought, when ill-adjusted, proceeds oblivious to a demand of harmonization. Kant's reference to inner sense, as a pure form of intuition, is in reality a condition of objectifying thought. When ego-consciousness or the *cogito* concerns itself with some state (a feeling, mood, sensation, or attitude), it has already grown objectifying, reflexive. Time has become the phenomenal expanse in which to assign objects to their place in a chronic scheme of events. It is "inner" only by contrast to the spatial expansiveness of the already constructed object.[7] It is "sense" only quixotically since it is not entirely raw and yet to be processed. Autonomous time is the time of self-concern. It is thought's absorption in its own phenomenal appearance. It is the inside of a bowl curved back to enclose itself—perpetually filled by its dark reflections.

In the Direction of Inclusion

The heart's delay can be further understood in the phenomenon of inclusion. According to the "Egyptian" arrangement, in order to avoid precipitous utterance, speech waits so that it may comprehend the thought behind it. The comprehension of an interior intelligence of the heart provides the point of reference for speaking. What speech is for becomes evident. Awareness of the intelligence that impels an utterance transforms the words into vehicles for a nonobjectified meaning that they serve. The transformation of utterance is a return to original function. Lacking the orientation of the heart, speaking speaks exclusively for the speaker—the one by chance utilizing the function of speech—and through a logic of exclusion. It ceases to signify its own ambiguity and conceives of itself as certain and defined. When speaking is for the speaker alone, the tongue is the organ of the mind. Words make reference solely to themselves and the spade of insight never breaks through the semantic crust of things to turn over the soil of reality. In the fallow of grammar, utterance falters. Its task of naming the namable is forgotten. Speech leaves behind an opening to the world and grows inbred, thick, and stupid.

We can take a clue from the impulse of inclusion. When spirited by inclusion, a group may delay action until all voices are heard. To include all in council is not necessarily to exclude conflict but to arrive at a sense of the whole. Then, a different voice emerges. In speaking inclusively—not for the one or the other but for both—the heart can be heard. In the context, dis-solution of the excluded middle—with its assertion that either this is or is not the case—works a reconciliation where is least likely, at the margins of conflict. A new resonance is felt, not for that which is present but for that which is not. The banished, exiled, absconded other speaks, the one that speaks for all yet is none. Analogously, the faint utterance emanates from the silent heart. The emanation turns toward the world through the word that signifies a purpose of significance. It speaks of that which takes precedence, a reconciliation of differences that negates no difference. It speaks of subjectivity.

As a phenomenon, inclusion expands to fill the time needed to arrive at a sense of the whole. Unlike thought, inclusion does not leap ahead to negate the presentation of awareness. Instead, inclusion remains enfolded in the wings of immediacy, not quite present. Its nontransparency respects the ambiguous nature of speaking. Not reliant on "clear and distinct ideas," inclusion does not define the present in such a way as to render it commensurate with itself. Presence remains that which escapes definition—even a "that which" brings a greater degree of determinateness than in actuality. Inclusion, it could be said, is the action of absence "in" whose field the infinite array of things can be contained. The inclusion of opposites—which inclusion effects—then is opposed to the exclusion of oppositions, as thought would have it. *Time is thought's greatest device of exclusion.* One minute necessarily excludes every other minute. By contrast, inclusion includes thinking, made evident by this very thought that I am proposing. Yet the proposal of inclusion by the heart, thought finds disruptive and threatening. An unboundedness so opposes the conditions for thought's self-replicating mechanism that thought comes to a stop. In the cessation prompted by inclusion, time blinks and in its privation every other moment is included.

How does a moment of inclusion arise? From conflict to inclusion, the shift is not preordained. This much can be said: it is initiated by attendance to conditions in their actuality. The rigors of immediacy precipitate a perception of the inner sense whose trajectory is a radius of the heart. If sensation engenders a language, then inclusion articulates an organically felt immediacy as the ground of the word. What is spoken, born of a somatic intelligence, emanates from the cave of the body—voice itself—in search of audible means of expressing its truth. A growing correspondence between the attention and the "primal language" of the soma eventually realigns the conflicted members of subjectivity in accordance with a template of wholeness. The template, from the keep of the heart, is raised again toward heaven by the lift of the word, speech itself. Even the silence of the keep is thus beholden to the word. It is this direction that my words now explore.

Approaching the Time of Delay

Thought's functional beat, its retrieval of past conditions to propound future ones, is auto-mation itself; *automation,* in its root, meaning a self-willing. The kernel of contradiction between the will and what is given as sheer mechanism, the rhythm of thinking, defines subjectivity on this level. The contradiction is akin to that of the musician's desire for music from the vibrating string of his or her instrument. "Willing" in terms of the automatism is fundamentally a willing to replicate conditions that have obtained, namely, those of the forward throw (the *pro*-jection) of time. "Willing," it could be said, is epiphenomenal, an echoing effect of thought's functional rhythm. It is real but not quite real. Against automation, nothing breaks the sur-reality of the will like delay. Like a drag on a moving vehicle, delay affects the velocity positing and repositing the self-making conditions. Delay is a hindrance to the smooth rhythm of thinking, a recurrent friction (sand in the gears, a spoke in the wheel) that disables the operation. The stream of thought harbors the illusion of clear sailing, no matter what. The minimal action of delay proves otherwise. A small retardation disturbs out of all proportion to its magnitude. It can bring fragmentation to the underlying pulse of thought or even an arrhythmia like cardiac arrest. Therein a vulnerability in thinking is exposed, that its predominance is susceptible to a slight incursion, and ceases. In a momentary halt, the saga of the automatism and autonomy comes to an end. When the force animating thought returns to its place, abandoning the *cogito,* retentive memory lapses and gives ground to another remembering. Under its influence, that of the heart, thought speaks in a different way, by way of the wholeness of speaking, the holy word.

Delay approaches the mind from behind, from the rear. To be hailed by one in delay means to be called back, to turn to look over one's shoulder at something already passed by. The rearward approach marks a direction radically different from that of automatic thought, perception, and action. Spatially, to heed the approach of delay requires the reversal that Plato describes in the allegory of the cave. In the image of *metanoia,* contradictories abound. The space one looks through toward the approach of delay is a space never traveled. No traveler passes that way because of its inaccessibility. Delay belongs to a region that never presents itself to thought except through . . . delay. Thus, the time of delay is likewise never inhabited. It is uninhabitable desert, supporting no life, no somatic exigency. Its remoteness, however, is not that of a prehistoric past that leaves no record. It is removed since it is of a time not produced by thought's production. No project can allow one to pass that way. The gates are barred, the temple is forbidden. Belonging to "anarchic" time (Levinas), the delay predates the world's appearance and therefore remains intractable to evidence denying its existence.[8] It could also be called "anarchaic." The delay through which the heart speaks is buried beneath the time of the world, below yesterday, today, and tomorrow, beyond the clockwork. Its very slackness or passivity defeats the sleek ballistics of time's arrow and offers proof, contrary to Zeno, that the infinite divisibility of time is far less significant than its infinite frangibility. Delay shows, by the way, that there is time for the arrow to get to the other side. It proves that time's fragility has nothing to do with death but rather the unremitting voice of life issuing from the heart. While it is true that from the wreckage of thought, another vehicle will be constructed, launched, and projected onward, delay will abide like a reef below the waves, awaiting another moment. In thought's anguish over the concealment lies its hope for remembrance of a speaking that is whole.

Teleology and Delay

The delay that I speak of is not born of a reticence, hesitancy, or vacillation. On the contrary, the delay is full with purpose, is purpose itself. In delay is found the *telos* of thought and speech. I am not thinking of the purposive will that is a byproduct of thought's autoeroticism. The automatism of that will is craving, compulsion, and obsession. That will fosters impulses to perpetuate thought's obscuration and keep the mind confused. Yet the willed phenomena are perceived to be the best expressions of one's subjectivity, results wrought by the springs of desire: we herein encounter the phenomenon of autoeroticism. In its account, one enters the world as a "free agent" in order to pursue ends through appropriate means. Attainment is a confirmation of one's election to a world that is just as one conceives it. The complex of desire and achievement is the perfume of allurement, continuously enticing the subject into dark woods like the whip-poor-will's taunting song. The purposefulness of delay, by contrast, announces itself as a random event that impinges on the mind from without and goes against the desired order of things. Purpose camouflaged as purposelessness: this necessarily belongs to an intelligence that I have already mentioned. "Random" disruption destabilizes one's assumed identity. Since the nature of habit buries itself in the sediment (Husserl), a shock, as Santayana says, is needed to break the hold of identification.[9] Under the wraps of thought's deep, habit assigns meaning to phenomena and the world of phenomena springs into place—while the soul sleeps! But when the river bottom of automatism is scoured, assignation becomes unmoored and floats to the surface. Concealed congruence of thought and object, word and thing, yields to a discrepancy between the meaning and itself—a schism in the bedrock of meaning. There is a gap between thought and reality. Does one follow the gaze down the abyss? In any event, the perturbations in the self's identity are in the reach of delay's teleology. It is through the purpose that the attention strengthens, an anxious tremor, and reveals its form as a question. Thus it has been said that interrogation and inquiry are step-children of delay's firm resolve.

The question *is* the invasion of purpose but a purpose not yet my own. Interrogation delivers the shock that reduces the automatism and the *cogito* to rubble, though because their heart is not with but in a different place from them (like a folktale ruse), they easily survive the blow. On examination, however, the "inner shock," the question, the enigmatic designee of the heart's purpose, points to a way of initiation, a *principium.* Strangely, the beginning of or initiation into subjectivity necessarily implies a "way," as indicated by the deep association between *initiation* and the Sanskrit *yana,* way. If the way could be directly stated, it would state the heart's purpose in delay. This would be to make the statement commensurate with thought that takes a stance, knows the status, and holds to a standard—and this is impossible. Such an impulse places responsibility on a par with disclosure—and this is impossible. Yet, to be responsive before owning the ability to respond to the shock of disruption, the interrogation, the summons, is to hold oneself open to the heart's purpose. That responsiveness before responsibility may be no more than a lack of refusal, the negation of a negative, not yet a true positive, but even this serves to illustrate the indirect nature of the way. Only with the advent of responsibility does the way open, disruption coincide with anticipation, purpose of delay join with volition of the subject, and the nonlinear procedure become the *modus operandi.* I speak of these matters later.

"Do not forget thy blunted purpose, Hamlet," the ghost of the father admonishes. If the purpose is other than vengeance, but still a purpose not yet his own, the speech makes it sound possible to remember and then finds Hamlet culpable in his forgetting. This is not right. Hamlet is unable to remember because the memory cannot be remembered, though he is still culpable. Memory of the purpose is necessarily dim, dull, without the luster of thought's natural light, Descartes's *lumen naturale.*[10] Its eruption is disorder in a series in contrast to the automatism of thought, and ambiguous and opaque. Dostevsky's description of the "exceptional, vague, and enigmatic" makes reference to the imprint of delay in the corrupted linear of the word. A command not to forget the purpose, in its impossible fulfillment, brings on the mood of anxiety that places the subject ever more at the disposal of an unknown call. What is forged in the darkness cannot be called "memory" but a kind of vulnerability on the far side of control, a surrender, a sacrifice. The anamnesis differs from the retrieval mechanism of thought's function particularly in its acceptance of the mind's irresoluteness and its striving to ally itself with a higher faculty of intelligence. One could say that it is the action of the organ, still embryonic, that is capable of carrying a question—of officiating at one's own initiation into subjectivity. Such a capability is no less than that of momentarily stopping thought's functional beat and entering into the pulse of immediacy, sensitive to Throth's word.

Craned backward, the mind in its extreme tension meets the other than thought. Could the unstable posture be called embodiment? The extraordinary condition subtly alters the *cogito,* thought reproducing thought, in a way analogous to a stretch's altering the body: sensitivity is included. There, an impress of the heart's delay passes and, like the caress of a beloved, lets one surrender one's customary evasiveness. There, preserved in the original language, the anarchaic word circulates throughout the soma and is let circulate once the guard is abandoned. Like a word on the tip of the tongue, language can "almost" be a memory, yet is not. It is a shadow of experience, the way that the fragrance of a pine forest dissipates, grows diffuse, but is not lost after one has left the woods. The shadow trails the systole and diastole of thinking, a murmur, hence, an enigma. In the murmuring shadow, the purpose of delay is repeatedly voiced and voiced repeatedly until thought wakes to take notice.

Chapter Two
Memory

Delineation of a Task

Thought has a shadow. Thought is shadowed in its function, throughout its projection of the phenomenal world, by a task. The task that thought keeps secret from itself, both taxes—that is, burdens and slows—and touches—that is, is tangible and affective to—thought, for that is what *task* means in its root. The secret task pulls at thinking, turning it round. Like any secret, it wishes to be told. Like any shadow, it wishes for the light. Fundamentally, the task is to comprehend its own secret and shadow. This can be put in another way: the task of thought is to comprehend the delay of the heart with the understanding of obedience.

The task surprisingly presents itself as a task of memory. *Mnemosyne,* memory, mother of the Muses, has a vision of the delay inscribed in her flesh. For the Greeks, each Muse is informed by, and becomes representative of, the word rising laggardly from the heart. Through music, epic or lyrical poetry, dance, or the others, a Muse expresses in its specific form the latency that I am exploring. The vision is preserved to this day in the English word *memory,* from the Latin *memoria,* both of which contain the particle *mora,* delay. The English word *mora* refers to a unit of metrical time in poetics equal to a short syllable. *Mora* finds its place in words such as *moratorium, demur,* and *remora* (the suckerfish, thought to delay the embarkation of ships by sticking to their hulls.) In its original sense, *memory* is derived from the particle *men-,* which makes general reference to the mind, plus *mora.* Thus we find *memory,* in its basic sense, as denoting a *mindfulness of the delay of higher-order intelligence as it makes its way to thought.* Chronologically, in reverence to a Mnemosyne faded, and her function weakened of linking the source of meaning with thought, memory was reduced to an act of retrieval from the storehouse of past. A connection between memory and an ever-renewed fount of meaning was replaced by a connection between memory and the remains of events. Clio, once Muse of history, displaced Mnemosyne and provided a record and account of events of other times. *Mora* is forgotten, memory, a thing of the past, and memorization a substitute for a subtle awareness of the divine speech within humanity.

In conception and performance, the task of memory is impossible. That from which meaning arises necessarily escapes the net of temporal order since it is not constructed by thought. Meaning, though given, has never been presented to thought. The gift of meaning belongs to anarchaic time, a priori time (though not

Kant's temporality), a time without a present. Meaning belongs to no present, has never been present, will never be present. Since it is the gift that involves no presence or receptivity, meaning remains enigma and incomprehensibility. Yet we are commanded to bear it in memory in order to commemorate its givenness. *Memory's task is to remember the immemorial.* If the immemorial exists at all, its existence is a perpetual threat to the persistence of memory. It is that against which memory is armed and organized to avoid, the surd erupting in the series of rational numbers. Though an impossible task, to remember the immemorial is also inescapable. Thought cannot escape the immemorial any more than speech can escape the silence. The immemorial is the darkened underside, the tain, of the cloud of memories, nostalgic and anticipatory, which, when seen from below, is obvious. No light of the mind penetrates the memory without also adding this quality of visible absence to thought. Yet because the mind looks down from its perch, brightness alone appears. The immemorial stalks memory the way the blind spot stalks vision. Uncannily at moments, a portion of the visual field disappears from view. Similarly, a gap appears in memory when a name cannot be recalled and the face is obvious, and the ambiance, and the familiarity. Then a tense striving to remember over and against the lack of recall may evoke the immemorial. But this provides only a rough analogy. The immemorial calls us to task as a remembered absence, as an objectless recollection, as a caesura in a review of the past. In searching my mind for a figure, I recall that Orpheus, on leaving the underworld, moves toward the immemorial as well as that which is lost when he turns to look back.

Whatever is memorable can be remembered. The memorable—whether of dates, times, names, ideas, or precepts—though often a task of memory, is not the task I speak of here. To bear in memory what cannot be remembered is to bring in the subject of the ethical. The fundamental task of memory, to remember the immemorial, belongs to the ethical. This is because the task is precisely to remember the ethical subject, the one who ought ethically to be remembered because it is impossible to remember. The ethical concerns itself with the embodiment of a memory that repeatedly escapes retrieval of thought by thought. Often enough, ethics is spoken of as acting on principles implanted in memory—for instance, "Do not lie." The study of these rules and their implanting involves the moral development of a person. My own discussion centers on a different approach to the ethical, that by way of initiation. Initiatory ethics concerns the process whereby a memory of the immemorial can become incarnate and the subject of the ethical be fleshed.

Memory of the Immemorial

The broad equivalence between memory and thought was first noticed, as I said, by Locke who saw that if one took away the retentive act of remembering, thinking would become vacuous. This marks an important modern discovery: that to reproduce thought, it is essential to retain the conditions that produce thought. Then, the retained memory must be leapfrogged futureward to allow thought to occupy a new position, or like not a frog but a snail that rides forward on its own secretions. The discovery was augmented by that of the oscillation between retention and protention, explicitly noted by Husserl to whom credit is due for formulating the functional beat of thought in these terms. Historically, however, Aristotle, in whose time the task of the immemorial memory has not been entirely lost, lays grounds for the question. In *De Memoria et Reminiscentia,* he asks: "Why should the perception of the mere impression be memory of something else instead of being related to this impression alone?"[1] This is a riddle that teases its sayer. After rejecting the notion of a distinctive impression of memory itself (since that would involve an infinite regress), Aristotle concludes that in being a "likeness" of something past, an impression "presents itself as a mnemonic token."[2] His annoyance is compounded when he adds to the question-begging response by noting that memory is itself a function "of that faculty whereby we perceive time."[3] But the conundrum stands even when the question is begged. The sense of likeness in comparing a present impression to a past one results from an act of retention by which the conditions giving rise to the first impression are held on to. Without the retention, no such likeness could be experienced. It is because he clearly saw the anteriority of retention that Husserl was able to derive the perception of time from memory rather than the converse.

When memory is reduced to a retentive function, to remember the unremembered becomes a problem either of capacity or of will. Its solution is a matter of mechanics or volition. The first attributes the unremembered to a shortage of memory storeroom (the most widespread trope for memory) or poor retrieval of the goods stored. The second holds that the memory is not wanted, knowingly or not, and therefore discarded. Deletion, distortion, and partial erasure of unpleasant memories illustrates the work of the latter. Either kind of unremembered memory can be remembered with the aid of proper practice. In Neolithic cultures, the mechanical capacity of memory was extended by exercise to phenomenal bounds with mnemonic devices. In our own tradition, the *ars memoralis* of Simonides and Cicero utilizes a visualization for training in retention of text. With respect to unwanted memory, various techniques of undeleting suppression have been formulated by psychoanalytic methods, often following the pathways made by archaic practitioners. In neither case—suppression nor nonretention—however, does the unremembered properly lie beyond memory. Each is a particular region within the memorial, access to which has been temporarily crippled. Each is more of the same in memory. Perception, once remembered, becomes part of one and the same memory store. This is as it should be, for the unremembered here corresponds to a lapse of memory. It is, however, different with the unremembered that gives subjectivity its task in memory. That unremembered cannot be retained because it represents no lapse of memory, but rather its annihilation. That the unremembered cannot be retained because its assault on memory is precisely the onset of the task to remember.

I remember that I have forgotten. The formula records the explicit form of the fundamental task of memory. With urgency, the subject is located within a realm of forgetfulness, in the unremembered, and is summoned to an awareness of a gap in retentive memory. The summons is issued from the far side of memory, a side that recedes no matter what phenomenal feats of memorization are mastered. The summons from within amnesia, moreover, occurs whether the subject lives in ignorance of the task or strives ardently and earnestly to meet it. The immemorial defeats any approach by memory, just as the infinite defeats all naïve attempts to count it out numerically. Neither to strive to bear the task nor to withhold it from memory protects the subject from being called to task. Relentless, the immemorial watches over thought, secretly preparing the moment of annunciation. Through the address, the subject is returned to a memory that cannot be kept, yet bears the essential relation to the heart of subjectivity. There, the subject is articulated, word by word, by a speaking that engenders the meaning of subjectivity. Through the influence of delay on thought, the subject is recalled to the task of embodying the divine word.

I remember that I have forgotten. In stating the noncoincidence of memory with thought and in asserting a domain of memory immune to thinking, the statement maintains a nonequivalence of two "I's." The I that remembers is not the I that forgot. Yet both are I. That I, subjectivity itself, encompasses or comprehends both the lapse in memory and the comprehending of the lapse. The lapse is the inevitable surrender to impossibility since the task of memory is impossible to discharge. Succumbing to the impossibility of the task, the automatism of thought reestablishes itself and continues its subvocal narration of events, *I think this, I feel that, I am doing this, I am undergoing that.* The inner intonation accompanies the functional rhythm, playing on it, extemporizing, accenting, syncopating, stylizing. It fills the space of memory to the extent that one mistakes its *I*-saying for subjectivity itself, whereas its voice is necessarily partial—in the "Egyptian" arrangement, thought not fecundated by inner intelligence. The collapse of awareness into thought thinking, the *cogito,* is Descartes's insight, from which we, as Cartesians, suffer. Suffering can be automatic and automatically deleted, hence, without value with respect to the task of memory or the ethical. Or suffering can be meant, weighed, and acknowledged as bearer of the question of delay. The second alternative inevitably encounters the fact of the second "I." The I that remembers, by contrast, partakes of the immemorial in its response to the task of subjectivity. That I remembers to repeat *I am,* from which follows the ten thousand words and the gift of language itself. Through the word, the subject is related to the others to whom language has been presented. That *I* is a member of a community of subjects and through communion with the others it both remembers its task and receives consolation for forgetting it. I speak more of this later.

The Other-in-Myself

From within, the immemorial pecks at the shell of memory. The once-unbroken surface becomes cracked. From the interstices, first awareness of the summons of subjectivity emanates. The other-in-myself, the *I* that partakes of the *I am,* is initially responded to. It is other in that it is *I* but not the one I call myself. It is other than the *cogito.* Its otherness reveals the dissimulation of calling myself "I." To the revulsion of dissimulation, the subject cannot remain indifferent since self-identity is critical to the project of thought. In the milieu of a fractured identity, an identity that has ceased to fully coincide with itself, the subject is summoned to the task of memory. Subjectivity is cast beyond the pale of the possible, for it is commanded to join the immemorial to memory. The synthesis is of incommensurables. How is an impossible synthesis, a synthesis of noncompossibles, to proceed?

Augustine in his *Confessions* asks a similar question. "But where in my memory," he wonders, "residest Thou, O Lord, when residest Thou there? What manner of lodging has Thou framed for Thee? What manner of sanctuary has Thou builded for Thee? Thou has given this honor to my memory, to reside in it, but in what quarter of it Thou residest, that am I considering."[4] Similarly, one might ask what is meant by the interior of memory. If the metaphor of a physical storehouse is taken literally, then the interior is location of the place holding the articles of memory. To specific a place "in" memory for the immemorial uncovers limitations of a literal approach, for the interiority occupied by the unremembered memory is a threat of sudden collapse, an implosion of structure. Memory in the manner of a storehouse sets things into storage for the sake of preservation. It is happily and smartly at work, maintaining an identity that coincides with the remembered world. Could it be said that its success depends on outflanking a vague apprehension that gnaws from within? The inward presentiment indicates the immemorial. That Augustine's memory of the divine dwells *in* his mind is an erroneous supposition, an ill-founded belief, an unsettled fear, a concealed terror. Unmanifest, the manifestations prefigure a foreboding. Divine memory haunts the memories of everyday things as both a nostalgia for innocence and a terror of amnesia. Divine memory, abrupt dissolution of the order of things, is a theme of myth. Semele, daughter of the king of Thebes, for instance, wishes to know the identity of her lover. When she is finally granted her wish and gazes on Zeus undisguised, her flesh is instantly incinerated. The upsurge of the immemorial is release from bounds of remembered things. Boundary momentarily disintegrates, including "I" that holds bounds in memory. In the place of the placement of all places is the displacing energy. The sheer disruptive force (*dynamis*) that we are summoned to remember—and be remembered by—rises spontaneously from within a remembered word or image and in its combustion we again are recalled to the speaking that belongs to Thoth.

My memory cannot give passage to an interior intelligence that would inform thought. If there is blockage, to that extent the immemorial remains alien, lurking beyond the bounds of *my*self. If the immemorial is remembered, no act of memory on *my* part serves to achieve it. The remembering is something I am subject to, the way thought is subject to pangs of guilt or hunger, itches, throbs of desire, or pulses of exuberance. Though I am prone to ambush by the immemorial, it is precisely in the assault that the task of memory is met. For then, I am not detained by *my* memory, I cease to coincide with *my*self, and I give *my*self over to a nonretentive remembering. The ethical dimension, which is primordial, lies perpendicular to our Western tradition's prevailing view. In a Protagorean vein, tradition has it that ethical concerns never overrun the humanly possible. What ought to be done supposes that it can be done, or otherwise no subject is ethically responsible. The school of thought collapses the ethical into the autonomic, that part of the self-will that makes a law (*nomos*) for itself. In rationalizing of the ethical and reducing moral bounds to those revealed by consciousness, Greek ethicists rejected an older tradition in which the ground of the ethical was said to lie beyond the possible. To bear the immemorial in *my* memory is precisely what I cannot do. Yet, since the ethical commands me to try, if I do not, I fail to meet my responsibility. My responsibility stalks me like a curse on my generation. I evade it. In the inevitable confrontation, in *my* effort to do the impossible, a melting occurs of the self-will, the perimeter of my autonomy becomes penetrable, and I am helped into a remembering beyond *my*self. I am in that moment dressed in the skin of a responsibility not my own but one that owns me and at the same time my own skin.

I cannot find a dwelling place of the immemorial in memory, yet it finds memory. It not only finds memory but memory, the retentive aspect of thought, is founded on "that place." The response of memory to the *I remember that I have forgotten* is that which finds that memory has lapsed. Yet the inadequacy of memory to the task needs not to be conceived as a quietism or nihilism. Far from it. Repeated striving toward the impossible provides a receptivity different from the passivity in the storehouse trope. The receptivity differs from that of the window to sunlight, and also from that of the will to conditions not of its own making. Through repeated effort, memory begins to subject itself to other influences and to modify its defined function. That fixation of thought is not inherent or permanent is the obsession of bearing the immemorial in mind. The obsession is a sign of real hope. For the transformation of subjectivity through active memory makes the designation "initiatory ethics" appropriate. Practice of the task "Remember yourself," in its total impossibility, opens the way to an embodiment of a memory beyond the identity of the self-confirming memory.

The immemorial is an undeniable "fact" of experience by which slackness of memory grows repulsive. Inadequacy of memory to bear in mind the heart's delay inaugurates an authentic inquiry into the mind's functioning. The line of questioning confronts thought's automatism, autoeroticism, and autonomy, and the dynamism of the functional beat with an accusation. Failure of thought to coincide with itself and memory to catalog its own content is a blessing on subjectivity since it leads the subject to an interior sensitivity. Unthought, unwilled, and unremembered, sensitivity invades the mnemonic lodgings, and like Attila's men, ushers in a new way of speaking. No longer is speech to the self by the self, an autoarticulation, sometimes vocal, sometimes subvocal. Now through the fluid medium of sensitivity, speech is inchoate. Returned to the origin, speech once again is able, as Adam was, to name the animals, the *anima*-ls, the ensouled beings of the world—and through naming to bring them to existence. This is the speech of Thoth, the speaking of the divine heart, to whose delay thought grows sensitized. In the speaking and through it, subjectivity is finally embodied and given voice.

Judgment in the Pans of Justice: Intentionality and Eroticism

Summoning, the heart's delay brings judgment that, as I have said, weighs memory and finds it wanting. The pans do not come to a balance and the element missing both corresponds to an imbalance in functioning and points to what is necessarily missing. The pans are too "heavy" with thought. Thought is lopsided with its projects that lend it weight and leave it impervious to a "lightening" through other functions of subjectivity. Yet the judgment itself is balanced or makes reference to a balance point since it derives from an equilibrium of human affectivity, sensitivity, and thought. The balance, moreover, does not begin and end with subjectivity. Balance, on the contrary, derives from an integrity higher than thought, through which the subject is related to a community of subjects, and to which the community is obligated. Justice is meted out in the failure of obligation and is measured by the pans being too full of thought.

The judgment concerns memory's exclusiveness and selectivity. The delay of the heart accuses memory, and thought in general, of a systematic practice of eradicating elements of the subject. For one, memory of the delay is deleted, as though an intruder at the gate of things remembered. Exclusion is apparently beyond the control of memory since it has to do with that which retention itself serves: the intentional posture of consciousness. For this reason, the judgment is rejected by thought as untimely, unfair, inapplicable, irrelevant, "not taking in all the facts," fanatical, or unduly harsh. Force of rejection equals that of a call for a radical transformation of consciousness, a loss of thought's self-identity, annihilation of the *cogito.* From the standpoint of an awareness that mediates the matter of presence, the judgment is staggering. It amounts to abandoning representation of immediacy—constructive thought and language—and giving way to the responsibility of speaking. Small wonder that thought remains defiant. To cease self-justification would open it to risk of relating to a power greater than it. Self-evidence would overwhelm proof. Descartes's Archimedean point would crumble, and the whole world fall back into the origin.[5] Defiance is not the only voice. Under accusation, the subject may admit its forgetfulness, bear testimony to the immemorial, and receive an imprint of the heart's delay. One could call this act "confession."

The selective action of the attention (noticed by William James) led Brentano and Husserl to formulate the doctrine of the intentional character of consciousness. The doctrine establishes that consciousness is *always* consciousness *of* some object. Both discoveries refer to the focal action of everyday consciousness. The action, one could say, is the essential spatializing act that is counterpoint to the temporalizing act of thought's functional beat. Focus establishes the grid of coordinates that Kant recognized as the outer sense, the sense of the exteriority of the world. Through focus, consciousness "targets" an object to the exclusion of the remainder of the field. Focusing or focal ability differentiates a foreground from a background aspect. Focus locates or situates a perceived thing within the differentiated foreground and against an undifferentiated background. Once located, the object can (theoretically) be assigned an identity that distinguishes it from the rest of the world. It becomes a "this." The result is extremely important. It completely disambiguates one thing from another: "One name, one object." Given a settled identity, each thing can be reidentified, selected out as one among other identities, and finally retrieved from memory. Gone is the queasiness of immediacy per se, whose "stuff" is absolutely plastic, amorphous, and perfectly mutable, in which each thing moves through all things. The vertigo of the moment has been relegated to poets and lovers and replaced by a "principle of the uniformity of nature." The order of objects endures and the future will be like the past.

Why should intentionality be the supreme device of consciousness? One vaunted outcome of a selective attention, an attention that can grasp the object, is paramount. Until location is a settled matter, it is impossible to actualize the object of desire. Agency and that which follows in its train—automaticity and autonomy—are still potentialities. Their time has not yet dawned. The ineffectiveness of desire, the impulse to fantasize, the intoxication of possibility: this, the tree of autoeroticism, leads to a maturation whose fruit is focus. For each branch of the tree incurs a suffering, an enduring of incompleteness. The endlessness of what might be is as Tantalus saw it: the torment of grasping for the unreachable. Within the sentence (never to attain, only to dream of attainment), patience conditions the growth of concentration. From the ground of the undifferentiated, the object is made manifest and stands forth. Until then, the law of the excluded middle did not apply since no thing is both one and the same. Now, logic shines forth, a new light, and is able to say when a thing is and when it is not. With logic, the realm of discourse of objective reality springs into expression. This is not an engendering of dispassion. Discourse is ultimately at the disposal of erotic choice, the capability of seizing on one, as opposed to the other, beloved of *eros.* Discourse speaks thought's autoeroticism through its own spontaneously arisen child, desire. We must not forget that *desire* in its own roots attests to the action of shining forth, ultimately, of the stars, and is of great interest in augury, in reading the language of objective reality. The connection between what is longed for and what is "spoken" by the world is preserved for us in the intentional act of consciousness whose teleology is desire. The stellar light of desire illuminates the field, permitting us to focus now on one thing, now on another.

Intentionality, furthermore, constellates a point of view around *my*self. That is, it draws together light from the distant source of desire, gathers it, augments its brightness, and gives it the appearance of a source. When Descartes comes across the phenomenon, he calls it the *lumen naturale,* the light of nature. Such light cast by intentional consciousness, the *cogito,* might better be called *lumen volens* to clarify its true source, the human impulse to objectify for the sake of retaining in memory. The light of desire is contrasted with the *lux dei,* a visibility that antedates visibility of phenomena that constellate *my* point of view. This light, from beyond the farthest horizon projected by thought, from beyond the edge of the world, resides mysteriously behind focus and becomes visible whenever defocusing occurs. It alone makes manifest the boundaries of the *I* whose point of view is its own. Through the display, thought's obsession with intentionality is repelled. Thought is not thereby cured of its obsession, any more than recognition is a "cure." And subjectivity is not thereby hollowed out of *my*self, any more than recognition "empties" the mind. But the light from beyond intentionality stroboscopically fixes the phenomenon of lighting and the mechanics of projection. Arrested by the stroboscope, intentionality and the automatism cease to dominate and the subject is prepared to respond to that which precedes autonomy. Almost as a by-product, the illusory nature of intentionality's "source" is unveiled.

Behind the Object's Back

The lag in delay is that which, in relation to the intentional and differential object, remains undifferentiated. The undifferentiated background dallies just out of reach of the object field. No amount of focus brings it "forward." It shuns manifestation as the dark-adapted eye shuns light. Progressive disclosure of objects has the field recede like a faltering horizon. From the undifferentiated, both sameness (*tauteron*) and difference (*ta heteron*) issue forth without affecting the dalliance. Since the undifferentiated has no place to go, its composure lies in its being laggard. Being behind itself, it never catches up with itself. Delay is able to abide in the time it takes for the heart's communication to makes itself known. In that time (*in illo tempore*), from beginning to end, the heart's delay does not know itself and has invented no storehouse of knowledge.

Assignation of Meaning

Intentional consciousness, consciousness of the object field, is master of assignation of meaning. Assignation is a double movement. By assignation is the object brought out of what lags behind, out of the Egypt of nondifferentiation. The page is one of wonder and miracle, full of signs and interventions—but rarely celebrated. The festival would require a retelling of the story of exodus, crossing of the Red Sea of surdity, and a desert life sustained by the divine word—a hearty feast. More widely commemorated is the fact that by the handle of assignation, the object is grasped—con-cepted since *cipere* is a taking or holding—for the sake of memorization. In marking the things of the world with meaning, assignation prevents their slipping again into the background. Outside of the intentional field, objects disappear without a trace, and though new conquests bring new objects, we continue to live on the ruins of the past, meanings partially or totally lost to memory. Only assignation preserves meaning from the shifting sands of ambiguity, which neuters difference and leaves objective knowledge prey to dissolution. Ambiguity, the blurring of boundaries, the marring of distinctions, the rise of vagueness, is the phenomenal twin of noumenal nondifferentiation. Proliferation of record-keeping technology demonstrates our human resolve to block the slippage of assignation. Archives, libraries, repositories, and memory banks insure against loss of meaning by keeping documents ever open to inspection. Fear of a new burning at Alexandria has made us deposit copies in a growing number of sites, invent cross-referencing devices, and develop without end the algorithm of retention.

To mark the locale of things, assignation turns to the sign. Assignation does not so much devise the sign as put it to a novel use. One could say that intentionality moves one step beyond nature, which already has its secret bower of signs that covertly await discovery. There the "natural" sign marks a thing so that it might take on the character of a phenomenon with a place in the object-world. To uncover the sign brings the thing into prominence, where it stands forth from the background. Consciousness therein divulges the secrecy of signs and negotiates their passage from the otherworld to this world. Its capability is that of a guide. Consciousness leads the secret sign from invisibility to visibility, a psychopomp, a Hermes. Or, to use an audible image, consciousness is a medium that is spoken *through* but does not speak. In a preintentional role, consciousness remains true to the basic meaning of the sign, *signum,* that which is followed. The signum was the standard of a grouping of soldiers, borne high in the front of the line so that everyone could follow. Similarly, without intervening, consciousness follows the process of the sign's disclosure. In its concealment, the signum possesses authority to command obedience from consciousness, and in obeying, to bring consciousness to express a new meaning. If the totality of signs can be considered a language, the oracular quality of the speaking entitles us to call it a language of discovery. Such speaking speaks with words obedient to Thoth.

The novel invention, its human indecency, of intentional consciousness, its assignation, lies in a reversal that it enacts. In place of the constant obedience to the sign which the medium must maintain, consciousness now commands the sign to "stand for" the object. In lieu of respect for the object's secrecy, now the sign denotes, declares, and publicly declaims the object. It rips it forth from its hidden bower and profanes its concealment by regimenting it in a stock of other objects. Whereas before, thing and signature occupied different levels, now, in a show of equality, sign and object are interchangeable. Thing has been reduced to designation. Signs become objects of a sort, "linguistic objects," objects made so by speaking. Objects are signs of a sort, "nominal essences" (Locke) that refer to other objects the way a road sign points to a distant city.[6] The reduction of sign to object can be pointed to as the singular achievement of assignation. It does for language what the elimination of the nonmaculary field does for the attention. Both represent a selectivity of focus and as such a blinding of receptivity and obedience. To obey is reduced to nothing more than a replicating of the object in a language that, folded back on itself, constantly deletes the fact of its blindness. Obedience is reduplication of experience by means of the word. Through assignation, language comes to speak about itself. Its dialogue is about the discretion of idioms, not about things. Plato's prophecy of the *Phaedrus*—that language entails a loss of memory—has been made true.[7] The way to remember the word that, though delayed, rises from nondifferentiation, without assignation, in its own time from the heart, has been lost.

Somatic Linguistics

Evocation of a memory of a primordial task is apparently blocked by a vocabulary constructed by assignation. The vocabulary, its syntax, designations, themes, and motifs, is at the service of the retentive impulse. It is constantly guarded in expression. It constantly guards what enters through impression. The tight circle of language must be kept "pure" lest it cease to have coincidence with itself in the mirroring of word and object. In the narrow space across which designee and designator stare, thought remains entranced. What is real and what is only a sign of the real? In the question, a presentiment of constriction is born again and again and requires quelling. On any occasion, the devil of disruption may burst the perimeter of thought, to speak *sotto voce* a command never to be stated, to remind of a memory not remembered. The antecedent to intentional consciousness and a nonselective attention occupies a place just behind the eyes and obtrudes whenever there is a relaxation of the will. As stiffened by assignation as thought becomes, abandon waits without impatience. It is more patient than passivity. Just as suppressed motives of daylight appear in the dream, so the task of memory takes on a form within the controlled speech of assignation. Any word, any locution, any intonation, may unblock the forgotten sting of the immemorial.

The speaking of assignation is preceded by one in which obedience of consciousness (as opposed to the rules constructed by consciousness) is still possible. Rising to the surface of intentionality, the nondesignating word passes through the medium of the body in a wake of sensitivity. In terms of the languages of consciousness, the "in-itself" precedes the "for-itself," the latter necessarily being a constriction of the former. The vocabulary of the in-itself, is given in the soma, the body's life. Its speaking is sensitivity. Sensitivity, a somatic responsiveness to differential influences, is uniquely capable of preserving and maintaining communication of the heart's delay. Unlike thought, it is not charged with autoeroticism and therefore is not obsessed with the retention of the elements of its own story. Unlike thought, its language has not been constructed in order to commemorate its own achievement: the invention of a self-referential language. In sensitivity is a submission to a speaking not its own, in which the sensitive voice does not distort what is being said by its self-serving repetition. If there were no voicing of the soma, would a word be communicated from that which is ever ready to speak? In the unique character of the sensitivity lies the possibility of remembering the immemorial. The connection between memory and the soma is preserved to this day in our language. To re-member at its root refers to the skin or membrane (*membrum*) that covers the living body, permitting material to enter and leave. A memory capable of bearing the immemorial in mind lies within the body's life, in the speaking of sensitivity, as it gives voice subvocally to the word rising from the heart. When the subject remembers the life of the body, it meets the condition necessary to fulfilling the task of memory, of remembering the immemorial.

Chapter Three
Embodiment

> At some time removed from the beginning, Horus, whose task was to oversee humanity, decided that an adjustment was necessary. The sacred interval of delay, that provided for the fructification of thought before premature utterance, was being lost. The strength of the scribe of the intelligence—the mind—had been growing. The basic correction that Ptah had earlier wrought was, however, sound. Only a "reminding factor" was needed. To this end, Horus took on the symbol form of a falcon. His ethereal body came to rest on the nape of the human neck. There a guardian, he touched a most sensitive area of the human body. Gradually, a warmth roused an inner awareness of life. In this way, Horus was able to quicken an interior sensation whose action was inherently receptive to the communication of the heart. The moment of sensitivity thereafter constituted the pause crucial to thought's fructification. Sensitivity become known as the "keeper of the divine word."

Somatic Awareness and the Life Body

The body of life, the *soma,* is *sui generis* and made new by the attention that passes through it. The soma differs radically from thought, though thought continuously annihilates the difference. In a parallel way, consciousness in-itself differs from consciousness for-itself yet is rendered by the for-itself as the same. In thought, the attention is taken up by the functional beat and grows retentive, grasping the objects of its own illumination. It becomes intoxicated with brilliance and craves certainty that derives from the bright lighting (rapture of the light). Consciousness accommodates to the focal area and shuns opacity; it is for itself. Does it not operate only with objects that draw the light and deactivate itself in regions bereft of objects? It no longer attends to undifferentiated orders. Consciousness becomes enthralled by the same, that is, the same bright light of the object world. That which is other than thought—the different—is excluded from consciousness. Hence, somatic consciousness, which belongs to the in-itself, elicits no thoughtful acknowledgment. The body as fugitive. The Cartesian legacy is that, to the *cogito,* no body presents itself that is not the concept of body, the *res extensa.* To the body, however, in its noncartesian posture, no concept can grasp its immediate reality. To the body, thought is the culprit that repeatedly lures the attention from abiding in opaque immediacy.

The new and different, novelty, the occasional breakthrough of the other in the sameness of the same, takes place within the soma. The sensation of life—vitality—is the basic datum. Receptivity to it gives expression to novelty. Whenever thought is permeable to vitality, the new enters into the self-enclosed chamber to work a great or subtle difference in ideas, concepts, and designations. In spite of the opacity of sensation, the caress of the body warms the mind to the fundamental fact. Somatic awareness, gradually or all at once, articulates the hesitant voice of retardation: the heart. It does so articulately without dismay, distortion, or dysfunction. Not as fixed concept but as moving field, sensation circulates in the soma along a pathway that leaves no trace. Because there is nothing to take hold of, the interior sense precludes conditions of a permanent identity. Because objectification must be relinquished prior to entry, each and every return must be made afresh. To carry a drop of quicksilver on one's fingertip is an ancient image of the skill of the undertaking.

The ongoing circulation of somatic material, the *hyle* of Husserl, is inscribed with the sign of delay.[1] Whenever thought turns toward the soma, it receives an impression of a movement *already underway.* In its reversed image, thought finds itself late, joining up with a process that began at an earlier time. It itself is a laggard that comes upon an act *in medias res.* It finds itself behind the tempo. It faces the fact that an event took place before its arrival, and that, hence, thought is not first on the scene. Through the soma, thought encounters the heart's delay and, as with all things, attributes the delay to itself. It nonetheless experiences a retardation of its own tempo—the functional beat—with respect to the timing. In the discrepancy which takes the mind to the verge of submission, the soma communicates the proto-word *delay.* In a near surrender of its autonomy, thought is impressed by a tempo other than its own and by a time not of its own making.

In itself, the circulating *hyle* appears as its own cause, *sui generis,* without beginning and ever present to occasional gaps of thought. When thought comes to a momentary stop, when—like an arrhythmia of the cardiac muscle—its functional rhythm skips a beat, the soma calls attention to itself. In response to the call, there arises a kinesthetic awareness, a consciousness of vitality that moves over pathways ordained for it. The consciousness introduces no new objects but an aura of difference. When the aura affects the reactivated mind, it engenders a novel thought. Even when kinesthesia stays within itself, however, it provides a sense of renewal and difference. The providential new breath or pulse of life imbues the soma with voice. The voice of the soma repeatedly speaks of the provenance of things. Through the speech, the origin is articulated and articulation given a genesis. Whether thought listens or persists in refusal, the speaking exerts an influence on the self-replication process of mind. The time is ripe for the "transcendent" to be conceived.

That thought cannot conceive the beginning of somatic awareness has strong implications for the ethical. First, within the soma, movement originates at a point removed from where thought joins it. The "beginning before the beginning" that refers to the self-encircling pattern of energy already describes the limits of reason alone. A zone that thought discovers but cannot enter informs and moderates the ambition of autonomy, which is to derive the subject from thought. If there exists a human function immune to thinking that nevertheless exerts a force upon thought, the mind is already in contact with an external condition to which it is obliged to submit. Contact with the soma transmits a summons from the greater whole to which thinking belongs and of which it is only a part. Second, that the kinesthetic flow presents itself as without beginning or end demonstrates an alternative rhythm to the stop-and-go staccato of thought. Spinoza suggests the ethical be a meditation on life, not death, that is, on a movement that never ceases rather than one that perishes and must begin again. The already-present (*deja la*) character of somatic flux draws consciousness for-itself to it and imbues thought with a sense of imperishable life. Thought remembers a thought that it cannot retain: that in a resurrected body lies a pathway toward its own transformation.

Remembering the Sensitivity

In itself, sensitivity travels easily throughout the soma, free of impediment. Access to the soma is, however, impeded and made resistant because the *cogito* is incapable of retaining an impression of imperishable life. That sensitivity has a function independent of the automatism of thought is by thought denied. From the act of denial, obstacles are "placed against" the quieting of thinking, a condition necessary to a cooperative link of mind to the whole. Preemptive claims of the automatism are felt on both sides of the failed relation. For one thing, *soma* is objectified as "body," onto which is projected blame for intruding into matters of thought. To body as demon, alien, and distraction is attributed the loss of self-will and the collapse of the autoerotic enterprise. Body becomes carnal, "flesh." The fall from the body of life to the corpse (which Descartes the grave robber coveted for dissection) inflicts subliminal discomfort, nervous dis-ease, and organic illness on the objectified cellular tissue. Their chronic character is a miasm into which thought wanders and is lost. A light-footedness is necessary before the attention is sufficiently disencumbered to join the sensitivity. Accomplishment of the fleetness is dependent on a momentary cessation of thought. Subordinate to the automatic rhythm, the attention is halted, gravely slowed, and unable to keep pace with a movement of sensitivity. When, however, momentarily no longer confined to the limits of reason alone, it is attracted to the soma and rekindles an awareness that predates each and every category of thought, including permanence and eternity. In such awareness but totally without category is the sense of the immemorial.

The face of refusal, the deaf ear, is turned away from the sensitivity. How can a communication from the *hyle* be heard? Only because, in exile, somatic awareness waits with a patience beyond patience. In the stage of denial, the ethical is exilic, diasporic, nomadic. It is the ethics of the desert, the pathless path, awaiting no formulated principle or precept but an ambiguous sign. It is that of the outsider, peering from the mountain top at the promised land "over there." On the basis of a latent scoptophilia, thought establishes laws (auto-*nomos*) for ethics that, though born of a longing, add to the gravitational weight of thought. Imperial postures and the imperious habit of positing per se gain support in a milieu where calculation and adjudication are needed for implementation. To figure the right thing to do turns thinking toward the self-willing region, the automatism, effectively sealing off access to the soma. Weighing reasons, attributing causes, determining means to an end, citing precepts: these are the many facets of "reasonable" rationality. A rational decision requires a rationing of the attention by which means the solicitations of the soma are excluded. Tensed and contracted, the body is repeatedly sacrificed on the altar of desire. The first act of an exilic ethics: to seize the knife held threateningly above the flesh and disarm the *cogito* abruptly, shockingly—disruptively.

That resistance faces away from the sensitivity expresses intentional consciousness's obsession with the production of a state. Consciousness strives mightily to produce for-itself the same state of consciousness, always a consciousness *of* a state, or else risk a summons to judgment. Within the sensitivity's independence from thought lies a prefiguring of the ordeal, of thought's confrontation with its automatism. I will look into the *epreuve* below. For now, I want to say that a tensed and knotted body is the price of avoidance, which represents the cost of selective focus. Breaking the obsession and ending the avoidance take place by turning around the resistance to face the other way, toward the sensitivity. The initial and greatest movement of the ethical is to submit to the beneficent touch of sensation. Then the strictures against the body expire and are abandoned. All that had been deafened—breath, pulse, and interior sounding—becomes audible. The initial impulse gives voice to the soma. Awareness brings to speaking the very shell of resistance which softens and grows porous with language. Even the resistance becomes articulate. Such is the reversal that sensitivity can work, from mute refusal to an eloquence that forgives the desire not to be heard.

"Only memory begets memory." The relation with somatic sensitivity is not a heroic exercise meant to strengthen the self-will or broaden the mind's horizons. Nor is it an intellectual attempt to solve the problem of embodiment. Rather, reinstatement of sensitivity is an act of memory—though not of a retentive character. To permit the kinesthetic flow through the organism is to re-member the body, to repeat the archetypal act of Isis collecting the scattered parts of Osiris's body. Osiris had been dismembered and the pieces distributed over the land. Through an act of compassion, Isis, his sister, locates each and reassembles the whole. Osiris's body is therein returned to life. The primordial speech of kinesthesia reiterates the original recollection of fragments by which the organism is reanimated. The interior sensation sympathetically recalls the soma's sense to itself and itself to that sense. It restores the body's memory of a tempo in which the soma is intermediate between the divine word and thought's task to remember the immemorial. Interior to the sensitivity is a sympathetic remembrance of that which lies beyond all things memorable.

Audibility and Sensitivity

The role of a sympathetic intermediary is missing in the play of the automatism, its self-replication and autoeroticism. Forgotten by history and a historical account of cognitive exploits, a sympathetic intermediary nevertheless plays the part of joining the incommensurables, thought and the word of the heart. Without an intermediary of outstanding sympathy, the word resounds unheard in the desert of nondifferentiation, a quality not yet qualified. To it, no response is or can be possible, hence, the responsiveness of the subject is muted. Hence, a responsibility that awaits response is ineffectual, in the way that a dream decision is.

How does the soma fill the missing role? The sympathy of the soma is not a feeling of pity for thought's closure. It is not an affect (an event of feeling) at all nor a sense of mutual understanding. The sym-pathy of the soma is its *patience-with,* its capability of a passivity sufficient to endure the impression of the interior voice. Its characteristic movement seeks no end and does not concern itself with any attainment. It conveys no agency at all. Its unique ability to bear the voice's spoken interior is entirely due to the absence of any ulterior action. Being utterly passive, inner sensation acquiesces without resistance. This is a double-edged sword. It submits, as I said, to its own annihilation under thought's program. It lacks means to protect itself against assault and domination. But also, it is unreservedly submissive to the inner word's spoken quality and responds by conveying that communication without modification or revision. In this way, the sympathy of the soma is *for* the delay of the heart. The sensitivity sympathizes inasmuch as it abides patiently with the one who lags behind, at the same time not disturbing the one who races ahead. If Orpheus had had the benefit of a sympathetic intermediary, the impulse that robbed him of Eurydice's presence would not have distracted him from his intent.

That the soma bears an imprint of the inner voice means it is *like* that voice. That the soma is able to speak to thought means that it is *like* thought. In itself neither thought nor inner speaking, it rather is the body's own essence, an energy specific to embodiment. Though its double resemblance, the sensitivity gives thought a form that corresponds to that which interiority speaks; it is, in medieval terms, the *dator formarum.* In its likeness to thought, sensitivity is persistently misidentified by thought as thought. To thought, likeness is a species of the same. In its likeness to the word, sensitivity can be mistaken for the organ of inner speech, the physical means of articulating that which is inwardly spoken—even though the soma is a mute transmitter of voice, a medium, a channel. If speaking or thinking were its virtue, sensitivity would cease to exhibit the utter passivity required of a sympathetic intermediary. Thus its kinship is with the ear that listens patiently with absolute receptivity and fidelity to the message.

Embodiment

Fulfillment of the role of sympathetic intermediary depends on the ethical distinctness or independence of the third from the other two principals. The feature in fact is an expression of the utter passivity of the soma. There are two striking things about inner sensation. First, its character of already-present gives testimony to its anteriority to thinking. Whenever the intellectual automatism is broken and the attention de-liberated, the interior body welcomes consciousness as one long awaiting the return of an exile. Second, somatic experience does not derive from voicing an inner word since for long stretches it gives no evidence of communication with the other. Indeed, to thought it *is* the other, and in any event, is the other before the Other is vocalized. Relation to the inner voice must, as any relation, be established before the sensitivity can be "spoken through."

Phantasia

The utter passivity of the intermediary—its ethical virtue—has made inner sensation prey to thought's retentive impulse or, in Husserl's terms, consciousness' intentional function.[2] Suppression or appropriation of the soma's vitality is each a result of disdaining the sympathy, a refusal of consolation. Without its actual and independent presence, thought clings to surrogates of somatic awareness, *doppelgangers* or aliases that pose as sensitivity. The distortion of somatic awareness in its ethical position has a history which is repeated in each individual biography. This is worth repeating. Originally (and in early Greek tradition), the five senses each have a distinct object while all partake of a shared substratum. Each sense is a potency (or more literally, according to the intromission doctrine of cognition, a faculty of the soul) awaiting its actualization by a cause, namely, the object. The eye, for instance, is the potency to see the object while the object is the efficient cause that actualizes the eye's seeing of it. The objectified world is constituted by an interplay of the two, eye and object, and provides *dianoia* or discursive, conceptual mind with thought. But the object-world does not coincide with the life-world, which arises from the action of the shared sensory substrate, the "common sense," *sensus communis* or *koine aisthesis.* By the time of Aristotle, the discovery had been lost and we can read of his rejection of "common sensibles" in *De Anima.*[3] The *sensus communis* designates the inner sensation, the self-perceiving aspect of the body of life, in its informing aspect. Its traditional name is *phantasia.* Following the intromission account, *phantasia* as potency is constituted by an act of *phantasm* and only thereby becomes an organ of the soul. *Phantasm* is an individual event of sensitivity, its rousing itself to a threshold of intensity sufficient to defocus and deselect the attention. *Phantasia* itself is related to the translucent, nondifferentiated background common to all objectified sense experience. As *phantazein,* it is the constitutive principle or power to make the world manifest. It is that which through its utter passivity allows the world in object form to show. One could say that if *nous* is pure awareness (consciousness in-itself), then *phan-*

tasia is *nous* looking through the body's senses. *Phastasia* is embodied *nous,* disclosing what is present to the organs of external sense.

The deletion of the ethical intermediary is an event that repeats itself until all relation to inner sensation (and perhaps the sensation itself) atrophies and is extinguished. This is a severe loss to the ethical. Though independent, the *phantasm* or the "event" of sensibility also exerts an influence on thinking, *dianoia* or discursive awareness. I have described at length the disruption that it can effect on the automatism of thought. Every event has an efficient and a deficit form. If conditions for a disruptive shock do not obtain, the *phantasm* gives rise to an image utilized by memory or imagination (*eikasia*). This is the degenerate form in which *phantasm* becomes apparition, figment, or illusion. It is a token reality. By the time of Kant, memory and imagination are overlapping functions, sharing a common basis. Imagination is figured and reconfigured after-images of *phantasms* retrievable from and storable in memory.[4] Becoming an adjunct to retention, the *phantasm* loses its capacity to link the two levels of consciousness, the inner word with the automatism, the in-itself with the for-itself, and *nous* with *dianoia.* The magnitude of the loss cannot be overemphasized. With the degeneration of the *phantasm,* thought lacks means of responding to the summons of the inner word, the task of memory, and the responsibility of the subject. It suffers an ethical incompleteness that lies at the root of all particular forms of suffering. Disembodiment of the ethical gives rise to the need that I feel to reexamine the terms under which subjectivity is commanded of us.

The developments that I describe make up a history of consciousness in which ethical meaning is progressively eroded, up until the present age when autonomy, the self-willing automatism of thought, is gauge of responsibility. An inner content specific to the ethical, inherently disruptive of thought's function, is no longer able to work its action. According to the history, the source of ethical meaning remains intact (since it is unaffected by our refusal of its power), but its link to humanity has been broken. Sensory experience, once touchstone to the task of memory, has become leaden, objectified. The physical world is nothing more than a means projected by thought to see out its own end, namely, reproducing the conditions of the same. Untainted impressions cease to be available since the attention now automatically selects interpreted schemata. The "flower in the crannied wall" bears no signature of an underlying unity, but rather offers itself to an anatomy of genus and species. It is different when a relation with the soma is vital and repeatedly revitalized. Then, the physical world introjects fresh data that dislodge thought's habitual reaction. While they evoke an impulse to retain, impressions also awaken a sensation of embodiment. The two distinct contents present themselves at one and the same time, one to the automatism and one to the sensitivity. Preserving the connection with the ethical, the double action of an impression proves that sensory experience is in itself not "aesthetic" but a secret doorway that communicates inwardly. Shunning the senses in the name of the ethical is, therefore, a symptom of a broken world rather than its remedy. To search for an inner content of sensory experience offers a way to remember a responsibility to the other-than-thought.

Proximal Speech

The other touches me first in and through the body, though not directly. The inner word, incommensurate with thought, is spoken first to the soma and only then communicated to the mind. In breath, pulse, sensation, and vital energy, the other speaks its word, to which I owe an absolute response. Muteness is tantamount to abrogation of duty. The word spoken is the *arche*-word *I*. That the word *I* is spoken to me indicates that as yet I am other than myself. The obligation that binds me—whether capable of responding, whether bound completely by intentionality—is to speak that word back, to exchange on the matter of myself. My incapacity does not free me from the debt owed. I am so indebted to the word that speaks to me that the obligation can be met only by giving my word over—even "unto death"—to the other. In the pledge of a subjectivity that I do not and cannot own, I do not so much clean the slate as add further to my obligated condition. Only in the moment in which the other's word speaks through me have I met my responsibility. Only in the eternal moment, when granting passage to a memory of the immemorial, is the other borne into the world of physicality—sound, sight, touch, and the verve of embodied being. Only then have I "remembered myself."

The other's touch, at my elbow (in the form of another human being) or in my breath, brings me to the verge of the ethical. Until now, its lack had gone unnoticed, along with the suffering of the unattended. Obsessed with thoughts of "should" and "ought," I had been obeying their directives. Although the notions did not differ from nonprescriptive thinking in cause or quality, matter or end, I took them to derive from ethical sources. Now, at the gentle, firm insistence of the other's touch, the soma seethes again with life. There is a gap in thought, prescriptive or not. In the emptiness, the attention opens to the circulating *hyle* the way a hand opens to meet the other's hand. The inner sensation, once established, turns responsively toward the silent source of touch. The extent to which it abides in responsiveness is a measure of its nearness to the ethical. In proximity lies responsibility. All irresponsibility derives from distance—the *cogito's* presumption of extension. In proximate sensitivity, in stillness, a word is spoken. Its communion has more in common with a pressing touch than the audible word spoken across a distance. To receive the spoken word has more in common with taking the other's hand than hearing a distant voice. In proximity, what is spoken registers in immediacy. Therein lies the possibility of responsibility. Immediacy, however, is a condition of the body of life, the intermediary. As soon as the communion is shared with the third, with thought, a distance is traversed. In distance, the possibility of responsiveness is diluted, not negated altogether. Yet in distance, the demand for responsibility remains undiluted, even though immediacy no longer works its wonder. This is the situation in which I commonly encounter the delay of the heart (*kardia*).

Unadorned Touch

The other's touch on my body may enter by way of the physical world, through Aristotle's proper sensibles or sensible species. How are they to accomplish the feat if they are entirely taken up by thought? Objects of sight, taste, hearing, smell, and tactility evoke at the same time an event in the common inner sensible (*phantasia*), an impression that belongs to the *communis sensus.* The former automatically trigger inferential thought (*dianoia*), which begins to cross-index the presented object with ones represented in memory and anticipated by imagination (Kant's schematic analogies of experience).[5] The functional beat is thereby reestablished. The source of the cross-indexing is irrelevant. Whether thought dwells on the sublime or the mundane, the sacred or the profane, it is engaged in reproducing its own identity. If the other's touch turns only my thought in a compassionate vein, it has not yet touched my body. Though I am then thinking in categories of proximity, I have not taken in an impression of the other as touch. A claim to conduct myself in ethically acceptable ways lacks the agreement of the sensitivity, and beyond that, the sentence of the heart. Accountability is limited to terms of the self-willing subject, myself, not to one over which I have no authority, much less absolute authority. I fall short of the ethical.

When conveyed by sensory experience, the other's touch has a different origin. Although masked by dianoetic thought, an impression (*phantasm*) of the inner sense is evoked simultaneously with the production of a sensible object. Although Aristotle argues against it, the common inner sensible is the necessary condition for shared sensory object, as when I smell what I also see, and so we possess common proof (if needed) of inner sensibles, and even their ubiquity. The impression serves to actualize a perceptive faculty of inner sense (*phantasia*), which embodies recognition of a pre-sense, of that which is perceptible and temporally prior to the impression of interior sensation. Antecedent to sense, either outer or inner, is inward speaking by whose articulation of the *arche*-word *I* the primordial call to responsibility is repeated. Through saying *I,* the *arche*-word speaks the other. As long as I think myself "I," I am not yet *I.* As long as I take myself to be the same, I am not yet other than myself. Only when I join without reservation with the other can I also speak the *arche*-word as my own. The noncognitive impression of touch actualizes that sensitivity that bears an echo of inner speaking. The other's touch reaches so deeply into me as to awaken the voice of the absolute other. In the whisper comes the summons to recall me to the task of memory.

In its inherent plasticity, the "sense" of sense experience is a neutral movement toward a destination—a vector. The movement can approach or recede from the other. In either direction, it is a misconception that sense experience is immune to ethical considerations. An incoming impression has the potency to arouse dormant powers of memory, powers buried within the soma. If deflected by the intentionality of consciousness, an impression will be put into the service of an illusory freedom that supports the subject's fable of self-creation. Guilt and bad conscience then foster an obsession with "should" and "ought to." If, however, the impression activates the kinesthetic flow and restores the subject to sensitivity, the quality of attentiveness serves a different master. Then, the inner sense experience bears in its "subtle body" a voicing of the heart that it uniquely is equipped to convey. The approach to the other is through a series of doorways. The final doorway, on the very threshold of the ethical, is approached only by entry through the initial doorway, sense experience. To that extent, "the senses" are prefigurations of my destiny to join with the force of the other.

The Matter of Empirical Experience

Sensory experience in service of thought's function assists in reproducing conditions for retentive memory and projective reality. It is cut off from a duality in its own movement and, furthermore, lacks discernment regarding its loss. If cognizant, it would need to deal with grieving. The dry-eyed, unmourned sense experience of Locke, Berkeley, and Hume walks indifferently away from the imperishable *phantasia.* Their tradition presumes the heavily conditioned (and hence, heavily processed) version of a sense impression in order to retain an "authentic" content because it has been richly endowed with intellectual structure. Sense perception is able to convince itself that the loss is worth no tears. Still, we can admit that to process original sense experience is to derive a less complete, less substantial, and (using Hume's word) less vivid product—a derivative, in short. The loss is nothing that belongs to the sensible object itself, as if an essence had been removed and its desiccated form could be rejuvenated. Instead, loss belongs to the one ignorant of sorrow, for then the eliminated common sensible can animate no disruption of the automatism and no defocusing of the attention. The "second nature" of sensory experience, in whose depths the other speaks, has been denatured and the intermediate realm intrinsic to sensitivity, forgotten. Second nature has become "gentle custom," mere habit, a "having" whose product is a replication, very far from the nature that literally "is about to be born."

The forgotten second nature of the senses, lying to the interior (the *eso*), embodies a self-perception. The embodied self-perception or *proprioception* proceeds through a circulation of sensation "just beneath" the body's inner surface. As intentional consciousness defocuses, as the attention is more available to join in, proprioception intensifies and becomes concentrated. The more fully activated *phantasia* is better attuned to a speaking that summons it to judgment. It is thus better able to let the speaking articulate that which is being called to remember—

to a thought grown absorbed in its own self-serving project. Yet while proprioception serves as an intermediary between opposites, it is independent of either, at least as independent of the *I* of the heart (the *ego eso* of the *kardia*) as an entity can be. Subject to influences of both thinking of the mind and speaking of the heart, proprioception can move toward either rigidification or transformation. By contrast, when transformed, the second nature of the senses offers a response for which inner presence (*parousia*) speaks. It becomes as it were the inner ear into whose labyrinth the word *I* is spoken. It has become the co-respondent.

The conjoining of a nonintentional consciousness ("consciousness in-itself" or *nous*) with the inner sensation is transformatory. The shift, a matter of incremental penetration, requires gradual subsidence of thought's functional beat. The more disrupted a continuous replication of retentive memory grows, the more attention is given to the kinesthetic sense. As a striving to bolster the automatism falters, the relative independent (the *deja la*) of inner sense shows itself. Further intensification deemphasizes that which is being disclosed (which is a "subtle" object) and places stress on the disclosing action. The increased power to allow the phenomena (*phainomena)* to become present is the effect of promixity, *approximation* in its original meaning. The concentration of interior sensation results from its nearer communication with the speaking of the heart. In nearness, composed by hearing, it corresponds to the speaking itself. As the *I* speaks and announces the *arche*-word, the interior of sensation is voiced and in a function parallel to that of the voice box carries the word outward toward audibility. *Nous,* the disclosing power, has made itself manifest through an agency intrinsic to the soma and is heard. Responsibility has been given a moment's birth.

On the Breath

Through voice, the breath manifests. Given that to render subvocal impulses audible requires pneumatic movement, we can say that the breath actualizes the potency of speaking. Inspiration and expiration conspire to supply a form that allows voice to appear. Though I refer to ordinary speaking, similar considerations must apply to inner speech, speech that rises from the heart. By analogy, the speaking requires an "interior breathing" to render it sensible. Such interior breath is a feature intrinsic to processes of the soma. Somatic processes undergo an arising, a flourishing, and a perishing—for the essence of breathing—and an awareness in contact with the soma must register the cyclic fluctuation. Analogously, pulse, heartbeat, and the on-off firing of autonomic nerve synapses express the discontinuous character of somatic reality. The "word made flesh" is a word whose inward intonation is not marked by permanence and immutability (properties wrought by thought) but by supple, living modulation. As long as awareness imposes categories on the speaking, voice is muted and made mute. Such awareness remains partially under the domination of thought. As soon as awareness is imbued with interior breathing and grows incarnate, voicing takes place.

That the heart's word sounds within a somatic awareness unencumbered by reflective elements goes against mainstream tradition in the West. It is important to emphasize that the role of the soma has traditionally been marginalized, propagandized, and made heretical. It is a dangerous thought. Aristotle's rejection of common sensibles is an early awareness of the fact. That rejection is appreciatively revised by Thomas Aquinas, who while affirming the distinction between inner sense (*phantasia*) and the imagination nonetheless disparages any intermediary role of the former. *Phantasia* for him belongs with sensitivity and imagination, with the rational, discursive faculty. To that extent, he agrees with the view extolling somatic awareness. Interior sensation, however, holds no special promise with regard to transformation. It remains forever obscure, indisposed to transformation, and deaf to the summons of the heart's speaking. It may evolve to a blurred "self-sense," but no further refinement of its capability to communicate the inward breath is possible. Soma is a dead end. The Thomastic prejudice in favor of reflective and retentive means as the sole approach to articulation of the inward *I,* the *eso ego,* is apparent. Only from the mind's eye does the light of clarity (*lux dei*) shine. Only through inferential reason can a true assessment of God's word be gained. Subjectivity remains absolutely reliant on thought and rational discourse vis a vis an inquiry into obligation and responsibility. The *phantasm* has once again become fantastic.

The Organon

Embodiment is, therefore, an earning, not a given. What is given in potency, a capacity for perception, an organ of knowledge (an *organon*), must then be actualized. The Thomatistic error involves a confusion between gift and effort. It is correct that both interior sensation and the means to perceive through it are given. Both the *phantasm* and *phantasia* are gifts, of very different sorts. Without a work toward actualization, however, potency remains dormancy. One could make an analogous claim about the eye as a capacity for sight. Although visual impressions are given along with the eye itself, unless the capacity to see is fully exercised, sight is untrained. An underdeveloped sight would be unable to discern objects that the well-sighted take for granted. It would lack appreciation of refined objects in art and symbolism. It would remain "blurred." It could not differentiate between real and illusory things. Similarly, an inner sensitivity, if unexercised, remains in a raw, undeveloped stage. Untrained, it is unable to discern objects or discriminate between things presented and things imagined. In its mere potency, there is a kind of truth to Thomas's claim that inner sense is akin to the imagination—even if the truth is self-serving of the automatism of thought.

Is it too far-fetched to understand the development of an embryonic capacity of sensing as an entry into the ethical? That disruption of thought and restoration of consciousness to the soma as a critical part of the process? That without a special effort, the abnegation of reason and its dream of freedom cannot take place? In any event, ethical work initially moves against a resistant automatism and strives to liberate the interior body for purposes of discernment. If the ethical concerns the task of memory and is meant to complete our fragmentary subjectivity, what is required of us?

Chapter Four
Initiation

The Ethical as Potency

Initiation is the force of the ethical brought to bear at an appropriate point. It is, therefore, twofold, a summons and a response, and is no less than twofold. Though a summons issues from the heart, it may do so vacantly without benefit of a response. The delay in that case extends to eternity and if (for want of the requisite wakefulness) the ethical is not involved, the word in solitude resounds in the desert of lamentation. Yet even at that point, even when the summons fails to engage the ethical, the subject is spoken to, bespoken, and held responsible for a void of responsiveness. The fact is the terror of the situation. Responsibility lies in wait to ambush forgetfulness and draw the subject back into its skin in order to face the ordeal of judgment. Such is the nature of summary justice. There is no latency between omission and accusation. Responsibility does not vanish when one closes one's eyes. In fact, it is the blow that forcibly opens them in the face of an almost inevitable enticement of sleep. Crack of the whip, prick of the thorn, turn of the thumbscrew: the blow is caressingly gentle in relation to what it helps avoid, but in itself, initiation is not a pleasant affair.

Responsibility remains a potency, intact or atrophied, in wait of a response that which will actualize it. Memory of the response, with the associated lapse in thought's automatism, recalls the heart's delay to mind and animates perception. Remembering to respond becomes the subject's chief task vis a vis entry into the ethical. To bear the memory for a consciousness resistant to solicitations of judgment is a work preparatory to the ethical. It is important to point out how strange it is to speak of preparatory work—work prior to the ethical—as itself toward but not yet *within* the ethical. Aristotle for one takes it as a matter of course that training in virtue is virtuous and that no hard line exists between the virtuous act of a novice and that of an adept. But the approach blurs the point that the subject must *enter into* the ethical and that such admission is an achievement. The fact is that the ethical lies at some distance from what must be prepared prior to it and that preparation is no guarantee for success. The subject not yet responsible is summoned to responsibility and regardless of his/her responsiveness is held accountable.

There is occasion to offer a response to awaken the potency of responsibility. I do not, however, say that the summons is continuously spoken, for continuity itself is a term of thought, thought-constructed and compulsively asserted. This much is known, that the summons is issued secretly, apart from matters of thought. Though served on thought, the summons is secretly issued by that which lies anterior to the inferential mind. No inference, therefore, can penetrate the secrecy. Yet the secret is out in the open. It is an open secret even though *summons* in its root meaning suggests a hidden reminder, an admonition or warning not necessarily meant for intentional consciousness, or rather, a warning given despite the heedlessness of that consciousness. *Summons* derives from *sub* + *monere*, to warn. The secrecy of the summons, moreover, is not to be construed as a discretion or confidence, as when information is kept from someone felt to be unreliable. Then, facts are intentionally withheld to some end as a stratagem of thought. By contrast, though the summons is withheld from no one, few are receptive to it. In its annunciation, by its nature, it differentiates subjects by the quality of their receptivity. It sorts and divides. In action its secrecy is found since *secret* at its origin has to do with separating one from the other (as in *cernere* from which also come *discern* and *concern*). The anxiety that anticipates the secret reminder—the task of memory—has to do with being chosen. That for which one is chosen is subjectivity itself and there is anxiety because subjectivity separates, divides, and is decisive. I walk into the secret subjectivity of the *I* with "fear and trembling." Subjectivity has been chosen and I am now commanded by an unknown *I*. Much hangs in the balance: I am weighed by that to which I am responsible and over which I exert no control. That is the formula for anxiety.

The Moment

The point at which initiation is brought to bear is inherently a decisive moment, a moment of decision, a moment, period. The moment is the secret summoner. For when we look within the *moment*, *mora* is secreted, the Latin word of delay. *Mora* is the delay. According to our proto-myth, for the sake of the subject's integrity, Ptah creates *mora*, the delay of the heart. *The creation charged with preserving our subjectivity is the moment.* Since the creation lies in being made manifest, we can say that through momentary manifestation, in each and every occasion thereof, subjectivity is summoned to fulfill its task of memory. That subjectivity falls short is reason for lamentation.

The moment is the integer of initiative. Through the moment, initiative is brought to purpose, and through purpose to fruition. Though this is true, purpose and fruit lie on the far side of initiative and not with its essence. Initiative concerns opening as opposed to finishing, embarking as opposed to arriving, starting as opposed to completing, and motivating as opposed to achieving. Through its intimate connection with timing, the moment grants initiative a foothold in the world. If the moment had not been created, subjectivity's potential response to the word of the heart could not be actualized since no means of engaging the field of actuality would have been available. The subject of delay itself would be a vague story, a possibility, a riddle with a lost meaning.

As an integer, each moment expresses not a part but the whole of initiative. There are no partial initiatives just as there are no partial moments. Each initiative is necessarily of *this* moment. Each moment contains provisions for responding to the summons as well as the summons itself. As integer, the moment is precisely what binds command inextricably together with initiating force. This does not guarantee an actual response but that response always shadows summons. The moon, even when not full, is accompanied by its own darkened part.

Through timing, the moment puts the delay of the heart into play. The moment is lavish with delay and spares no expense in displaying it. This is because the word in itself arises at its own pace, which is languid in respect to the heroics of thought's speech. There would be nothing spoken of the heart's reticent admonition were it not for the moment, which is other than and outside of constructed time. The moment that languishes is timed to coordinate the heart's rhythm with that of the clock. It is the "gear" that regulates the joining of reason with compassion and binds them both in the skin and nerves of the living subject. Since the joint is elastic and can expand or contract, the "size" of the moment is variable and its variation gives measure of the subject's need for response. Yet it is the heart that voices need since delay itself is an invention of need, a needful invention devised to announce the absent heart of subjectivity. The heart of delay is in need, and as in Plato's gentle myth, from the subject's resourceful response, desire for remembrance—which is a kind of poise—is born.

The dimension of the moment, its length, width, breadth, and height, is the time it takes for the heart's word to "catch up." The moment's duration is exactly sufficient for the double action of the heart's addressing the subject and the subject's initiating a response. If it seems insufficient, that is because the moment has been cut, fractured, and broken—and thereby annihilated—not because there is not enough time. The sufficiency is an expression of delay inasmuch as the moment "holds back" until every opportunity for initiative has been spent. Though big with opportunity, the moment is not always big. Always, a quality of attentiveness is the decisive factor. Attentiveness separates wasted opportunities of whatever magnitude from those seized. In this regard, it is accurate to speak of attentiveness as a species of exigency.

Initium

It follows that initiative is subjectivity's part in initiation. It is that which gives form to, the *dator formarum* of, initiation. Closest to subjectivity and, therefore, farthest from the summons, initiative is the more difficult to articulate. Or rather, the burden of articulating initiative gives an indication of its distance from an enunciating force. Initiative is the ablative of summons. Mainstream thought from Aristotle to Kant and beyond follows the line of least resistance, avoids investigation of subjectivity's contribution to an inward dynamic, and concentrates on that which is anterior to the subject.[1] Thus, the middle ground occupied by subjectivity itself is left blank. The neglect is transposed into mainstream accounts of the ethical. In the first, the peculiar attraction to the subject to virtue is left a mystery. Why should excellence of function be such a lure to subjectivity whose responsibility lies on the far side of function? To the second, the good will's receptivity to the categorical imperative—an unconditional command of the ethical—riddles us to this day. Yet, in the matter of being better disposed to the summons is subjectivity itself put in question. What is needed is an understanding of how the subject is informed about and gives form to the awakening word, and in particular, to the initial phases of response.

Initiative is at its root the *initium,* the way in. When we examine the tropes of *in*wardness, we find among the earliest how Orpheus travels the *initium.* His sojourn corresponds to a search of the inner world for his beloved Eurydice. He persists, succeeds, and accompanied by her continues along the *initium*—though now in a reverse direction—with a single admonition. The summons makes it mandatory not to look back. The rest of the account is well known. Orpheus forgets himself, turns behind, and suffers a loss of memory regarding that for the sake of which Eurydice lags. In the lapse, his entire monumental effort of gaining entrance to the inner world—his initiative—is obliterated. Forgetfulness wrenches his beloved from him. Orpheus cannot regain entry, can no longer travel the *initium,* and is confined to the outer world. He is bereft of a distinction between the two worlds and discerns no doorway. The gate of the *initium* has been sealed and hidden from view. For all intents and purposes, Orpheus has been stripped of initiative. Walking the earth a shell of his former self, he can no longer move inward because for him the *initium* has ceased to exist.

Besides being the way in, initiative also is the movement, the wayfaring, itself. The *initium,* on this account, does not preexist the subject's passage along it. The movement, that which moves, and that along which the movement takes place, come simultaneously into existence. For, when we examine the trope more closely, within the root of *initium* lies the radical *ei-,* as in the Latin *ire,* to go. The Orphic journey describes what takes place when the spark of subjectivity erupts, awakening discernment of a doorway between the two worlds. Bursting into flame, the scintilla of consciousness enters or reenters the inner domain, where the beloved waits. *Movement, moment, initiative.* A circle of terms becomes apparent. Here, as we saw the delay, *mora,* hidden within the moment, so too we find it hidden within *movement.* At the origin, *movement* refers to a specific release from rest. *Rest* in this context should be understood as stasis or constraint, the condition of rigidification or fixity. Rest is a negation of free mobility. The specific slackening of form comes in urgent response to a communication from "behind the lines" that has "sneaked up" and taken one unawares. Movement is a passing over unto passivity but a passivity other than rest, more passive than rest. Correlatively, initiative involves an undoing of conditions that impede a movement communicating delay. In the trope of Orpheus, the impulse to look back, to reactivate the retentive/protentive rhythm of functional thought, needs to be undone. Thus, initiative is neutralization, paralysis, cessation, stoppage.

The specificity of release to which *movement* refers is a temporal one. Release lags behind constriction, a faithful partner that obediently follows. Yet one glance from the constricted form turns it into the same. This Medusa-look of thought freezes the free temporal flow, full of rampant ambiguity and vagueness of immediacy, into the unequivocal timeline of the object world. After follows before as in a fixed military march. Chronology makes a debut, both the diachronic and the synchronic. There is always an event coming "next." But when the laggardly accompaniment of release is not interfered with, its action comes as a delay timed to "sneak up" on its preoccupied companion. When least expected, the formally timed pace is commanded to go slack and become informal. Initiative co-responds with the absence of anticipation. Initiative per se is agreement, nonrefusal, correspondence. The name of its locus is the moment.

Substitution

Initiative engenders a tempo appropriate to and sympathetic with its originating impulse. A child of need, it embraces a capability to actualize what it seeks, such is its resourcefulness. Once disbanding the time constrictions of thought, it enters into synchrony with the kinesthetic flow of the soma. This is because the impulse to initiate is directed toward somatic awareness, toward the embodiment of the inner body. Its tempo gives to initiative its properties of nonlinearity, recurrence and proximity. *Andante,* a movement that has been surreptitiously lagging behind thought "catches up" and like Zeno's tortoise overtakes time that has raced by. The paradoxical velocity of initiative has do to with the fact of time's preoccupations. The temporal hare has once again misjudged the state of affairs. Thinking itself "ahead," the mind falls asleep, only to discover itself "behind." In a leap to awareness, the "hare brain" sees the workings of a time it has not invented. Zeno's Eleatic model of temporality illustrates how, in the duality of tempos, the slower is able to overtake the swifter. The time-clock of production dreams of a triumph over mortality, only to wake to its own loss. In pitying the fact that time has run out, constructive time surrenders to another tempo from whose origin is issued the initiating summons.

Initiative brings change—specifically, the change from rest to movement. The change—subject of Zeno's paradox—is other than substitution. Substitution is re*place*ment of one condition for another, in this case, its opposite. The first takes the place of the second. The second is in lieu of the first. Substitution does not take into account the fact that movement originates on a level higher than the condition it meets. The higher reduces the lower to zero in the process of engendering a shift to motion. When that which moves encounters that which is fixed, the latter is annihilated. There is no place for its stasis in the force of dynamism. The latter necessarily results in an entirely new place. The result is a difference in substance and reality. By contrast, *sub*stitution, one thing standing for another, presupposes a sameness of level. Substitution belongs to the logic of the same, which governs the community of sameness produced by thought, like a table standing in for a chair. The upheaval wrought by the force of initiative forbids the application of the logic of identicals. To the despair of thinking, disruption summons a different way of response—a response of difference.

Cessation of the functional beat of thought, vacillating between retrieval and projection, uncovers somatic awareness. Illusory movement—the *trompe l'oeil* of the mind—is displaced by the hyletic flux within the soma. The latter is no stand-in for the former since it is not a product of substitution. Circulation of inner sensation is on the contrary the manifestation of initiation. It is a registry in which the movement of inwardness is inscribed, arises in its own time from the heart, and comes to rouse the dormant organ of perception. It is the first and most immediate record of the purposiveness of consciousness in-itself with respect to our embodied form. This is not to say that the inwardness of subjectivity may undertake other rapprochements that do not arrive at the stage of sensitivity. These "probes" remain so to speak on the far side of being. At the same time, to say that our perception is given through the form of the body, through the "fact of incarnation," makes it sound as though this is as far back as we can trace the provenance of initiative.[2] The conclusion lends itself to a new skepticism in which direct acquaintance with "pure" consciousness is either not possible or no longer meets with initiative per se. But we must not lose track of the fact that sensitivity is already a *result* of initiative, an early fruit of the summons that initiates. To limit investigation to the field of results is to fall into a shallow consequentialism. It is to veer from an initiative whose resident god is of doorways and entrances toward one occupied with that to which they might lead.

Nonetheless, though the origin of initiative—a first response—lies beyond perception and sensitivity, in the systole and diastole of consciousness in-itself, we must not lose track of the importance of embodiment. To put the matter another way, the soma is the doorway to origin and itself may be penetrated to varying degrees. One can say that there are degrees of embodiment or distinct "bodies" that possess different capabilities of perception. To each body belongs a different attentiveness. Since a fuller impress of the summons requires a freer movement in the soma, the higher degrees of embodiment permit greater initiative. The practicability of initiative, if at all possible, lies in a resensitizing of the organism. In this way, greater penetration can occur by the force of initiation.

Annihilation

The fact is that the subject's initiative is never enough. An incompleteness afflicts it with a genetic disorder. Recognition of insufficiency opens the door to a different quality of response. Only then can a full conjunction with the side that is initiating force—the summons—take place. On the bridge of conjunction where *tertium est dator,* initiation proceeds. There, both the "I initiate" and the "I am initiated" obtain. There, subjectivity is inducted into the ethical and the ethical becomes incarnate in subjectivity. The word of the heart, *I,* is truly spoken by the lips. In annihilating its insufficiency, initiative, an active force, paradoxically undertakes that which is most alien to it: to become passive before that "to which every knee must bend." The undertaking by which initiative loses itself in order to complete itself to a higher degree is one of daring and greatness. It corresponds to the subject's ceasing to say, "*My* initiative," and instead giving over to "Let me be initiated." This change is hardly one of substitution, of my giving my place over to someone else. A complete annihilation occurs of the one whose place it is and of the place itself. It has been said that other than by substitution is the subject initiated into subjectivity.

In default of recognizing the inadequacy of initiative, the subject continues to "pound on the gate to heaven," demanding entry. In this case, the subject lacks a comprehension of nonsubstitution. The subject's own initiative needs to be met by a force that annihilates both subject and initiative altogether and thereby initiates the subject into its own secret subjectivity. The encounter is fraught with risk and contradiction. Without the subject's undertaking initiative, there is no hope for initiation. With only the subject's own initiative, there is also no hope for initiation. That by setting its initiative equal to zero, that by participating in the nullity of its effort, the subject is in peril of falling into quietism. Quietism substitutes resignation in the absence of movement for voluntarily suffering that absence. Quietism errs in not recognizing that only through an awareness of suffering does the subject enter into the secret of its own subjectivity. This is precisely the contradiction of nonsubstitution. The subject's "little spark" does not give up its place but rather the place and the one who occupies it are utterly destroyed by the word of the other. Induction into subjectivity is by a force that absolutely disrupts and destabilizes the will to initiate so that nothing of that will remains. If it is correct to speak of *from,* from the nothingness is an entry into the *initium* of subjectivity offered.

Quietism, "nothing to be done," awaits the coming of the messiah while denying any role to the subject. Initiation into subjectivity "just happens" as spring comes or the new year arrives. A confusion between denial and submission parallels that between substitution and nonsubstitution. Quietism refurbishes the bleakness coloring the insufficiency of the subject's initiative. It thus fails to prepare the way for the unknown upsurge that drowns the subject, dissolves its illusory identity, and draws the secret subjectivity into response. Its complement, activism, is guilty of the opposite error. It assumes that by intensifying, concentrating, and refining one's initiative, the decisive moment may be approached, at least asymptotically. Activism, "always to do," thereby repeats the same error as quietism, namely, that of substitution. A clearer, more precise, more fluid, or more inclusive effort, it argues, must be substituted for an unsuccessful one, and so on, until the result of initiation is achieved. The despair of activism is that one can never leave one's place without forfeiting the opportunity for initiation. The mounting tension of achievement blocks an appreciation that an abandonment of will is needed to divulge the secret that the subject bears in its breast.

Between the Charybdis of quietism and the Scylla of activism, a way opens to a memory of the immemorial and the word that is necessarily forgotten as soon as spoken. The memory of the *arche*-word, the *I*, does not and cannot belong to the subject. As much as the subject longs to remember, the memory poses a great threat to its self-concept. In the moment when a possessive impulse dies and memory takes possession of the subject, the secret of subjectivity is told—but not to the subject who has ceased to exist as subject. To tell the secret for all who have ears, its narration, is to complete an intrinsically incomplete initiative, for the one who was subject is thereby summoned to respond *subjectively* to that which unconditionally commands its obedience—to the source and keeper of the immemorial. Into the moment, there is a great celebration of silence.

Annihilation and Substitution

Initiation is the bridge on which the imperative of "my initiative" is conjoined with the prayer of "let me be initiated." The momentary conjunction of contradictories is so incendiary that neither active nor passive voice survives. A new voice, a middle voice, thenceforward speaks. As the voice of initiation, it speaks secrets (since novelty is always a secret until it grows old), and of the secret lying coiled in the heart of subjectivity.

The secret of the reticence of time, *mora,* the delay, is that into which the subject is initiated. Inasmuch as a secret is a discernment, initiation involves knowledge into the separation of one tempo from the other, the inner tempo that lags from that of manifest time. Initiation repeats the story I have told of the triune deity and the original design of the heart's delay. In the account, thought-constructed time passes too swiftly for the inwardly voiced word to be heard. To alter the condition, a new temporal arrangement allows comprehension of that spoken prior to all conditions. The secret of *mora* contains the inner meaning of the three terms central to my study: memory, movement, and the moment. Initiation into *mora* opens a passage to an incontestable memory of the immemorial and thus permits response to the summons from the far side of being. At most, initiation confers responsibility to subjectivity. Prior to initiation, the subject may be bound by rules, precepts, and conventions, but all are products of thought. The subject may *think* itself responsible but there is no more substance to the thought than to delusions of freedom.

In thought's functional beat, its retentive and protentive phases, time-experience is defined by its dying away. Decay, ruin, decomposition, dissolution: the memory that retrieves elements of the past is woven with the colors. Gradually, retrieval accumulates particles of the mortality of things. In fading memory, an impression of death is given. Objects exist in their perishing and perish in their existing. This is the veil of impermanence. When we look more closely, however, a second aspect is hidden within the first. The hidden aspect is pronounced no more strongly than in language. If we take account of the radical origin of words, also lying within *mortality* is *mora.* Concealed in the obvious is the heart of delay. Here we find a deepening secret of initiation. That the delay resides unto the mouth of death may give us pause. For the fact speaks of a secret death that lies within what we call death, a death anterior to mortal death. The secret death is the subject of all initiation. Knowledge of a death inside death is *eso*teric. It grants subjectivity a new relation to dying. Such initiation is not *about* immortality; it provides means to immortality itself.

The skin of responsibility awaits me prior to birth but is not inhabited until the event of initiation. *I* lacks the pulse of responsibility until the constructed self awakens to a knowledge of nonsubstitution. In the discovery, the subject is incinerated, with nothing remaining. Yet the incandescence embodies that which was being sought: a "body of actuality" (*corpus dynamis*), fit to inhabit the epidermis of mortality. Is this not the enigma of subjectivity? Until initiation, the initiative to remember the immemorial impedes the incarnation since it proceeds as though initiation were based on intentionality. Repeatedly the function of retrieval is substituted for the point of memory's task. Only when retention is cast into the fire is the debacle of substitution combusted and a living skin, able to respond to a command, Remember! uncovered. In the very body of blood and bone, a response to the summons proceeds without interruption. The movement of subjectivity, a barely audible murmur of the *I,* redounds in knowledge of the secret of death. Inheritance of the secret is nothing other than the skin of responsibility. *I* knowingly participates in the slackened tempo—and its undying overtones—that arises from the heart of myself.

The subject is summoned to remember a body that it had before its birth. The riddle of the memory is posed to a candidate for initiation. Its solution involves casting aside thought definitive of "body" and pressing into the sensitivity of an inner and substantial body. Obedient and responsive, the soma bares its anarchaic secret, a secret more archaic than *arche*-time, and thereby divulges the reason why one is to remember. By the act, the subject steps into the skin of an obligation awaiting subjectivity since time immemorial. The patience of obligation combusts the subject's identity in a restive, restless, never-ending, undying consciousness whose command is never matched by a subjective response. Nonetheless, to turn the subject toward "true north" is to undergo the secret death and to emerge living as another, as a responsible other.

Apperception and the *I*

As initiate, the subject is alone entitled to utter the *arche*-word *I.* This is the sole privilege of subjectivity and mark and remark of its responsibility. In saying *I,* the initiate binds itself to an obligation that it has never agreed to, has done nothing to incur, and cannot be fulfilled—an obligation that waits in ambush at birth. Yet, binding is also like binding a wound since it stems the flow of anxiety over one's irresponsible ways. That one is no longer in the dark about a purpose other than one produced by thought, eases dread of separation—a great deficit of any intellectualist ethics. Nonetheless, that one, if called, can say, "Here I am," does not lessen the burden of responsibility. If anything, to be inducted into the company of responsibles deepens the impress of obligation, for now a memory is lodged (as Augustine puts it) in subjectivity, and thought and obligation face each other in utter transparency. There can be no hiding the fact that a personal memory persists only in the shadow of a memory that antedates the person. There can be no hiding that fact that the former is subordinate to the latter.

We need to be clear about one more thing. In the enigma of initiation, thought and its productive mechanism are not annihilated. Lobotomy is hardly a transformation but rather the vacuity of one. What does take place is elimination of the subject's confusion over the pronominal first-person. Ordinarily, the grammatical form is taken to refer to a substantial identity that controls the productive automatism and is protagonist of the world-picture. The first-person ascribes to itself a freedom of choice, predominantly, a freedom by which to direct (or select) the attention, and argues that its existence is a "necessary condition for the possibility of all experience whatsoever." The transcendental unity of apperception, Kant's concept of a first-person whose claim to absolute necessity is that it *could* accompany any experience, is the ultimate device by which to preserve the illusion.[3] That apperception is required by a logic of thought production does not annul the fact that somatic awareness antidotes the absolutism. The transcendental unity of apperception is a mask beneath which thought congeals within its own limitations. But the eyes of the mask are blind until pierced through by the enigma of initiation. Then, the initiate, who sees through the mask, annihilates its opacity and beholds the naked face. When the fantastic claims of an apperceptive first-person subject dissolve in sight of an unremitting obligation, thought is ready to serve. When sensitivity dispels the valuation of a transcendental I, the mind begins to wrestle with the angel of nonsubstitution. In the struggle, thought is wounded in the grip of the other.

The initiate's entitlement waits patiently in anarchaic time for the subject to claim it. The subject owns the entitlement before all else, and after claiming it, no longer possesses it. The meaning of being chosen has little to do with title and privilege. To bear memory of the immemorial and to comprehend the heart's delay is to participate in an inner, reverse movement of the world, that which opposes the direction of entropy. Set before subjectivity, that is, consciousness in-itself in relation to the subject's functions, is the enormous and incomprehensible opportunity of participation. That an entity of our scale is called upon to assist in the preservation of totality is surely another way of describing the initiate's entitlement.

Chapter Five
Discrepancy

Equanimity and Intentionality

In *The Confessions,* Augustine turns his attention to the utterance of the heart. There he meets the riddle at the center of a lengthy investigation of memory, reading, and speaking—the matter of confession. "But how didst Thou speak?" the question is.

> In the way that the voice came out of the cloud saying, This is my beloved Son? For that voiced passed by and passed away, began and ended; the syllables sounded and passed away, the second after the first, the third after the second, and so forth in order until the last after the rest, and silence after the last. When it is abundantly clear and plain that the motion of a creature expressed it, itself temporal, serving Thy eternal will. And these Thy words, created for a time the outward ear reported to the intelligent soul whose inward ear lay listening to Thy Eternal Word. But she compared these words sounding in time with that Thy Eternal Word in silence, and said, "It is different, far different. These words are far beneath me, nor are they because they flee and pass away; but the Word of my Lord abideth above me forever."[1]

Augustine is riddled by the language of difference. Difference is plainly the difference between *levels of language,* between what is "far beneath me" and what is "above me forever." Difference in levels apparently results from the abiding articulation of the other, the force of which continues to act rather than to "flee and pass away." But in what manner does difference speak? It cannot be in or through "ordinary" language, the language that passes itself off as our first or ordinal tongue. For that language belongs to thought and thought has co-opted meaning and placed it under the law of identicals for the sake of productivity. When words speak, they describe states of affairs that belong to one and the same level. Meaning expresses the intentionality of consciousness for-itself and depicts the objective realm and the space-time continuum. Reference is to things which ring round to form "the world." At the center, the selectivity of attention (as the necessary condition to "all possible experience whatsoever") commands the appearance of objects without ever showing forth itself. In ordinary language, thought guided by rules of substitution and synonymy dictates how one word can be replaced by another without loss of meaning. Such guidance recognizes that the universe of discourse compasses one level and only one level and that, therefore, parceling up the universe by parsing the words encounters nothing different but only the same. The recognition is a stick with two ends. It mixes peace of mind together with a suffering of separation and abandonment. It is calming to know that as far as language extends, one will not fall off the edge of the earth. It is despairing to suspect there may be no source of truth beyond the limits of language.

The calm of language. To speak of the calming effect of words is to note their lack of energy. They do not sting, prick, grate, burn, or abrade. As Hume puts it, in lacking "force and vivacity," words express only the imagery of associative linkages. As a function of the automatism, they fail to convey impressions that energetically specify the moment. Within the web of reference, energy is subdued and contained by lines of synonymy. Along each line, as meaning is passed from term to term. In the interweaving, energy is attenuated inasmuch as it no longer disturbs thought. Patiently spinning the web, the mind gains assurance that speaking will send no seismic shock across the universe of discourse, nothing to signal anything other than "this is the case." Words may denote, refer, ascribe, or partake of many other speech acts, but always they defer to the rules of synonymy. Since it postpones disruption of the productive mechanism, deference to synonymy preserves the equanimity of intentionality. Or more exactly, disguises it from view. "Synonymy first, synonymy at all cost!" is the banner of an intellectualist language that quells outbreaks of difference before they unsettle and disquiet thought.

Difference is not the language belonging to the higher level, a language spoken into the "inward ear," of the silence of divinity and the altar in the heart—of the *fiat* itself. That language, which commands absolute precedence over all saying, retains its inaudible, protoverbal character as consciousness in-itself. It is a language of nondifference, communication of undifferentiated, uninformed energy. Its speaking is both prior to manifestation and manifestation itself. In the course of its word, various concrescences of meaning become apparent. They have the power to affect things, including the words of the mind. Deference to synonymy is overturned. The language of thought is violated like a house by thieves and the possessions of intentionality strewn about. The overturning of deference disrupts an intentional attitude. Disruption is a most significant event, the *event of signifying* itself. Disruption, the terrorist who annihilates the palace of intentionality, expresses the language of difference. Difference is to thought-constructed speaking as antimatter is to matter, negative space is to space, or a black hole is to energy. One speck brings about an implosion of meaning, the fallout from which summons consciousness for-itself to remember its task of memory.

What Augustine reports is that one level of language is to the other, less like assonance and more like dissonance. Not only do they not mix; they react combustively with one another. What is said by our lips is unsaid by that which speaks through us. The difference is unspeakably unsettling. More expressively, difference unspeaks. It unbraids the lines of synonymy and unravels the weaving of the world-picture. It is the nocturnal hand of Penelope who undoes the tapestry by night that she braids by day. Object of its undoing is the automatism and what it undoes is the speech of thought, the words of which serve a single end: to maintain the mechanism of retrieval and projection. An intercession of language from another level is a cog in wheels of the machinery, a sabotage. An act of a forcible stoppage. The functional beat of thought comes momentarily to a stop and the timing of an interior speaking grows audible.

The Autoerotic

In Augustine, perception of the difference between levels of language evokes a penitent tone. That he should want to do penance results from perceiving a discrepancy between the act of his speaking, mentally or verbally, and the speaking of the heart. Penance bears fruit of understanding. The discrepancy is not remedial. Nor does he seek to remedy it. To suffer the discrepancy, therefore, only brings repeatedly renewed remembrance. In wake of suffering passivity, he again and again returns to the task of memory and bears the immemorial in mind.

Penitence does not arise only from a lack of responsiveness to difference in levels. But in his case, Augustine recognizes thought's calculated strategy. In its autoeroticism, thought desires to protect its own speaking from a disruptive language of difference. Thought's love of self-replication and its ceaseless repetition of the conditions of its own reproduction lead it to obscure a different speaking. Do not Augustine's words "flee and pass away" describe exactly the protentive and retentive phases of thought's functional beat? The continuance of his mind is deeply threatened by a momentary cessation in its self-speaking that has been so concealed that any mention of it is deleted from language.

Thought's autoerotic character seeks its "immortality" through unending speech. The echo by which thought listens narcissistically to its own beauty is a debased form of inner speaking. It is Locke who first innocently uncovers the phenomenon, so closely connected with the problem of retentive memory.[2] A continuous stream of language pours from the fount of the mind. Fragmentary, accidental, imagistic, and associative (as Hume puts it), the stream is a major attraction for the attention, which then gets submerged in the waters. The mental murmur, following Locke, is that of an absent-minded thinker trying to keep in memory that which endlessly slips away. Individual elements and their relations may make little sense, but the ploy of commentary on experience passes for an exercise in memory. Like the absent-minded one, there are mistakes in retention, faulty deductions from association, mislabeled images, and extravagant expectations. The murmur moves in an eccentric direction, dodging questions of its own purpose, yet in its flamboyant persistence, giving birth to its own voice.

Desire whispers distractedly about its own discourse, with the vaguest reference to what is really happening: the phenomenon of degraded inner speech. Through its freedom of association, speaking thereby propounds the illusion of freedom—an important achievement. Freedom lies in thought freely associating, one thought conjoined with, overlapping, superimposed upon, or intertwined in another. The chimera of "freedom" is exposed by Hume, who finds it masquerading as its opposite when he formulates laws of mechanical association, contiguity, resemblance, or causation; yet deficient inner speech appears to go to where desire leads it. In a sense, its meandering is to be understood as an end in itself. There is nothing beyond desire that desire wants to secure. Nothing beyond desire is desired. Perpetually itself, desire seeks its continuance. Acting as the "emotional arm" of thought, desire perpetually seeks assurance that the mind will be constantly entertained by it. In anxious quivering of the need to be reassured is the internal monologue that passes itself off as freedom. "Freedom" as obsessive neurosis. Freedom as compulsion.

Does desire explicitly desire the corruption of language or is this a particular failing of desire and its incessant murmur? Augustine is sensitive to the question. Occupying itself with a running commentary as it replicates its automatism, thought is deafened to the word of summons. The language of the other, which is nonsubstitutable and does not substitute one meaning for another, speaks with a patience greater than patience and is not heard as long as the interval of delay is occupied. Its rumbling, discordant voice speaks from beyond the pale, but no sound reaches an organ of hearing. No flicker of responsibility takes the matter of heart to the subject. The heart suffers in solitude and the anguish of its silence does not penetrate the thickets of desire. Augustine's anguish is not yet that of the heart but of one who perceives debased inner speech for what it is, a pollutant. He wishes to quiet the autoerotic impulse enough to heed that of which the interval of delay speaks.

Equivocity and Assignation

The two levels of language differ in meaning and the difference is not expressible in terms of ordinary language. If it were, difference would be reducible to synonymy. The difference is a difference of noncongruence, one meaning to the other. In noncongruence, the right hand can never coincide with the left without invoking a higher level in which a reversal can take place. Though the two levels share points in common, the words of the higher are not readily communicable without distortion through the lower. Difference behaves like a field gradient of electrical potential. Upon discharge, it is capable of annihilating what is below. In this way, ordinary meaning, assignation, is uttered just ahead of a vacuity that shadows thought's speech with a thunderbolt of meaninglessness. Meaning attempts to outrun the phantom of destruction, but with vain effort. A stutter on the tongue of intentionality is audible to a keen ear. At the margins of speech, with an unyielding exactitude, a discrepancy appears. The very phenomenon of assignation brings the death rattle of discrepancy. Discrepancy rattles in the hollow of meaning and speaks the death of signification through the drumroll of the higher.

That the essential relation of a word with its meaning involves a discrepancy means that ordinary language is equivocal. Discrepancy identifies the hidden equivocation of intentionality, which intentionality hides from itself. In professing no end other than itself, intentional consciousness must cultivate an inattentiveness to subjectivity, to consciousness in-itself, and to the mechanism of focal selectivity. Speaking in an intentional voice, a word and its assignated meaning are the same. *True* means true, *sincere* means sincere, and *transparent* means transparent. No schism between the two can be tolerated because the self-replication of thought, thought's automatism, depends on word reproducing meaning without variation. Since a slight ambiguity in meaning throws the mechanism of production into disarray, deviation from univocity is assumed to be a defective mode of production—not a difficulty with the machinery in general. By means of a *lux fiat,* intentionality creates a vocabulary that "fits" the reality that it describes like a map, the landscape. By means of the ploy of nonsubjectivity, assignation in ordinary language deletes the speaker whose identity is interrogated through the truth of the speaking.

Equivocity is the quaver that reveals a denial of self-interrogation. Disambiguation of utterance requires a deafness to the quaver. Deafness to meaning deformed by the voice of another language is required to force disambiguation on the audience. The cost of univocity is great. An absolutism with respect to language obscures all trace of noncongruence. Lost is the point of the speaker's speaking. Only when speaking ceases to propound the sameness of word and meaning does the question resound: Who is the subject of speaking? Through whose lips are these words uttered?

The gap in signification ("things just don't add up") summons an attentiveness for the most part bound up in production of thought. The attention is inherently imperatival. Its imperative is incommensurate with the amplitude of experience, which is ordinarily quite small. A floating sense of absence, a dull inadequacy, an irresolute mood, the gnaw of dissatisfaction: nothing important is apparent yet the semantic fabric is rent and the air resonates with interrogation. That which speaks in deviant meanings speaks from a worm hole in the universe of discourse. Deviancy evokes anxiety over the enigma of meaning. The one spoken to is in awe of the one who speaks. In the margins of noncongruence, the subject is commanded enigmatically to complete a task never agreed to and to meet a responsibility never promised. The subject is further upended by the task of subjectivity: to remember a meaning found in no lexicon or encyclopedia—of the heart's delay.

A rattle of discrepancy beneath spoken words unnerves the dissimulation of the speaker and leaves assignation subject to a new measure. Utterances now "don't add up" and their variance reveals a prevarication. The one who speaks may intend the truth but truth does not cooperate. It evades, escapes, puts on disguises, simulates. The speaker bends the truth or approaches it, falls short of truth or distorts it. Truth no longer appears available no matter how carefully words are framed. The very intention to tell the truth, the whole truth, and nothing but the truth is inadequate and its adequacy only feigned. The one who pretends, suddenly alerted by discrepancy, is laid bare. *Pretension is the extent of intentionality.* Intentionality exposed to the skin of the subject reeks of dissimulation—the declarative mood of sameness. Truth, by contrast, is in the imperative mood. The commandment of truth rattles its saber and cuts through the speaker's words which, hollowed out and discrepant, lack the spine of purpose.

The Law of Identicals

Discrepancy hollows out speaking and makes a hollowed-out rattle in the throat. The sound has no more meaning than the sound of the body's nervous system or blood circulating, but its resonance admonishes the speaker. It warns that univocity—substitution of the same—is an illusion and that without the illusion the center of intentional consciousness cannot hold. In self-replication, thought constructs a language that assigns an identity to the speaker. The speaker *is* that one who uses words in an identifiable way, with an identifiable intonation, gesturing, mannerism, articulation, and vocabulary. In being spoken, words reproduce the speaker's identity. At this level, the speaker is an epiphenomenon of language. Within the orbit of speaking, the speaker is the same as a certain idea of self. The law of substitution of identicals reigns supreme. For the speaker, a set of synonyms may be freely substituted without loss of meaning. The speaker persists as a dispensable syntactical locus, a gesture that language makes toward grammatical convenience.

But discrepancy warns against the validity of substitution. Take away substitution, and belief in a real reference for the word *I* also goes. Hume was upbraided as a soulless agnostic for his observation that "I" is nothing over and above the bundle of perceptions defining any given situation. For him, the I is defined by the expanse of inner and outer speaking called forth by a situation. A self-subsistent *I* is an unwarranted inference created by the illusion of language. The groundlessness can be deduced, as Hume does, by considerations concerning the level of language. But more serious reservations arise when difference and the other level are taken into account. Then belief itself gets hollowed out by discrepancy. A persistent low rattle of emptiness in the flow of speech unsettles the speaker's assignation of the self-concept. A hidden meaning, oracular and riddling, begins to speak through the conventional I. That "I" is only a grammatical particle and not a reality opens the question of an identity more real than syntax.

Hollow-sounding words. Specious, shallow, without claim to validity, language grows vacuous. What discrepancy takes away in a moment cannot be gained back save by self-imposed oblivion. Momentary annihilation of duality of speaker and utterance by a disparity between word and meaning brings the automatism to a stop. Lack of a substantial identity to the speaker provokes an anxiety—if I am not myself, who is speaking? The drumroll of discrepancy is harbinger of interrogation. The subject is interrogated by incomprehensible words arcing from a higher level and speaking in strange tempos. In the root meaning of *interrogation,* words "stretch their arms out between" the two levels. They destabilize the cognitive beat, invade the interstices, and fill up the rest between thoughts with restive silent inquiry.

Since such words speak in a language not translatable into that of thought, the subject's experience is a foreigner's. To be addressed in an unknown tongue: this is the otherness of language. Language no longer prepared for the reproduction of thought or involved in its autoerotic fantasy. The harsh sound of the other in language disturbs the monologue of thinking by pushing debased inner speech to an extreme. In trying to figure out assignation, the speaker is constantly attempting to stay ahead of dissociation. An incomprehensibility of language—the word of the heart brought to mind—dislocates the speaker from its assigned identity. With the substitution of synonyms for the speaker cut off at the root, the speaker as subject is suddenly isolated, alone. At the same time, solitude throws the speaker open to a lack of proximity. If assigned identity defines the speaker, who is he or she? Strange words come from afar. They speak commandingly in an unknown tongue. Alone, the speaker is near to nothing, shorn of substitution, vulnerable. The speaker is ready to listen to discrepancy.

Choice

Alone, cast onto a foreign shore, the one who speaks is called to uniqueness by a uniqueness. The words *alone* and *unique* share a common root. In response, the speaker ceases to be a locus of replacements governed by the law of identicals. When the same is no longer represented as a biographical, biological, cultural, or psychological property, anxiety over the question of subjectivity intensifies. No disclosure regarding the self allays it because disclosure is reducible to substitution. Although that which is disclosed about the speaker can take the speaker's stead, the solitary subject can exchange places with no other one. By participating uniquely, the subject is other to all the rest that remains the same, dissimulates, feigns to be itself but may be replaced by likeness. Not subjected to sameness, spoken to by unknown words, the subject is chosen, placed apart, made to bear the yoke of the other, and differentiated from the indifference of the same—the way a leper differs from the community of men. So addressed, the subject becomes . . . jew.

The breakdown of thought-constructed language summons the speaker to the other-than-the-one who speaks. This, the enigma of speech, is ruled from a level beyond that ruled by synonymy. The one is commanded to join in with the other, to wear the shirt and walk inside the skin of the other, to endure the labored breathing of the other, to suffer as the other suffers. Even though the other's face remains unknown and unknowable and even though the stature of other is incommensurable, the subject is ordered to wipe tears from the other's cheek. The command precipitates a breakdown whose critical proportions explode the limits of language as known and of speaker as speaking, and from the ashes arises a choice. The very concept of a forced choice—a choice not one's own—reveals the scale of the crisis. One is given to put on a choice of life in the desert of suffering, a suffering not strictly one's own. One is forced to decide against one's assumed identity, the alias of self, in favor of that which is other than identical, that which annihilates identity. Not to change places with the other nor to take the other's place—both of which are impossible—but to forsake an assumed biography for a reality beyond all hiding: the directive of the other-than-the-one. At the breaking point, the disruption, there is no choice but to be broken.

Uniqueness as other-than-the-one: this means that uniqueness is impossible as long as synonymy, substitution, and the law of identicals are in effect. The suchness of any one thing is ruled out by the fact that an entity is a mere placeholder. Its replaceable nature is a solution to the nagging problem of universals, a preeminent syntactical dilemma. No listing of universal traits, even if infinite, suffices to yield a unique particular since the particular can always be substituted for by another grouping of universals. Utter particularity does not belong to a language of thought construction. (Solution to the problem of nominal essences.) Only in the breakdown of the one, where its synonyms dissolve, does uniqueness come forth. In the breakdown, words from another level command in their specificity and terrorize in their quiddity. They are words of the other-than-the-one, a foreign tongue, a lost speech, the way ancient Hittite is a lost speech. They remind as thought constructs cannot, for they restate the task of memory, the immemorial, the forgotten word of the heart. In their summons to the lack of summons and their judgment thereof is their terror.

Until the subject responds in uniqueness, there is discrepancy. Even after the subject in uniqueness responds to the summons uttered in an unknown tongue, there is discrepancy. Before, discrepancy concerns the hollow in speech. Now it concerns the hollow in response and how vastly less responsive it is than what is commanded. Attachment to the identity assigned by language continues to exercise its spell. Individuality, the unique of uniqueness, therefore, continues to be a fugitive state. It persists only in its passing away. Its tense is "is not yet." Yet it is not to the future, as the fugitive tense might indicate. Instead, it opens to the past, to the anarchaic past which predates all pasts of record and history—the past before human origin. It is, therefore, a bridge to that which is not—not because it still is withheld from being and may somehow yet reap the harvest of being, but because it has nothing to do with being or nonbeing. It is a bridge that no one can pass over and still remain the same, yet a bridge that one is commanded to pass over. As long as one is subject to discrepancy, one remains a fugitive to responsibility, skillfully evading the summons, forgetful of the task of memory, living under an assigned identity, an alias, a pseudonym. Even after giving up one's fugitive status, like an addict, one remains prone to relapses of indifference. Only attainment to individuality, to the unique of unique, annihilates the bridge of the fugitive, the one who speaks and forgets, and binds that one everlastingly to the other-than-the-one.

The Correlate of Intentionality

That there is a discrepancy between I and myself skews the entire field of signification. Husserl observes the same when, in his Paris Lectures, he says, "True being, therefore, whether real or ideal, has significance only as a particular correlate of my own intentionality."[3] Two equalities are involved in the statement. First, being equals being disclosed. For Husserl, an attentive concern for the objective world lights up the front of things and allows their being-there to manifest. The backside is not yet manifest and represents an idealization of being, one that can be realized simply by one's walking around to the blindside and perceiving the object from that point of view. Second, "I" equals my own intentionality. The identity of consciousness for-itself, the one who says "I," is nothing other than the attention selectively trained toward this or that object. *Attendo, ergo sum.*

The two equalities are in reality refractions of one and the same equality, namely, I equals I. The marshaling of sense data into the *noesis,* together with the bulky intellectual apparatus of focus, supports the assignation of an identity to the I. Put another way, the language as a whole is utilized to shape a self-concept. That which is disclosed in turn discloses the subject of thought and perception. "Subject" is the vanished viewpoint from which "object" appears and is, therefore, defined in totality by the objective world. In terms of linear perspective drawing, the vanishing point, that toward which all "parallel" lines tend, is the counterpart of the artist's eye. The marriage of being (the vanishing point) and intentionality (the artist's eye) is happy and complete. But what happens when I no longer coincides perfectly with itself? The illusion of three-dimensional space collapses under its own weight. When the *arche*-word from which the pronoun *I* derives drives a wedge between the wedded partners, then the illusory I collapses. From the gap, a consciousness not devoted to thought production weighs the I's claims to self-identity: the ordeal. The shape of the *I* begins to warp. The reign of terror is that "I" in fact equals "not-I," an impossible equation. The decomposition of intentionality, its return to basic elements, is also the deselectivity of the attention, the rejection of assignation as a language. This is the terminus of correlation, in

Husserl's terms, when objectivity is cleaved from thought and conditions of reproduction fail to obtain. Parenthetically, from decomposition comes hope. The terror is also an awakening to delay and to the heart-word.

When the "I" that I say does not add up to "I," the totality of meaning slips off its moorings. The things of my world—my chair, my pen, my house, my character, my ideals—fail to mean what they mean. The synthesis of perceptual manifolds (Kant) does not imbue sense objects with their customary signification. For, that upon which the scaffold of meaning rests is not an impersonal, nonpronomial consciousness but, as Husserl notes, "my own intentionality." Regardless of its permutations, intentionality always is the representative of I insofar as I is a self-concept. Once intentionality is pierced through by speech of a higher level and the I subject to question, assignation suffers a *cris de foi.* The hidden strategy of imagination becomes visible and a buffering of the self-concept no longer disguised. The fugitive flight of meaning, into a future when again it might yet come into being, leaves the I bobbing in its wake. In the instability—the vulnerability of an identity pierced by enigma—muffled word from within the interior can be gleaned, for then is there a quiet awaiting the implosion to burst.

Self-identity hounded by an absence of meaning constructs proofs and demonstrations of meaningfulness. Like Io fleeing the gadfly over the Caucasus, thought turns evasive to avoid the truth of its situation. Proof of the continuity of the world offers continuous assurance against an imminent collapse of meaning. Need for assurance brings the concept of evidence to center stage. That which is "completely seen" (*e-* plus *videre*) shows itself to be real and substantial. The evidence lies in the *phainomenon* and proves the docility of a nature that submits to the light of consciousness, the *lumen naturale* or the selective attention of the for-itself. The history of philosophical inquiry, as Heidegger argues, is of the *illuminata,* that which is illuminated and made evident.[4] That which is seen, according to tradition, alone can be said to be, since being is fully constituted by the disclosing consciousness. To bring out into the open, to wrest from the darkness of nonbeing or make manifest, defines the bright circle of awareness within whose compass the world appears. Such appearance makes evident what has been obscure to mind and itself provides proof of being, of being's continuance, and of worthiness of disclosure. The very act of disclosure settles the queasiness of a self-identity prone to destabilzing forces the way oil settles a roiling sea. For the demonstration that *there is* something retrieves the I from the abyss of the holy word and restores confidence in a language of proof, syllogism, and conclusiveness. Safety in speaking is guaranteed by insistence on disclosure.

Justification

Is that which turns the inner ear toward a language indifferent to proof? Until the shock of discrepancy, the subject is awash in a comprehensive language of justification that is essentially self-justifying. The "I" not congruent with itself skews the totality of signification. But skewing represents no defect of signifier, signified, or signification. Justification operates perfectly for what it does. It avoids the sudden slip, blank, bloop, gaffe, or misnomer since a momentary decompression of speaking renders the pretense of retention audible. The pre-tense is not intended but is the warp and woof of intentionality itself. It is the preparatory tensing of consciousness by which field comes into focus and the one who focuses, obscured. It sets the stage for retentive memory and the "functional beat" of thought. In and through the tension, two momentous acts take place. First, a world-out-there is given boundaries and filled with objects: the space of retention. Second, time is "stretched out" into its tensed form, past, present, and future: the temporality of retention. Accounting for the objective "spatiotemporal continuum" disguises the pre-tense by establishing a constituting consciousness as absolute and absolutely beyond disclosure. Discrepancy as a deposition. It dissolves the absolute imposition of a consciousness—a positing consciousness—obsessed with light and blind to blindness. In the dissolution of a totalitarian language, a language bent on total justification, the body's opacity once again holds secrets the keeping of which is a speaking. The secret language, a language that keeps secrets, speaks without disclosing. It is summary and imperative. Its speaking is an unspeaking. Its obedience is not to the law of identicals but to difference. It is apophatic. Having no need to divulge, it declares nothing and hence preserves everything.

At no moment does discrepancy "come to light." That is the meaning of saying that discrepancy arises from beyond and shadows without ever catching up with assignation. Discrepancy is not a phenomenon. Hence, it discloses nothing about the speaker or the spoken. What is said is left to mean what it means, only now with a crystal of acid on the tongue. The sourness of signification as a project turns thought's "palace of wisdom" to ashes without revealing an alternative path. The lurid lack of disclosure brings thought to defend itself against the far side of speaking, speaking of the other level, the level of the other. Thought itself closes off the province of disclosure from the guerrilla other. Since the barricade is subject to disclosure, inferences may be drawn concerning the source of the other's summons. The inferences (like proofs of God) may convince the mind of the need to stop. Or they may provide no benefit other than to exercise the language of justification, which is of no benefit to the task of memory. In either case, they fail to represent discrepancy and its cleaving shock. The givenness of discrepancy is that it is unfor-giving. It forgives nothing about thought's attempts to penetrate or to ignore its secret. No bribe buys its tongue and no disclosure reveals its essence.

When justification comes to a stop, justice is served. A fugitive and tensed flight at the apprehension of discrepancy is momentarily stayed. Just there, with all adventitious motion stilled, the summons is given. A nondisclosure whose tongue is necessarily "vague, exceptional, and enigmatic," the summons is the interval it takes to weigh thought against the task to remember. To the side lacking in substance, it adds a suffering—the ordeal of self-will. Desire, autoeroticism, the automatism, the illusion of freedom: the insubstantial elements are weightless beside the obligation of subjectivity. Not to adhere to a responsibility inherited by birth (a birthright) is to flatter the automatism with the belief in its dissimulation. The justice of irresponsibility is swift. Its ethics of desperation, isolation, and finitude provides just retribution. No other justice, even God's, could be harsher.

Chapter Six
Search

A Language of Return

"Why, I beseech Thee, O Lord my God? I see it in a way; but how to express it, I know not unless it be that whatsoever begins to be and leaves off to be begins then and leaves off then, when in Thy eternal reason it is known that it ought to begin or leave off, in which reason nothing beginneth or leaveth off. This is Thy Word."[1] So Augustine asks thoughtfully about the meaning of *asking*. He wants to understand an *asking* that lies on the far side of thought, an asking of prayer, deep interrogation, and responsibility. When one asks in thought and at the same time seeks contact with a level beyond thought, what impulse prompts the words? Asking of this sort does not pose a problem, formulate a question, or entertain a query, though problem, question, and query might be the outward sheath. The correlate thought process derives from an interior attitude that seeks to relate to that which is spoken in the heart. But since the spoken word undergoes an interval of delay before it manifests as a thought that it itself does not produce, the essence of the asking remains secreted. It is the essence, *search,* that Augustine wishes to be more available to.

There is a hint of a secret asking in the word *search. Search* comes from a root which in Greek is *krikos* and Latin, *circus,* and carries the sense of a ringing or circling movement. Search has to do with the secrecy of a language of return. *Return* is the language that Orpheus spoke on his descent to the underworld, Hades ("the invisible"). Retrieving his beloved Eurydice, he continues to speak it as he leads her back. At a critical moment, the language of return is taken from him or he forgets it in fear: he turns in precisely the way that he was ordered not to in order to look at her. The circle symbolizes a total, completed movement, *out from* as well as *back to* origin. The latter is return. A language of return speaks from a wholeness that cannot be represented in thought. The language of thought, ordinary language, expresses an arc that indicates movement *out from.* This is the underlying theme of projection that specifies thought's functional beat. Intentionality, the automatism, and retentive memory also belong to the same theme. To search is to search for the other arc of the circle. It is to strive to complement the incomplete language of thought and being with a language of the other. *Return* is a language with secret powers. We know that Orpheus could quell storms and sedate monsters when he spoke. To search is to be prepared to listen to the word, spoken over an unknown interval, that has powers to animate a life adrift in the underworld.

After a falling silent, there is a speaking out. After a falling behind, there is a catching up. After a going outward, there is a coming inward. After a dissipation, there is a concentration. After a forgetting, there is a remembering. After movement into manifestation, there is a corresponding movement back to the unmanifest, from the phenomenal realm back to the noumenal. There are the two arcs of a language of return. Intentionality and the automatism of mind concern the former inasmuch as they construct and project objects of the senses, audibles, visibles, sensibles, tangibles, and the like. Retentive memory is servant of the manifest, charged with keeping thought from oblivion and giving way to the other. The arc of phenomena is bounded by tenses of time and geometry of space and can be investigated by thought in all its dimensions. By contrast, the reverse movement, the noumenal arc, requires surrender of sense objects, welcome of common sensibles, an untensing of temporality, and release from the law of identicals. It requires a remembering of the immemorial.

The sector where the circle circles back on itself begins the return to the other's speaking. The point at which an outward stream of projection is annihilated ends dissimulation of the self-concept—its pretenses of freedom and self-governance—as well as an automatic reproduction of the conditions of thought in general. In the dilation of awareness, sensitivity is born. Does the path of inner sensation point the way back to a level where speaking evokes a power beyond thought? Certainly the intensifying quiet of mental speech seems to presage entry into the other with its imperative mood. A more complete transition to "common sensibles" and *phantasia* opens consciousness beyond the monologing for-itself, toward an unknown power. To cleave sensation from its object and restore it to a preconceptual animation embodies an imperative, not in thought but in action. The very mobilization of a sensitivity independent from thought's functional beat is a response to a command. The command is not uttered in thought but beyond and beneath, in the heart. Until the automatism is breached, the utterance is ineffectual, a voice crying in the desert. To breach the citadel of thinking is to give voice to a language of return.

Orphic language, that of return, points out an important feature of ordinary language. Thought construction, in its reliance on substitution and the law of identicals, greatly diffuses the power of speech. To impose substitution over the totality of speaking, thought exchanges an animating power for one of discourse. Discourse is able to describe the world in great detail after it posits sameness of meaning and object. Its mastery of phenomena derives from this basic position. Yet, loss of connection with its source limits its focus to the visible. Its oblivion to that which the focus focuses—consciousness in-itself—limits its speaking to what is already said, for all thought is in essence reiterative. To refuse the temptation of exchange (description for animation), the Orphic refusal, is a dilation of language. Speech immediately opens to the other. Poised on the brink of phenomenon, speaking commemorates its return to nonobjective expressiveness through the glorious and the subtle. Its memory diffuses throughout discourse and the causal realm in mysterious ways, as an exception to law and an enigma to the mind. Language returns and speaks of a time before time, anarchaic time, and through the illustrative mood, alerts the inner ear to the interval of delay.

Search is an approach to return. It is an approximation to the current of the other, that speaking of glory and the proximity of the heart. It forsakes the deadness (*le mort*) of description but not without suffering. For in substitution is certitude, the knowledge that one thing can be replaced without loss by a second and that no single meaning is indispensable. In the order of things for which Descartes martyred himself, the subject of speaking can be exchanged for a thought construct. In sacrificing a speaking that exchanges identicals for identicals, the subject faces momentary annihilation of signification. Totality of loss includes any meaning assigned to the subject itself, its self-concept. In the possibility of nothingness is a source of question. Its imminence and proximity kindle the flame that incinerates thought: *Who am I that I am reduced to this?* To endure the question is be animated unto the *asking*. It is to be called to task by the other who commemorates a time before time, and in the summons, to be returned to a life before life, a life that precedes death and mortality. It is to be summoned to the word of the heart.

A Winding Itinerary

The inward movement of search, its in-quiry, is itinerant. No pathway is fixed, no question set. The *asking* inherent in search is unto the moment. One who seeks seeks after an entryway to subjectivity. The entry is the *initium* and the search is for an understanding of the heart's delay. No direct approach, however, is possible, where *di-rect* has to do with traveling a straight line. A line is straight only in outer, Euclidean space, the space constructed and projected by thought. There, the straight line, shortest distance between two points, is of great conceptual utility. But inward travel cannot afford luxuries of straightness and ease. In proximity, there is a groping in opacity. The way ahead (*meta hodos*) is blocked and resistant. Since at no time is an approach straightforward, the itinerary is a series of stabs, thrusts, backsteps, leaps, pirouettes, somersaults, arabesques, turnabouts, and still poses. It meanders and wanders, devious and evasive, following neither rule nor regulation. Not guided by the rectitude of thought, movement in proximity depends on a sensitivity to another influence, influence of the other. Fluidity and fluency characterize its dynamism. The mode of deliverance is other than that of the causal order, on which expectation, prediction, and intention depend. The mode is far from trivial or accidental. For, only by virtue of the influence is movement toward the other-than-the-one possible. What will I call "the influence" if not the guide of subjectivity?

As long as movement is directed by outcome, it is not search. Outcome, the effect of a cause, belongs to the phenomenal realm whose axis of definition is that of causation. Kant felt the main accomplishment of his *Critique* was to rescue the necessary status of causation from the contingency Hume had ascribed to it. The difference between the two thinkers is not so much one of depth but of angle of vision. For Kant, the projective project of thought is necessary for establishment of an objective world that is inconceivable without causation. Hence, necessity of causation derives directly from thought's necessarily projective thrust. For Hume, by contrast, the world is given in objectivity, and in thought, which is nothing other than a mechanism that works associatively to picture it. For both, however, the realm of action brings one into contact with the phenomenal order and the objective world. Since to try to achieve an end requires an intentional object, action determined by result cannot be confused with search. Search abstains from an intentional outcome and through its poverty meets and is met with the other.

That which search overtakes is delivered by circuitous means. One day, it is found on the doorstep or by the windowsill. The day before, there was nothing. When the ear is turned directly toward the speaking, it recedes and grows faint. The same is true of stars when sight turns face forward. The indirection is the direction *in.* By turning the ear away, that which is not apparent and has no appearance to make can be heard. The inner arc of return speaks words evasively and deviously. Their very resonance is roundabout, like an echo over the lake at night. Is it one's own voice or another's? Is it inside or outside? By the words, the subject is under interrogation.

Between *itinerant* and *initiative* is a relation neglected were it not for the language spoken quietly before the beginning. There, one and the same root meaning indicates an entering and a wandering. That is to say, initiative is that which breaks the linear movement of thought construction, its di-*rection.* The rectilinear is the shortest distance between two thoughts. Thinking repeatedly strives to shorten the distance in order to maintain its illusion of continuity of production. When directness is disrupted and the gap between successive thoughts widened, the subject is in front of a nonlinear itinerary. Primarily, there is no fixed order of succession. That which is *next* is ordained, not by rules of distance but by proximity, which is unruly, without cause, surprising, and intimate. An itinerant subject follows an influence from beyond being, the phenomenal realm, and the causal order. Such successiveness is not of mathematical construction. On the itinerary, the subject is guided from one moment to the next without knowing it, since knowledge is necessarily an outcome of thought construction. Calculation will not and cannot determine the relation of succession in the case of itinerant movement. An indeterminate relation of subject to pathway has nothing to do with an objective order of things yet undeniably interpenetrates that order like an atmosphere. One stretches out one's arms or moves one's legs while breathing in the air and the way is different, even though the terrain is the same each and every day. One speaks and words do not match their meanings. Thought does not elide with thought and the gap cannot be closed. To be subject to an emanation from the farther side of the world is to be an itinerant one who at the same time seeks entry into the secret of return. It is not to refuse that which infuses the breath with a remembrance of things past before the past was or will ever be.

The itinerary moves in proximity. In proximity, in a nearness between one thought and its successor, there is the surd. Beyond ratio and proportion yet impinging on the mathematical line of thinking, an indeterminate influence finds its way with respect to phenomena. To follow an unmarked way back to the source of influx, initially one must respect the cessation to which thought's functional beat is subject. Through stoppage, the automatism is exposed and an organic sensitivity celebrated. Dissimulation of an autonomous identity is breached, along with its pretense challenged. In the opaque interior of the body is the ground for travel. Either it had been previously prepared or it had been always ready. In either case, through inner sensation the way assumes form. Inner sensation is the *datum formarum* through which the subject may be struck by an influence that arises from the far side of being. By its very attendance on the influence, the subject remembers the task of memory and the immemorial. In turn, the influence finds its place in subjectivity through an act of being remembered. Disintegration of ambitions, expectations, and goals follows from embodiment of the other-than-the-one and the compassion that thereby arises. The itinerary is a taking leave of the self-concept and a greeting of a subjectivity whose face enigmatically presages that to which the one is born. The feeling of departure is a longing for the other whose life has been hitherto neglected.

Dissimulation

Yet a wandering itinerary is the very opposite of a wandering mind or eye. The latter are symptoms of distraction, when the play of intentional objects sweeps the attention away with it, like the wind with dry leaves, an illusion of freedom. By contrast, the winding route is symptomatic of approach. Strangely, its wending is a surrender to necessity. Subservient to a concentration more subtle than that of intentionality, the itinerary renews openness to what is commanded of the subject. To the command, a choiceless response is mandated. In the momentary turnabout at which inhibition is suddenly released, a voice is spoken that has been fecundated with the word of the heart. The speaking is absolutely required and has been required absolutely since before the first thought. Nonetheless, it gains audibility only when the delay of the heart, the delay that stretches from the infinity before the past up until now, is acknowledged. At the joint between two levels of speaking, subjectivity is momentarily accomplished while in the throes of giving voice to an obligation older than place and time, yet as current as the vibrating larynx. At a mingling of levels, speech worthy of subjectivity's real destiny resounds. Its sound alters the face of the cosmos. Its sound brings about a revolution in the face of the cosmos—and meets the other's face.

In a certain sense, a wandering mind and its love of free association prefigure the itinerant path—just as an off-hand remark may prefigure a momentous decision. Giving over to mechanics of associative free play, the *cogito* distances itself from its retentive compulsion. It roams over objects of desire and in longing for their realization senses the fantasy. In longing there is an incipient distinction between *phantasia* and imagination. Although imagination lacks a concentration and is automatic, it is also a relaxation, an *allegro,* of the functional beat of thought. To an extent, it anticipates movement along an itinerary. By virtue of an attentiveness cleaved from autoerotic tendencies, the subject follows an interior sensation along pathways other than thinking. *Phantasia* is sensitive to an influence that speaks from an inner language. Although the influence is not obedient to causal law, its advent is never without reason. To heed the secret speech is, from the viewpoint of the objective order, to be subject to an indeterminacy. Time, pitch, and direction of that which speaks commandingly of the task of memory cannot be represented in advance, in the manner in which thought represents. *This,* the itinerant way, leaves its tracks in actuality through the actual steps movement takes.

An itinerary moves from moment to moment. Since the moment embodies the heart's delay (as *mora* is stowed in a truncated form within the word), routing is the antithesis of a straight line. Although one moment is "next to" another, and the universe is compact with moments (as Leibniz's is of monads), within the objective world, there is a gap. The path appears as a series of discrete points, like the flight of a firefly on a summer's night. There is a momentary remembrance of the immemorial, an epoch of forgetting, then another momentary remembrance. Interior to the moment, by contrast, the last moment still echoes. This is not a phenomenal sound, but the inward trumpet of the wayfarer. The *arche*-word *I,* the center of each moment, resonates uniquely in all moments. It is call to a memory that seeks to embody the imperative of subjectivity and to thereby serve out what is commanded. Each moment "forms" around that nucleus, like a raindrop around a mote of dust, and precipitates an event of meaning. The event is the mystery of return, momentarily completing the circle within the body of subjectivity. At a moment of nearness, the *I* that my search seeks to approach by "walking on my knees" reaches out to embrace me.

From simulation to dissimulation, the itinerary longs to break the ground of habit. Every apparent turn of direction belongs to simulation. The identity assigned to the subject by virtue of rules of substitution looms heavenward, blocking a view of any pass. Yet it is only simulation of the *arche*-word, a posturing that provides convenience and security. The moment's advent comes when the face of the other casts a pall over routine and jerks me up from my "dogmatic slumber." The other-than-the-one, the identity spoken in the *I,* catches me unawares, an incongruent entity, oblivious to my obsequious servitude, lost to journeying. Disruption rips open a way different from the ways of simulation and speaks in an anarchaic language of summons. The ground agape under the shock of command,

I am drawn to bow in atonement for the noncoincidence of myself with myself. As yet I have no words to speak in reply.

An Opaque Mortality

The proximity of search takes away the breath. In the vacuum of the outbreath, prior to any drawing in, a tenuous mortality resides. Perhaps it is the place of a life before life. In the brush with mortality, in the pneumatic interval, there is also the delay. Coiled literally in the mortal word, *mora* awaits either respiration or expiration with equanimity. The word spoken in the heart summons the subject to an appointment that cannot be broken. "Even if you die, come!" A force from the far side of being places a moratorium on all movement except that stipulated in its oracular sentence. The subject is admonished secretly of that which takes absolute precedent, but what specific act is required? What consequences of not heeding?

A proximate touch from within the soma discloses nothing because it is given in opacity. Like the deaf speaking to the deaf, utterance is understood by placing fingers on lips. Such uttering is in very opposition to shedding light on an identity and brings one up short, as though hanging on every word. The breath catches in the lungs and can go neither in nor out. As the self-concept withers from lack of ventilation, somatic awareness recollects an absence prior to any pretense or stiff-necked posture. Neither a here nor a there, that which is recollected cannot be brought together in a "final unity," yet obdurately awaits a reply. Woe to the subject who does not, for unresponsiveness reaps a harvest of dread and insouciance. Yet to abide between the outbreath and the inbreath is no option. In the impasse, between irresponsibility and mortality, a language of return speaks. Living in proximity and enmity to both, it seeks the *arche*-word *I* that energizes death as well as its opposite. In death, resurrection of life begins.

In proximate opacity, in a cave of the soma, the spoken mode is not declarative, for that would offer no better response than arrogance to the exigency of contact. To declare is clearly to state what is, an impossibility once transparency is surrendered. Within darkened soma, penumbral at best, the immediate need is for perception and sensitivity. Otherwise, one is bound to succumb to monsters of the deep, sisters to "summons," "admonition," and, more distantly, "*mnemosyne.*" For dread, if not recognized in the cloak of reverence, turns fearsome. Interrogatively—the alternative to declaration—one moves in nearness as with one foot extended as a probe. There is no luxury of sensing at a distance, since sight and hearing, the distance senses, are dominated by mind constructs. There is only to question each encounter as to whether it helps or hinders the itinerant way. The subject speaks a language of sensitivity whose grammar makes no distinction between *across* and *beneath,* that is, between *object* and *subject.* The proximity of touch touching itself (one hand grasping the other hand) prevents the subject from speaking the same and reverting to assignation. The difference can be timorous or fierce, but in either case, speaking conveys the heart's delay through the bruteness of the medium. *Brute* is *bruit,* a sudden noise—shock of awakening.

If it existed, a language of sensation, of proximity, would be close to the mother tongue. In the mother tongue, the gift of speaking embodies full knowledge of the heart's delay. Words are spoken, therefore, in consciousness of the time that a higher impulse takes to light on thought. Each word bears an impress of the summons to remembrance. Could we say that each word expresses an imperative not to forget the reason that speech was originally given: in order that the speaker listen and recollect the *I* who speaks through the speaker's mouth in words of the other? A language of sensation, by contrast, is already a contraction of the speaking of consciousness in-itself. Yet it is nearer than that of thought. In the negative, its speech does not posit, declare, or objectify. Positively, its somatic dynamism is pitched actively enough to be intermediate between the stasis of thought construction and the pure, uninhibited resolution of the in-itself. Words of proximity are not discrete units, linearly arrayed, with assigned significations. They are more mutable, overlapping, unambiguated segments that, in circulation, are capable of multiple meanings—all of which express contact with the higher. Spoken from a vertiginous height, the breath goes out and does not easily return.

Effacement

The search is set in a foreign land, where a foreign language is spoken. The locus predates thought's dynamism that produces the time-space continuum, the "a priori forms of intuition," and the world. From the locus, the heart's anarchaic word destablizes the timing of the present and the two Principles of Pure Understanding that Kant was most devoted to in the Transcendental Analytic, the "anticipations of perception" and the "analogies of experience." One experiences a gap beneath one's feet, a place where the ground does not come together. In shocking decompression of appearance, all secret monitions cry out. No longer whispers or murmurings at the margin of audibility, the summons cannot be ignored. That is the imperatival moment, the moment, plain and simple. There, the search of memory for a trace of the immemorial is motivated. In an alien land whose personal past has been mostly effaced, a watchfulness not given to easy identification does service. Effacement, the suffering of past life, is a resurrection of responsibility.

Watching goes linguistically in tandem with *waiting,* the action of a patience more patient than patience. Surprisingly, both can be traced back to an original root *weg-,* of being strong or lively. *Vigil* and *awakening* are other derivatives. In patience, the degree of activity is disguised, that is, internal. It is alien to our way of thought not to sharply distinguish activity from passivity. In fact, the most fundamental dualism of the West, Aristotle's division of theory from practice, derives from an earlier division between actor and patient, between one who effects change and one who receives it. From the theoretical, we get the noun—subject as onlooker—while from the active, that which the subject *does*—the verb. From the syntactical distinction, all major dualisms follow. Yet, in watching, the one who watches is not other than that which is being watched. This is because, in an alien locale, one's strength lies in an outward passivity so as not to cross the customs of the other and call attention to oneself. To watch is to decline all identicals that can be substituted for the one on watch. It is to pass beyond the identity of indiscernibles into discernment of a summons that disrupts all identity, like Joshua's trumpets acting on the walls of Jericho.

Coeval with the *arche*-word *I*, watching is its primordial accompaniment, a melody that goes with the articulating rhythm. *I* is spoken and simultaneously a consciousness watches and waits. During the interval between the word and its comprehension, the watching continues. Similarly, a melody carries on in the intervals between rhythmic beating. It is essential that the watching continue even during the time it takes for the speaking to find its understanding, which can be considerable. If it did not, the delay of the heart would be filled with an intolerable muteness. Longing for a sensitivity to awaken a memory of the task would be swallowed by the hungry maw. As it is, the time after speaking and before thought's disruption—the delay—is permeated by an awareness (more patient than patience) that awaits a recognition of what is said. In this way, a yearning for an opening of thought is cultivated.

Parenthetically, the watchfulness of watching is not identified by the gaze or stare of the eye. The unblinking eye tends to lose itself in a swelling field of vision and becomes enthralled by the objects it brings to birth. The subject is lost to the project of objectification. It must be said that the Medusalike nature of concealment and consciousness's feat of unconcealment (*alatheia*) promotes a hypnosis. The stare that "sheds light" on the world is mesmerized by the spell of being, that which appears upon coming out of hiding. The thralldom of being, the plenum of vision, and the unwavering eye: the three aspects define a history of metaphysics in the West. To watch, however, looks to a different direction. It is a glance that interrogatively penetrates a situation. It is an eye in movement that keeps in movement to avoid visual fixation and its love of the categories of permanence and continuity. The glance abides nowhere and practices disturbance on the fixed field. It is thus a foreshadow of a disrupting force.

Watching extends from an initial articulation of *I* through projection of the world. It fills the entire interval with its wakefulness. Of particular importance is its awareness of the language of thought. Thinking obscures the axes of justification and rectification on which mental formulation turns. Both try to straighten deviant thought as it lurches toward a discrepancy. Both maintain the lie of productivity: that there is no discontinuity in the world-picture. Both propound a concept of self that attributes permanence, autonomy, and identity to the I. A selective and focused attention presupposed by such a language neglects the soma, through which a summons is issued. A tensed, constricted body of life no longer gives passage to a memory elusive enough to be in contact with the immemorial. It is in default of remembering that watchfulness is on alert. It neither affirms nor counteracts thought's productive mode, but simply makes note. It brings nothing to the clearing yet clears the way for a speaking that summons one to a responsibility never agreed to yet at the same time absolutely binding.

Regulation and Forgiveness

If one searches for the exception to the rule, how to proceed? Rule and technique, guideline and methodology, are all products of thought's productivity. They, whose accomplishments are world building, are *the given.* If kept, the gift is a Trojan horse. It contains a power to destroy the potency of searching. The requisite organ, sensitive to an audition of the heart's word, will atrophy once the given are released, for they cast the seductive spell of being over consciousness. Consciousness will become for-itself and intentional. It will become focused on the given entities and gradually assume their form and energy. It will, in short, forsake itself, consciousness in-itself, and grow docile, civil, and obsessed with the light of the given. Identified with the given, it will forsake the responsibility of subjectivity.

Transposed into the sphere of action, the spell of being, its siren song, becomes the rule. The given is necessarily given "in accordance with." As Kant puts it, such a regulatory rule is a necessary condition for the possibility of experience, which is to say, the experience of a self-concept.[2] Without a rule of this order, there would be no unity of apperception, but only a distraught grouping of perceptual segments (patches of color, blares of sound, odors, rough surfaces, and the like), a potpourri, but no identifiable object of perception. Such a rule, as shaped by an intentional consciousness, is a devotional object. It serves to keep the subject who is focused on and entranced by being from feeling anything strange about the incessant repetition of spoken thought that proceeds in the brain. The monologue is simply a thoughtful worship of being, a shepherding necessary to prevent the mind from straying far afield. It is mentally spoken prayer.

When it comes to search, however, the given is that which is given up. In fact, it is given up beforehand if there is to be a search. Reference to a prior surrender is found in the original meaning of *for-give,* a submission prior to the gift that makes it possible to let it pass by without accepting. The for-giving is not an act of refusal, any more than, for example, a duck's back refuses the water. It is rather a mobilization of the attention that immunizes the subject against the spell of being, intentionality, and thought's productivity mode. The mind is for-given for its obsession, devout worshipper of what it is. It is for-given for its mental speaking, retentive memory, automatism, self-will, and avoidance of the heart's delay. For automatic attractions of its attention, thought is for-given, since the submission of forgiveness lends another purpose: to bear the task of memory to thought. For-given, given objects wear the abject cloth of poverty. They are poor vessels through which a richer, finer, more imperative tongue speaks. The given, which are given in order to be given up, also convey that which commands submission and offers for-giveness. Softly and with a caress, they speak the summons.

To proceed by giving up rules of procedure: a shedding of skins. Each level of epidermis leads to a new covering whose presence (which is pretense) asks to be for-given. Each act of for-giveness is a step away from the given that yet leads toward the given, for the given is not so much left behind as its charm temporarily removed. The spell of being, the intoxication with essence, and the lure of assignation are undone by for-giving a consciousness that cannot help but be taken. Piercing through the automatism yields to a subjectivity whose "identity" lives in breaking identifications. To discover that one is blindly following a rule of procedure is to break the back of the rule and leave it spineless. Over its prostrate form, with the scent of mortality in its nostrils, a body moves in a trajectory other than automatic. A source of motion, not the identity of identicals and beyond thought's productivity, brings subjectivity to a new pitch. In the urgency, with exigency, a search is reborn.

It must be said that the subject, in a for-giving that sheds skins, does not wind up an abject body, alone, and at the pity of the universe. Quite the contrary. For the one who relinquishes guises of identity, contact with reality waits. Such contact as can take place in sightless depths of the soma, in the cave of the Good, takes place when sensitivity is roused from dreams of autoeroticism. Then one is gripped by a summons to respond as is gripped by no other thing. The grip tears open the flesh of mortality and exposes one to a waiting that waits upon delay. There is the heart's word, speaking of a time before anarchaic time, that destroys the last integument before the one dons the substance of the other. The heart's word, speaking through delay, commands one to join in the other's suffering, maintenance of the other's integrity, upon which the subject's own depends. The joining is one without absorption, for one is one and the other is other-than-the-one. It is a joining at the hips, as twins sometimes are, and when separated, one dies. It is the duality of life, the productive and the antiproductive, that fortifies the flesh as well. A glorified body emanates like a new star cluster—the Twin stars, Castor and Pollux—and brings all the more glory to the whole of the whole.

"To forgive is to forget," which is to say, to let drop the retentive memory that actuates thought processes. The subject who embraces "active oblivion" is fortunate indeed. In the forgetting of for-giveness is an approach to the immemorial whose task confronts each and every subject like a Damocean sword. Being given and accepting the given is a necessary step toward for-giving. Objectivity is as essential to subjectivity as friction is to movement. To join in the secret way of return requires a subject first to appreciate the throwness of the world. From the poverty of the subject's situation, an urgent revaluation can arise in which given elements become letters that state, upon interpretation, the command of the heart.

Chapter Seven
Schools

Of the Olympian Muses, the Storm King's daughters.
They were born on Pieria after our Father Kronion
Mingled with Memory, who rules Eleutherae's hills.
She bore them to be a forgetting of troubles,
A pause in sorrow.

—Hesiod, *Theogony*[1]

The Hollow of Memory

Subjectivity is in need of "remembering itself." More precisely, subjectivity *is* the need of remembering itself, though not by way of substitution of identicals for identicals. Subjectivity is the need by way of disidentifying itself with the selfsame need, hollowing out need the way a vessel is hollowed out, in order to let blood flow through. It is hollowed out like a reed, so that a musical note, a resonance from a higher level, can take the place of the pith. Subjectivity is the hollow left when the need to be remembered absconds with the storehouse of memory, leaving only negative space.

Yet that which subjectivity is asked to remember—"itself" or ipseity—is no entity, *res,* substance, or being. The hollowed-out need is rather a hiatus or vacancy. That which "fills" the interval is a delay that separates the heart's articulation from its enunciation. If there were no passage through a human subject, the annunciation would ring loud and clear, with no retarding effect from the call. But the infinitesimal interval is an infinity through which the subject is summoned and must pass, and that makes the human necessitated, rather than a "transhuman" declaration. To fail and play dumb is to forfeit a labor that is one's "divine right" and by rights, therefore, the only approach to not only humanity but divination and divinization. The labor cannot be accomplished, at least by ordinary means, since the mode of achievement seals one off from the task of memory and sets off a striving to affirm something quite the same. If a response is to be actual, it requires nothing other than a sensitization to the need in question. If responsibility is to be actualized, it requires a sensitivity to the very impossibility, which is to say, to the interval of delay during which the word of the heart manifests itself as thought and is thought *of.* It is the need in question that "signifies" the delay to subjectivity. In subjectivity's need to remember itself lies danger of identification as well as triumphant responsibility in being a member of a community charged with bearing an immemorial memory in mind.

To respond to the need by deflating it—and thus to find oneself in memory—may sound odd. But in its roots, *need* records an ancient alliance with mortality since *nau-*, its Indo-European radical, means death and exhaustion, and thence, distress and necessity. As we ask, need of what? so we must ask, death of what? In the original atmosphere of death, one breathed the secret element that *mortality* contains, namely, *mora,* delay. *Mora* mingles with mortal life by means of the additive *ta-* whose sound signifies finitude and limit. Recondite knowledge of one's mortality then bred a patience more patient than death, for it disposed a subject to the course of delay and the acausal way in which the heart expresses its life-giving word. Far from a romantic, tragic, or nihilistic embrace of death for death's sake, acceptance of "mortality" sensitized a subject to an exigency that summoned one to the hall of memory wherein the pans of judgment were set to balance. Did one remember sufficiently to embody a true subjectivity, that is, an individuality? Did one remember *oneself,* One Self? There, though one would inevitably be found wanting in remembrance, the very deficiency served to hollow out the need in question and to awaken knowledge of the delay. Judged deficient in effort, the subject was more thoroughly exposed to proximity and made vulnerable by taking part, as a member, in a community chosen to suffer a memory of the immemorial.

At an early epoch, before historical consciousness, Hesiod alludes to the great sorrow borne by the community. He refers to the primordial condition of a memory, *Mnemosyne,* as one of a completeness that is forever elusive. How is memory—even cosmic memory—to carry the infinite woe of the immemorial? For one level of reality is thereby enjoined to be replete with the other, the spatiotemporal continuum replete with the articulation of the word of the heart, and retention of things replete with abandon of foreknowledge. Thus, remembering is twinged with forgetfulness as though God in the fit of ordaining cannot bear in mind the ordination. What can "Remember!" mean? For the injunction gnaws at the tongue that speaks it. The utterance reeks of betrayal and at the same time is necessitated from above. So, the objective world that cannot decipher the oracle clings to a univocal language rather than deal with a festering sore of the immemorial. One is witness to the contagion in one's neighbors—as one speaks with them—yet what is to be done? The riddling sphinx of memory has sent a black plague because no one is able to answer in truth.

Subjectivity ordinarily casts primordial memory and its sorrow into oblivion, and the sorrow turns to dust and is blown away as a shadow in the wind. This is the history of the subject of memory, with its progressive reduction to the personal and retentive. Memory becomes enclosed by remembered events, being their outer shell. Times leave pock marks, scars that deface the cornea of consciousness. They are there for future reference, the way a scratch on a lens is. The memory of a people or race is no greater than the sum of its separate memories, and conceivably less. Thus, collective memory shows no new way through the impasse. Without practiced vulnerability, a subject has little chance to join in the action of a memory that perpetually weighs itself in sorrow and finds itself outweighed, that is, outstripped by its task. An initiative toward proximity or an approach to somatic awareness, a response to the need that evacuates the need, embodies recognition of the need itself. It is interesting in this connection that Hesiod records the fact that the "daughters of memory" signify a return to the practice of remembering. That makes them channels of vulnerability. Their special excellence pertains to some special aptitude with respect to the subject's "remembering itself," some means of calling forth an irritation sufficient to disrupt the dream of *maya* that lulls the subject to insensitivity.

The Lethargy of the Subject

There are two "pauses"—two delays—in the welling great sorrow of *Mnemosyne,* as alluded to by Hesiod. He does not go on to say, as others have, that waves of sadness release the manifest universe from the unmanifest like a teardrop released from the eyes. Such a release would bring creation to existence in the way that pangs of remembrance give birth to character and destiny. Nonetheless, of the two pauses, one is efficient or mnemonic, the other deficient or amnestic. Hesiod mentions that the first twin practices remembrance in pursuit of the nine Muses, whose very name is derived from the same root origin as their mother's. Calliope, Clio, Erato, Euterpe, Melpomene, Polyhymnia, Terpsichore, Thalia, and Urania: each offers a discipline through which the immemorial can be uttered or traced. Not a specialized memory of historical fact (Clio), musical harmony (Calliope), or dance placement (Terspichore), but a remembrance of the task of memory: each is a matrix in which the subject can yield to the need to be remembered. Around the matrix flows the great sorrow of *Mnemosyne* unattended. Putting on the vulnerability of the Muse, the subject participates in the secret sorrow, its epigenetic quality. The participation itself—a rejoining with original, uncreated energies whose manifestation is sorrow itself—brings about a remembrance whose origin lies in the impossible, that is, in the transition that is Hesiod's first "pause."

But strangely the other twin, the second pause, also leads to the selfsame result. Sister to *Mnemosyne,* forgetting, or *Lethe,* takes the subject back to the protention and retention of thought, automatism, and identification with the world-picture. There, the law of substitution of identicals provides a continuous panorama of the self *as.* The self *as* anger or generosity, *as* pain or joy, *as* universal or particular: the content of the attention furnishes an identity for the subject. Limitation is the obscure product of autoeroticism since the subject can be no more than the thing attended to. The lethargy of the self is fabled. It cloaks the subject from the winds of chance and the arrows of injustice—and so is as potent as the ring of Gyges, which can be read as an account of Lethe. Yet the very cloak can open to a suffering, as in Aesop's story of the north wind and the sun. For, lethargy is susceptible to permeation and like an inert pod exposes a living seed within. Such is the toughness of the fruit of proximity, that which somatic awareness opens to touch, that it survives even negligent, heedless, or somnolescent thought. Then, it is the shock of touch that takes lethargy unawares and turns it "inside out" to expose its delicate interior, the way a grain of sand exposes the inner body of an oyster. Then, the sorrow of memory is visited upon subjectivity like a task of survival: undo the knot of lethargy or die forever. One hears in the body's forbearance the immemorial word. It speaks impartially through hardship as the pearl anoints itself with the infinite sea.

Memory and Community

Mnemosyne is perpetually in the throes of re-membering, that is, of bringing disparate memories unto a wholeness, just as a womb knits disparate embryonic tissues unto one organism. An event of unification rarely happens because it is always happening, and one infrequently pauses to take note. Nonetheless, without the action, things would fall into *Lethe,* forgetfulness, distraction, and the first and foremost loss would be the need to be remembered. *Mnemosyne* bears in mind the root meaning of *need* and its ally, mortality. Life is to be found in a hollowing out of the dead. The body that bears seeds of its mortality carries in its hollow a new life, the life of an unknown identity, an identity not constructed of identicals. Since *Mnemosyne* embodies its opposite, it also is aware of a necessary reciprocity with *Lethe.* In the fable, an angel touches the infant's lips to erase records of its preexistence and causes the indentation beneath the nose to be a sign of remembering. Memory and oblivion are systole and diastole, inhalation and expiration. Remembering the need to be re-membered, the subject again belongs to a community of the disparate parts in the throes of bringing forth a wholeness. *Mnemosyne* is the secret inner action that, like contractions in labor, accompanies the birth of the subject's memory, the memory of subjectivity.

In the throes of remembering the need to be remembered, memory is self-remembering. This does not mean that there is a substantial self, first-person pronoun, or self-concept, but a participation in speaking the *arche*-word *I.* It means even less that memory is self-reflexive, that it somehow remembers that it is remembering. The infinite regress and hall of mirrors has since ancient times been signature of the *cogito.* If what is meant by ipseity is a dwelling upon memory's condition of privation, such memory, it could be said, remembers *itself.* The "itself" remembered has been hollowed out so that its sorrow attends the influx of an identity that has nothing to do with identicals, speaks in a foreign tongue, and needs to be heard. That is, the itself lies in the throes of need, awaiting its maieutic. Its sorrow, which overflows its unspoken word like uncried tears brimming over an eyelid, spreads over the retracted skin of consciousness-for-itself, and warms it with the breath of compassion. The itself to be remembered awaits a sharing of sorrow the way a parent does when a child comes to see its own ancient suffering through eyes of obedience.

A memory that "remembers itself" incorporates a single crucial element different from memory laced with lethargy. The difference is not that of need (that owns both) but that, being in need, self-remembering eschews closure in order to scoop out the substance of need. Need is formication. It is an itching pain just beneath the epidermis, relief of which repeatedly scratches off the fresh scab and exposes raw surface to the air. Memory suffers from need. In the case of ordinary memory, suffering stems from the fact (as Husserl saw) that it can never complete itself.[2] In ordinary terms, memory strives to incorporate that which renews it—difference—and chokes each time that it tries to ingest its future. Though it cannot complete itself, it tries. The deficient striving expresses itself in obsessions that displace the formication. The ego's suffering remains contained in the automatism, in consciousness's obsession with the substance of suffering. By contrast, self-remembering hollows out the substance without neutralizing the need. Such a memory in its sorrow can embody the other-than-the-one and avoid a frustrated effort for closure. That which reserves a place in the one for the other is recognition of the other's sorrow. In fact, recognition is simply an impulse to speak the *arche*-word *I*.

Exchange

Memory as a bare storage function—under the trope of retrieval—is deficient. It flaunts a mechanical operation in order to jettison that which differentiates memory from other intellectual functions, its formal cause. The impoverished approach leads to a conflation of memory with forgetting, *Mnemosyne* with *Lethe*. The storehouse trope omits the essence of what memory has to bear. Lacking that, memory is degraded to a means of the automatism of thought, whose flare is to retain a fixed, objective system of signification. From the degradation, much follows, chiefly, elevation of ontology as a study whose primary deployment is against attacks of nihilism and quietism. The primacy of metaphysics in Western thought—the study farthest from an *exercising* of philosophy—follows the degradation of remembering to a mere fetching from storage. Ontology as vigilance. It is the mind's eye on guard, protective, defensive. Its positing is necessary to prevent the gnawing away of being by a relativism that severs relations between levels of awareness. The shrinking or receding of being that results from mechanizing the memory function places great stress on ontology. Yet ascension of metaphysics to the throne of philosophy dissolves an obligatory search of subjectivity for what is other in itself. There, metaphysics remains stationed, warding off guerilla attacks—initiated by the same guerillas that conspire with ontology to subvert the attentive concern of Western thought.

From these considerations, it follows that the *formarum dator* of memory cannot be a particular content or remembered contents "in general," for both presuppose a form-giving force. The force charges functional memory with its mission. The charge is not to inform but transform, not to infect with need (since memory already bears the contagion) but to address and be addressed by need. To attend to thought's need undoes the illusion of self-sufficiency and self-determination—that thought can remember history and a-history as well. Memory's striving for totality (which Kant attributes to a transcendental illusion of reason) is thwarted when it hits the root of vulnerability whose trunk is need and whose crown despair. Thought's running sore is that it lacks integrity and must devise a "plan" for integrating itself with "the rest" of subjectivity. The illness transforms thought's retentive habit. The ill know a sorrow that the joyfully vibrant lack. From the knowledge follows a scheme (or schematization) that bestows a new form upon memory since from that point on, memory has purpose: to hold a plan for integration firmly in mind.

Memory takes its proper form whenever one exchanges lethargy for wakefulness. But how does that take place? The one lifts the mantle of Hypnos—one of suppressed suffering—from the other's shoulders and with the other breathes the atmosphere of awareness. Or would it be more precise to say that the mantle lifts in response to a summons? In exchange, the subject is brought back to memory's task: to speak the *arche*-word. Response requires at least a dyad. "Wherever two shall gather in my name, I too shall come." But were there not two to start? Before, the one spoke and the other was mute and dreaming. After, each participated in the primacy of remembering, of re-membering the community of consolation who speak the *I*.

But to shift a dream of power from the other's shoulders, doesn't one take a great risk? And, moreover, a risk that is double? First, there is dismissal, rejection, and misunderstanding that may accompany a return to proximity. The matter of disrupting the functional beat of thought removes one from continuous production of the world-illusion. Furies of autoeroticism whose rage protects the illusion of freedom are poised to attack those who return to the cave after the rupture. Their form of reprisal is to ignite fires of self-advancement that drive the automatism in its ever-constricting circles. It is a break with production that then sears the illusion, which poses the second and greater risk; namely, that one abandon the question of the heart's delay. To lift Hypnos's mantle is delusional in this light. Proximity is viewed as yet another attainment rather than a responsiveness to the inner word. The quest appears as a fantasy as ordinary assignations of meaning quickly assert themselves. Here, one's fidelity is tested, or rather, the lack of a faith in work of memory is reconfirmed. How else is fidelity developed other than through its exercise?

An exchange as an all-important step toward responsibility of the subject, how is its basis to be understood? The basis is not given by substitution that regulates ordinary speaking and replaces one identical with another. Substitution yields a map of synonyms, an orthography of identifications that plots the subject in egocentric space. No one encounters obligation there since the map allows no provision for an obliging force. Yet to require an actual, physical "exchange" of one for the other, as Levinas does, sets the mark in the wrong place.[3] The one who changes places with the other is "hostage" to the other and must be willing "to take the bread from his plate" to feed (or the shirt from his back to clothe) the other. The acts are components of an ethics of martyrdom. One is to be willing to sacrifice the bounty (pleasure, profit, good fortune, strength, reasonableness) of one's position for the sake of occupying that of the impoverished other. On what basis does the one so meet the other? To relieve the other of the slings of misfortune and to see through the other's eyes and inhabit the other's skin, is to readjust the pans of justice. But in the nobility of martyring oneself, are the other's conditions changed, except materially? Which suffering is the other relieved of? To the extent that the martyr is ultimately moved by pity, so is Levinas's thought—a return to a Hellenic ethos in spite of Levinas's Hebraic tendencies.

How does the other suffer? There is material deprivation in which the goods of a life (food, shelter, health, reputation, etc.) have been withheld and hardship inflicted. And there is deficiency in a need to be remembered—in which the contingencies of life's goods are immaterial. The two faces of suffering cannot be interchanged, though they may be worn double. To take the place of the other—removing the shirt on one's back and putting it on the other's—is to answer to the other's material deprivation. The one is even hostage to that, both in the sense of being host (*host*-age) to and obsessed (whose root meaning comes from the same root as *hostage*) with deprivation. But the titanic event per se relieves none of the amnestic suffering, the suffering that robs the other of subjectivity. For the body's and psyche's wounds may play a purpose in bringing the other to remembrance, whose purpose is then negated in the name of comfort. To awaken sensitivity to the need to be remembered, wounds need not first be bathed and bound, but rather the attention animated sufficiently to doff its customary lethargy. For the one to lift the dress of forgetfulness and inject the sting of truth beneath the skin: that is to turn the other cheek to suffering.

The Scathe of Irritability

To rip off the swaddling and expose the raw nerve of obligation: is there not that to the exchange? Far from comfort or rescue, the one delivers the shock of memory to the other like a blow from the *dokusan.* To draw back the helping hand, unleash the scathing tongue, pour salt on the wound, or turn the light off so that the other will stumble about in the dark: these modes describe truth's famous unpalatability. The gift of bread from my plate, moreover, may cloak a dagger, which is the reason that Kant distinguishes acting on the basis of moral feeling from acting in accordance with an unconditional imperative. The former is necessarily hypothetical and heteronomous and mistakes the *telos* of exchange with its inner motive. Exchange inwardly removes *impedimenta* to an unknown responsibility. How exchange outwardly affects the other depends on external conditions and cannot be used as a guide to action. To communicate risk of subjectivity and "choice of oneself" is a task beyond knowledge. Perhaps the matrix of intuition, the maternal guide, the mother's sense of things needed—the mother tongue of the heart—can be invoked.

Whether the gods bless or damn with poverty depends on the story, a poor sage or a poor rogue. Impoverishment masks or reveals. A species of deprivation, persecution, may be drawn to a person as a cloak against responsibility or risk. What does the comfort of changing places with the other then provide? Far from beneficence, it removes the possibility of meeting the ethical meaning of suffering. Deprivation is a surrogate for the task of memory, the impossibility of which is a repeated irritant to the subject, is in a way the subject itself insofar as subjectivity is irritability. Substitution is one identical (deprivation) taking the place of another identical (the task of memory). But the peculiar and peculiarly trying action of exchange concerns a value that has no substitute. Exchange does not replace one thing, being, or entity by another, which is better, realer, or truer. It rather awakens one to the *irreplaceability* of a task that the subject is constantly trying to replace. Exchange awakens the subject to one's forgetting, in forms that *Lethe* assumes: avoidance, elision, erasure, deletion, compensation, deceit. To disrupt lethargy of mind, the one has the other stand forth in nakedness, in the persecution of nakedness. The one is then wakeful witness to the other's wakeful state, now unadorned by habitual impulses of adornment.

To exchange is to bring the subject of memory to the memory of subjectivity. The exchange excites a tremor to the productive arm (and army) of mind that is tensed toward continuity. So it must have felt to Abraham, arm held high with the knife of spiritual achievement. In the tremor, subjectivity does not present itself as a project in time, or even as an eternal project (as Kierkegaard might have thought), since subjectivity does not present itself at all. Something like a recognition of vanity—the vanity of memory's capture of the immemorial—must give rise to urgency. Destined to fail, the very failure breeds the phoenix of triumph by enduring. This is what exchange "remembers." Any real remembering is of the impossibility of "self-remembering." When conjoined with need, exchange opens the subject to forces able to help in the art of memory. To work artfully with the forces is to address the obligation of subjectivity.

Group Memory

Exchange, the upsurging other-than-the-one, has an invisible stipulation. It takes place only in group. This is tantamount to a boundary condition in physics. The condition stipulates that, although not necessarily present, a group of subjects, bound by a common pursuit of the task of memory, surrounds an act of exchange. Exchange is in relation to an initiatic body of knowledge. The group's identity is effective through its call. Since group size, composition, and training are accidental matters, a literal understanding of *group* is not helpful. We can experience an atmosphere that conveys a relation to the memory under study in "places of worship," sacred sites, and ancient "meeting places." Does constancy of purpose or repetition of aim leave a perceivable residue? In terms of its organic form, a group is an organ of speech. A group forms, articulates, and enunciates speech of a higher level that is the provenance of the *arche*-word, *I.* In speaking, the group is re-membered, that is, comes to a moment of understanding the heart's delay and is made whole. In the throes of speech, the group is related to *Mnemosyne,* memory that brings the fire of subjectivity. Each is "warmed" by the heat and moved to respond to the task of remembering.

Re-membered, the group unleashes a dynamism in which the "pitch-torch of wakefulness" is passed from member to member. At the point of transition, it passes from an exclusionary count in which the whole equals the sum of the parts, to an organic count in which the whole is greater than the sum of the parts. As a whole "body," the group awakens to itself and to each member. Awakened, it is properly the intermediary between levels of language and reality. Awakened, it links the productive/constructive mind with the attending one, intentionality with consciousness in-itself, and the automatism with will. If the body of life, the soma, is also thought of as intermediary, the soma is "body" of the group. A given subject's experience of somatic awareness is, from this vantage point, that of a cell in a larger body. A subject does not *have* somatic awareness but rather participates in an exchange whose outcome yields that. The truth of the fact persists even when awareness arises without any apparent group activity. In such a case, it is not correct to think that the group is virtual because it possesses the same substance as a congress of persons but "at a distance." How could it be that upon awakening, one finds oneself in isolation? To awaken is to awaken a sense of belonging and so, to find oneself awakened not only *with* but *in* the other.

How the automatism, its dominion over the body, and the circulation of memory, all relate provides a central focus of group dynamics. As the shroud of sleep lifts and the body receives an impression of consciousness in-itself, the subject undergoes a shift from the one-for-the-one to the other-in-the-one. Machinations of self-love, in which autoerotic objects of desire create the time needed to obtain them, subside. The objects represent the peculiar illusion of autonomy by which the subject "legislates" rules of order for its life. The children of the one-for-the-one (regardless of altruistic or empathetic postures) each strive only to realize themselves. Self-love, or the autoerotic, has an intimate connection with self-realization. In fact, the ethics of self-realization makes autonomy attractive as a position. In sharp contrast, to stop the functional beat of thought is repellent to desire and to the desire for self-realization. To surrender a body defined by concept and theory to the kinesthetic flow and to yield to the force of life carries an apprehension of the unknown. No pleasure of realization occurs when desire momentarily lets go the reins. What takes place when there is a question about pleasure? Through proximity, memory of that which is other than desire is rekindled. That which is the other, which exerts itself perpetually in poverty of self, commands an obedience to its summons. In the movement is found the other-than-the-one.

Other than desire, other than immortalizing the realized one, subjectivity is nourished through a meeting in which the other never succumbs. The other submits to the meeting but is never met. Nor is the lack of encounter a failing on the subject's part or cause for self-recrimination. Or, to put the matter another way, to have met the other *per impossibile* would mean to have become the other, thereby committing an act of betrayal. The peculiar folly dogs all approaches of absorption, whereby the subject is subsumed entirely under the category of the eternal. Is there here a disguised loathing for incarnate form, a meeting "under the skin," in the fold of the soma? Or a fear of disrupting the insular self, for the group convenes as the "body-image" breaks up and yields to the invocation of proximity? The other—who may or may not be my neighbor, my fellow citizen, my boss, my enemy—meets me "in" the kinesthetic flow as a fellow subject. This is no project of constructing a neighbor or citizen out of the "sense-data" of my experience—which may preclude any meeting. But if the two of us are in exchange, then we both awaken to the solicitation of the soma and its communication of the heart's delay. In the speech, neither of us utters a word of our own but both of us share the burden of articulating the *arche*-word, *I*. To root out a mute tongue and to exclaim *this* word revitalizes (as nothing else can) the movement that is subjectivity.

Intersubjectivity

Memory of the immemorial is intersubjective (Marcel).[4] It belongs to no subject, but rather, the subject belongs to it as it wends a way in the interstice between subjects. To regain a sense of belonging, the subject must relinquish a memory that is personal. Is this a difficult result for those who consider memory as of the subject? Is it not I who remember myself? A consideration of the event shows otherwise. When the subject is on its quest for subjectivity, memory permeates retentive (and protentive) tendencies of thought to summon one back from the isolation of autointoxication. These tendencies enrapture a subject with a sheath of "personal memory," an autobiographical account of desire. History is a narrative comprised of triumphs or failures to attain the object. In the account, memory of the immemorial roves beyond the pale, a marauder. In an enclave safe from risks of subjectivity, in a historiography, the one-for-the-one is secured—and imprisoned. Outside the pages, between one page and the next, an unscripted memory is ever ready to undo the text, the one-for-the-one, and consciousness for-itself.

Fugitive memory is one of limits, off limits, and from the far side of limits. Its limits, as Kant shows, are not established by the productive mind, but invoked by the mind's anxiety over the boundless, bounding memory. Exposing thought's impulse to limit (as Kant does in the transcendental illusion),[5] the subject in proximity is more receptive to subliminal penetration, to that which attacks borders and subverts liminal regions.

Not of the subject, memory of subjectivity is intersubjective in the way that amniotic fluid is not of the embryo. The memory is that in which each subject is embryonically immersed. Subjectivity is a shared subject (the way the air is) and belongs to neither the one nor the other but to both. Sharing subjectivity, the awakening memory passes back and forth, to and fro, as it makes its circulation. Although it circulates in proximity, through somatic awareness, and is shared in and by a group, such memory needs to be incarnate in a single subject if it is to be remembered *as subjectivity. The fact of subjectivity is its incarnation of memory.* The event of incarnation is not incarnation of *my* body, the possessive of objectification. It is rather of the soma in me, an inner body whose action disrupts thought and embodies consciousness in-itself. It is the voice of proximity and proximity is approximated through ordinary speech only when the subject's body is involved—when voice box actually speaks. The intersubjective, even impersonal, character of subjectivity puts the subject repeatedly at odds with a search for what lies beyond essence. Were it not for the enigmatic character of the voice, the subject would have no reason to accept contradictory conditions of truth.

Emanating from an unknown source within the immemorial, memory of subjectivity, intersubjectivity per se, ceaselessly violates borders of a subject's mind—like an obsession. Yet it invites synthesis in spite of thought's refusal of the other. Although thought attempts to capture it, the intersubjective proves immune to captivity and (unlike an obsession) cannot be owned. The thwarting of ownership provides a double lesson on the will. That a fugitive memory continues to defy thought demonstrates thought's unwillingness to accommodate itself to the other. But does not the back of the seam reveal, in the progressive acceptance of unwillingness, an inability to further will (as distinguished from autoerotic impulses), and so erode resistance to and shape receptivity to the other? *To will is to be obedient to the fact of intersubjectivity.* Disobedience, conversely, is the refusal of intersubjectivity. This is to say, memory proper in me is related to the other's memory (as is the other's to mine) and unless awakening the other is an aspect of my effort of remembering, conditions defeat me. The sobering thought that I am my brother's keeper means that vigilance toward the other's torpor is as required as toward my own, if I grasp for a fuller comprehension of "remembering oneself." The re-membered self is an impersonal group that includes both of us and does not even exclude the principle of exclusion, the one-for-the-one. Indeed, unless the one-for-the-one, substitution, and the automatism are included, the grouping is not an intermediary, which is to say, not a group at all.

Formal Cause

The group is the organ of memory. Memory of the heart's delay impresses itself upon the organ as formal cause or *dator formarum* of the act of remembering or *noesis*. The formal cause in medieval logic is also called the species because it takes a generic cognitive possibility and specifies the kind of cognition that takes place. The formal cause, as *intentum,* also constitutes the kind of cognition that the organ is having, or *intentio.* Thus, the group in its act of remembering expresses a unique intention that is specifically different from every other act. Informed by memory and performing the noetic act of remembering, the group serves the kind of memory by *pre*serving it. In subjects' continuing vulnerability to the other, a group *preserves* memory of a need to be remembered—to be whole and wholly available to the holy. Disparate persons in a moment embody a group—and are related to the group body—when impressed with the need to be remembered. In the incarnation lies the mystery of exchange and its gift of renewal. The contact between memory and the group's proximity opens both to a resurgence of fresh energies. Is not the distance from a personal, autoerotic memory clear? Only in a deficient sense is preservation that of a relic or a museum piece. In its efficient phase, memory maintains the vitality of a highly perishable life whose pulse indicts our negligence and summons in response a circulation of articulated intelligence.

Preservation of memory by dynamic exchange dispels once and for all the notion that memory is of the past, the old, the already decayed. The restricted notion derives the thought construction in which the past must be retained as past in order for the "functional beat" to temporize its constructions. Here is where Kant held that conception is spontaneity, but always and only in the matrix given by "inner sense."[6] Thought is incapable of dematerializing the matrix and interrupting time. The ceaseless narrative of a history replaces an organic vulnerability in search of renewed vitality. Just where time must have a stop, where novel energies inject themselves into critical conditions, memory refuses its relation to what is present and becomes degraded and insular. Historical narrative that tells of the ego's erotic conquests tends toward absolutism. Temporally, it retreats to an immemorial time, the time before any present time and need. A memory without need, even if boundless, is a memory strangely sealed off from concerns of subjectivity, a funerary memory. It is absolute in being absolutely closed to any expression of its power. Since its absolutism is that of being absolutely without need, it is absolutely needless. With such memory, there is no word of the heart and possibly no heart.

By means of actualizing the potency that is a group and "removing the shackles" from the organ, memory is awakened in proximity of subjects who accordingly strive to meet the need to be remembered. Through their striving, the awakening memory is revivified to the extent that the group is actualized. The latter is a process of stages and degrees. But no matter at how preliminary a phase, the group returns the gift that it has received. The summons, spoken initially at a higher level, eventually finds an obedient response at a lower level of language, in which coarser forms of expression generally occlude the call. By this route, the word of the heart is brought to the world. Object, thought, substitution, the identity of identicals: all are momentarily dissolved and in the amniotic solution become particles of a living body. The somatic body, a living order of memory, is related ordinally to body conceived by thought. The latter is the first body, born of earth and the other three elements. The former is the second body, born of the fifth element, the quintessence. In proximity, through the second or memory body, the actualizing force of immemorial time is rejuvenated through contact with the one-for-the-one.

Need on a higher level becomes necessity on the lower. What we understand as a summons is, on the level of its origination, an expression of a need to be remembered, an exposure to vulnerability. It is a heartfelt expression of self-remembering. The need, broadcast across the interval of delay, becomes an imperative for the subject. Subjective necessity is obligation To the extent that the subject feels the need as its own, rather than as an externally imposed precept, it joins in the original meaning as spoken.

Organization

The group as an organ whose potency is actualized by an informing memory, is, as the root meaning of *organ* tells us, a tool. But as a tool, the group is not merely a means to an end, a means to infuse memory of the immemorial into the realm of distraction and lethargy. The means encompasses only a downward arc of return. An upward arc involves, as we saw, rejuvenation of a need to be remembered, a fresh exposure of the vulnerability of *Mnemosyne* to the force of her pale twin *Lethe.* The repeated dis-membering of memory's need for integration, its amnesia with respect to a work for wholeness, is precisely what must be countered in the reverse trajectory. A repetitive thrust into proximity is the dynamic of proximity itself, through which dismemberment is recalled and repaired. Sensation of the ascending arc is a language in which *organ* also gives rise to the word *work.* In its originary sense, *work* refers to the group's obligation to restore integrity to the fundamental need of re-collecting memory of the immemorial. Work devolves from the mystery of exchange and the reciprocal passage of consciousness from the greater to the lesser and back again. Work concerns the pre-servation of memory, that is, service to memory of the immemorial before all else.

From the self-same source of meaning (*werg-*) as *organ* and *work,* another important aspect of a group arises. This is contained in the idea of a secret rite or worship. To preserve the need to be remembered, the group responds in proximity to a summons. Through inner sensation, the word of the heart is communicated to the collective subject of the group. An attentiveness commanded by the speaking is properly a "reverence for language." The long-sought-after responsibility to subjectivity is in the last analysis a matter of wonder and awe that obliges the subject to be within hearing of the heart's speech. That such impulses cannot be commanded in any ordinary way is obvious in their synchronistic nature. They are not deeds accomplished on command. Yet they are commanded of a subject by a voice not subject to conditions of being human. To heed the command is to attend to the speech of what is higher. Conversely, to fail to heed is to be subject to the awful judgment on a deficient heart.

Preserving memory, *work,* belongs to an organization of groups, an organ of organs. Hierarchically ordered, an organization is called a school. Schools provide channels through which contents of a memory of the immemorial may pass. Keepers of the mystery of exchange and the enigma of return, schools guard against the lethargic tendencies of mind through the practice of a "reverence for language." Yet there is no special speech and the rules of common usage are adhered to. The unsaid may be expressed proximally even through a banal utterance. A rare attentiveness can discern the heart's delay even in the commonplace. The *raison d'être* of a school is to guard against the force of distortion with respect to such knowledge. A school is thus the repository of "lost" knowledge since it concerns itself with a time that has never been present. A school is resident where what is missing is placed and given a place. In its knowledge of mortality and beyond, a school addresses the subject of actualizing subjectivity, and if authentic, conveys the summons of the heart. In its knowledge of vulnerability, a school invokes the subject's need to enter a work in reach of memory. In both aspects, a school is bulwark against deterioration and degeneracy of the heart's word.

Chapter Eight
The Guide

Hermes commanded his son to sow gold, that living rains might ascend from it.

—Aurora Consusrgens

Retardation of Guidance

The one who lags behind seems to be a follower subservient to the one who goes ahead, the guide. Eurydice trails after Orpheus as they leave the dark, unseen realm and in a similar position Lot's wife moves behind Lot as they leave the purgatory of Sodom. Because each partner flees the underworld (*Hades,* "the invisible realm," shares the same root as *guide*), we are presented with a reversed image of the event, a page *in verso.* The inversion may not be obvious until we recall that Orpheus had pursued Eurydice to the land of the dead, which, like the mirror's tain, transposes right for left and forward for backward. When we take reversal into account, that the laggard is the real guide does not seem unusual. The one at a slower pace marches with a fuller, wider perception. There, but not in the forward position, one can see the other. Eurydice or Lot's wife is more capable of perceiving direction and avoiding mishap and is, therefore, the one who in reality guides. The guide moves from behind and despite difficult communication with the forward member directs the procession toward its destination, toward a freedom of movement.

This is a good piece of deduction. It reminds us of two things: that a quicker pace does not, despite appearances, delegate one as guide, and that guidance in the ethical derives from a tempo so retarded that even an indefinite amount of time would not suffice to bring it up to the forward tempo. The retardation is such that, as Zeno proves, given as many days and years as are countable, no lessening of difference would take place. Difference is irremediable. Separating foremost and rearmost, dawning and twilight, an intervening interval forbids their commensurability. Having passed backward from the time of mortality, Eurydice as guide inhabits an earlier time, *in illo tempore,* a time never present to thought's time, anarchaic time. The mode in which she expresses her guidance, her utterance, is enigma. Her speaking is self-referential and opaque. It is the speaking of the secret delay, yet because she speaks to her mortal beloved, her words are simultaneous with their references and point to backward time. Orpheus's mind cannot decipher her and is mired in formulae. When the anxiety of the *aporia* drives him to heed a desperate thought, he turns his head in the forbidden direction—and loses his guide and himself. The story is a parable of the heart's utterance across the interval of delay. The summons comes in disruption's voice, bold or subtle but always enigmatic and exceptional. Unnerving the one whose pace leaps ahead with the speed of thought, its speech stands in need of an inter-preter, or else one remains frozen by the Gorgon. That the guidance of the guide falls on deaf ears without an intermediary, a go-between, is at once the dilemma of the heart's delay and the evocation of one's task to remember the immemorable interval.

The awful temptation of Orpheus: there are other ways to describe his ordeal. Take the one that Kant deploys. For him, thought's regulative principle mandates the mind's continuous productivity, an automatism that can permit no break in operation without relinquishing its authority. Regulative principles in general are rules for the totalization of totalities in the objective world. As the rubric implies, they rule thought, primarily neither by the content produced nor by the die that stamps the content, its form (a constitutive principle) but by ensuring nonstop production. That no discontinuity disturbs the totality that is "the world" is a result of a regulative principle—"a principle of the greatest possible continuation and extension of experience, allowing no empirical limit to hold as absolute," which exists "for the purpose of bringing systematic unity into our knowledge."[1] The principle is at work in avoidance, deletion, erasure, and elision of disharmony in thought's functional beat—as if it were a lash in the eye during silent prayer. A slight threat of interruption in productivity activates the regulatory mechanism to move attentiveness and concern away from the irritation, to select, "safe" areas, and thereby to forestall breakdown. Simultaneously, since the mechanism lies beyond "possible experience," it does not disclose itself. Through regulation, incursion into the objective world by a "nonobjective factor" is not perceived. So too nonrecognition of the nonobjective is not recognized. Thus does the regulative principle cloak its operation in the colors of dusk (when Minerva's owl throws off sleep) to throw thought off the scent of its trail. Perhaps only, as Kant argues, when regulation speaks out, turns speculative, and drives thought in a "metaphysical" direction does it reveal its concealed intent. But his conclusion itself is speculation.

Orpheus is faced with a terrifying dilemma. He is drawn to heed his beloved and yet at the same time, she exerts a destabilizing force on his thought. He wishes to obey her yet must seek confirmation of what she asks. The contradiction is apparent only from his vantage point. From hers, given the regulative principle's strong hold on the subject, Eurydice must first deregulate the automatism. An order so tenaciously affirmed by thought must yield to a radical incompleteness. Only in that way can a new order be engendered. The fissure, the maw of chaos or whatever name we attach to the disordering force, is peril to her lover. It flares up like dragon's fire and instantaneously reduces his mind to ash. The dissolution overwhelms him. Why? It applies extreme pressure to a correspondence theory of truth since it reveals the deficiency of a univocal assignation of meaning—that which thought assumes to be "the truth." Signification constructed so that the subject identifies with identicals means that the subject continuously remains one and the same, a cinematic illusion created by an endless repetition of a single still. By the artifice of continuity, the subject's singular truth is vouchsafed. Orpheus remains Orpheus, the self-made, self-perceived singer of song. The fissure changes all that. To fission is to give entry to not only the dragon's breath but its voice, the enigmatic voice of dissimulation. To let that be heard, Fury or Fate ready to enact justice, but a justice inhuman in its exactness: that is risk. In risk, in fission, in the momentary separation of one from the other—a momentary collapse of the identity of identicals—does the subject return to proximity and search out the humble passage toward responding. Orpheus ceases to be magical singer but rejoins the other-in-himself. This is his single hope of regaining Eurydice.

The Seal of Untruth

With regard to Orpheus's temptation, is there a "special" approach to rupture and risk that takes his proclivity for an illusory continuity into account? That accords his organization of the world with a legitimacy while still demanding its dissolution? Here, we are asking how the injection of equivocity into the subject's "regulation" of reality can thaw the lockjaw of literalism. For continuity is fundamentally maintenance of thought's self-identity—that product(ion) defines *self*—and once the identity of identicals proves to be disingenuous, the world is stopped. It would seem an ancient approach to "seal" within belief a certain deceptive matter which, when the belief is unsealed, serves to break apart the *cogito.* Because of the act of sealing, I would call the practice *hermetic* and that force released by the unsealing, *hermetic force.*

Deployment of hermetic force has always been a guarded secret because of its potency in antidoting autoeroticism and desire. Unstoppered hermetic force, in its blinding recognition of duplicity and distortion, brings a sudden shift from univocity to equivocity—as if the eye begins to see the back of things and the ear catch the voice that does not speak. When "the veil falls," hermetic force defies the subject to take up old themes once again. In their familiar places, clothes, melodies, books, and handshakes have turned to ash. In the beauty or terror of the remains, in tracing their outlines, memory is deregulated, a cosmic dimension restored. The *dis*-identification—the breakdown of substitution, I for object, object for I—sees unlikeness where likeness was assumed. In the central case, I am unlike the one I took myself to be. Primordially, *I was deceived.* The deception was self-deception. To unmake it, I must become responsible. While the subject undergoes a trial of recognition, Hermes stands witness for the prosecution. I am accused of setting identical equal to identical. Grave, poignant, disturbing, unremitting, Hermes the psychopomp, stands ready, with his cruel smile, to transport the one to "the invisible realm," Hades.

What is the specific action of hermetic force? We can try to approach it through an analogy. Take the familiar case of seeing through a *trompe l'oeil.* At first, one sees a bowl of grapes partially hidden by a curtain. The wind seems to be lifting the fabric to reveal some fruit inside. Afterward, one sees a picture made to look like a bowl of grapes. The curtain is pulled from one's eyes and the sudden shift discloses an illusion. But the gasp of revelation is a mere flicker of dragon's fire that flares when pictorial deceit is hermetically unsealed, for the ground of being is barely fazed by such optical trickery. Destabilization is minimal because the optical field, not the field of self, is affected. Aesthetic illusion belongs to an order different from the ethical, so we must not be misled by the analogy. Shucking the illusory self is not the same as shucking an illusory oyster shell. The former encroaches on the organ of perception more totally than does the latter. When the scales drop from the I engulfed by an ethical illusion, the subject is reduced to moral anxiety. It is not too obvious to say that *moral* contains *mora,* the delay. One is subject to moral anxiety because *I have forgotten again.* One has forgotten the guide is in the rear, spatially and temporally, and that the word of the heart is uttered across an infinitesimal divide that separates response from muteness. To the one who has lost the way, anxiety over the delay speaks in proximity, for the body suffers an apprehension of no longer fitting its skin. Proximally, the body can bear not looking back at phenomena—Orpheus's temptation—and heed the given direction. That which leads away from phenomena, back to subjectivity, is the escape route from ordinal and ordinary properties assigned to things. The escape is marked by fire from an alembic dragon, and the escapee is tortured and singed. In any escape accorded by delay, the primordial question of subjectivity prosecutes the subject as no matter of art's illusions can. By the tongues of flames, as in the Heraclitean "death by fire," the fissile character of self-image and its autointoxication is slowing and inexorably combusted.

The transition from mind construction to somatic intermediary to the heart's word is the pathway of hermetic force. Awareness of the force holds a double action. It is the light shed by the dragon's fire and also the reading by that light of the transformed material, an augury on the charred entrails of the beast. One can call the awareness *hermetic.* Like Hermes or Thoth, the archetype of inner revaluation, it does mischief to the autonomous, spontaneous play of representation, breaking production of form, deforming the time-dimension. Intervention also occurs in a double way. Hermes appears both as a player on the stage of desire and autoeroticism and as a force that materializes to stop the play action. Having initially exerted itself, hermetic awareness goes on to interpret the residue of the momentary destabilization of the regulative principle, when the sum of the parts ceases to equal the whole. If a language of totality and objectification is expressive of the principle, then the new awareness points to a language of fragmentation and exception. How does a speech of fragment and uniqueness come about? Listen to how Hermes speaks against the designations of the automatism and commends them to the crucible and flame. There they will be subjected to the heat of transformation. Only the most intense combustion of elements—fission—can yield new matter, *prima materia.* Meanings automatically assigned to phenomena there acquire novel properties, and following the hermetic force, become the philosopher's stone, that which willingly responds to the summons of the immemorial. Thus does Hermes sow gold so that living rains may ascend!

In Apology for Deceit

> We know how to tell many believable lies,
> But also, when we want to, how to speak the plain truth.
>
> —Theogony[2]

Deceit, untruth, duplicity, delusion, prevarication, lie: what value do these vile offspring of *Lethe* hold for a summons to responsibility that the subject draws in with its first breath? Why should the daughters of Memory—the Muses—give birth to misshapen, devilish creatures? One has only to look at how they unsettle univocal assignation, with its strong alliance to literal meaning and a correspondence theory of truth. For truth and univocity, word corresponds to object and object to word as one identical substituted for another, *x* for *x.* The law of the excluded middle defines a domain in which univocity reigns as absolute. Truth is a light that discloses phenomena as either a *this* or a *that* but not both. But the lighting of disclosure itself conceals (or plays at concealment!) a moral attitude, namely, that equivocation and imprecision are failings. To speak "out of both sides of one's mouth" or "blur the lines" violates a literalism of meaning and in turn draws a violation, often violently enforced. What deep insecurity gives rise to the fantastic (and fanatic) position? To grasp the rigoristic attitude toward duplicity, conceive the correspondence theory of truth as a large planetary body and each deceitful act, a small stone. The gigantic gravitational force exerted by planet inexorably pulls stone to its surface and effectively masks the reciprocal tug that stone exerts on planet. But the rigorist calculates the minute effect too. He feels that each lie tugs upon monolithic truth and threatens to pull it out of orbit—hence the guardedness about even white lies. The lie evokes fear of moving in a new orbit, and he refuses to believe that in fear lies the beginning of wisdom. It is for *Sophia,* a nickname of *Mnemosyne,* that the Muses speak many lies.

Under further scrutiny, does not moral rejection of deceit offer an apology for retentive memory? The implacable will that holds that a lie is evil under any circumstances expresses an extreme disregard for inclusion and an extreme concern for self-protection. The innocence, harmlessness, sweetness, lack of consequence, even courteousness of lies appears humane in contrast with the razor-sharp line. What provokes such wariness? Could a warp of deceit unravel the objectivity of the world-picture? The skein that binds the subject's autonomy, its autoeroticism, and its self-coincidence can likewise be snipped in two. It is cunning that knows deceit discovered equals discrepancy. The noncongruence of the subject with itself is a door open to its various simulations. Thus *Hermes duplex,* Deceit's double edge, hones anxieties of the functional beat of thought with regard to possible disruption, and so restores the subject to proximity through which the other speaks. Duping itself turns truth against truth and brings forth the golden seed of memory. Hermes, born of the Muses, duplicitous, dual, and deceptive, seed sower of a dangerous truth, an antitruth—or rather, an ante-truth. Hermes, born into a time prior to Apollonian reason, before phenomena, before truth *versus* falsehood., is child of lies and speaks no other than his pedigree. He is not offended by moral disapprobrium and caters to no standard when speaking his mind.

Deceit, perilous act of duplicity, uses fraudulent means to achieve an end and to trick one into belief. But belief itself, is it not also trickery? In the rich tradition that Plato inherits, belief is induced by phenomena and labors toward the false birth of pretension. Belief as arrogance of conviction. Belief as cherished self-possession. Belief tricks the subject into believing in a self-concept, or rather, that the self is a concept and nothing other. More precisely, belief is lure of the self-concept, a scent that tempts the subject into dissimulation, a magnetism that draws the subject into dissembling. Belief is exuded by the self (as protection is), an intoxicant distilled from the waters of *Lethe* that grants the subject its dream of substantiality. Belief is mere belief.

The conceptual manifold reinforces the delusion in ten thousand ways, for once the world becomes a concept, the equation of "self equals world" is true. To attribute nobility to a lie is to hint at how the lie turns belief against itself, using deceit to trick deceit. In the seamless realm of phenomena is thought's delusion concerning its own nature and function, and all beliefs that spring from thought's regard reinforce dissimulation. So long as thought is the same reproducing the same, it remains supremely heedless of the fundamental functional rhythm. The subject's credulousness is an effect of a hormone secreted by retentive memory. A belief-system justifies a need to retain data, information, and knowledge in the storeroom of the mind—and hence justifies a whole collection of allied faculty, problematics, pragmatics, explanation, criticism, evaluation, justification itself. The chicanery of belief dupes the subject into two fundamental errors, the second mother of the first: the subject thinks that its thoughts disclose the world and thinks that disclosure is the avenue of subjectivity itself.

From the fact that *conception* and *deception* share a common root (in *capere),* much follows for a study of the duplex of duplicity. For here is the duplex in action. In the play of representations of autonomous thought is an ingenuity that sustains our credulity and yet at each point we can become incredulous. The genius casts a spell over the mind's automatism and creates an anxiety to retain and project items of cognitive production. The duplex comes out in the fact that, by design, the spell is not entirely irreversible. The "artist" is restrained from exercising complete control since that is impossible. Come a fateful slip and the play is seen through, and Oedipus aware of his own wounds ceases *in the moment* to bow to the power of his mind. The new awareness, the duplex, is reason hidden in reasoning beyond all reasonableness. It uncoils at the speed of instinct to bite the handler: the essence of hermetic recognition. In the bite, retentive memory relaxes unto death and the play of autonomy exposed through a mortal wound. In a return to the flesh, kinesthesis, proximity of the other, response arises. In recognizing the mind's deception, the subject is seized by a responsibility that it never agreed to. Vulnerability incites the need to be remembered.

The viperous ways of the force mirrors and masks a curious relation that cure bears to disease. Hermes, inventor of medicine, is a homeopath who knows "Like cures like." Cure results from contact with that which is other than disease but is necessitated by proximity to disease. Difficult means are necessitated by the fact that infinite ease—that which is other than disease—cannot be directly solicited. Through the presence of a mysterious *tertium dator,* the combat of likeness with likeness yields a fissure through which the force of unlikeness can appear. Even a momentary advent of the force equilibrates the subject, according to a balance that antedates any imbalance. By virtue of unlikeness, homeopathy assures us, delusion is not incorrigible and the subject recalled to a responsibility not incurred by any agreement or choice. The debt, however, has no mitigation and no treatment has power to cure the fundamental condition of indebtedness.

Belief

In Hesiod's rendition, the Muses herald speaking the truth by speaking believable lies. Modern ears take the theme for poetic license, the play of poet with the literal meaning of things. But ours is an anachronistic reading of a responsibility that Hesiod knew to be far more grave. To speak the truth with the help of lies is the special office of Muse-inspired work. For the poet was Hermes' persona and, therefore, psychopomp incarnate, guide to the path of subjectivity and its terrifying cloak of responsibility. It is the dangerous knowledge of hermetic deceit that the Muses declare. Deceptions whose charms break the listener open and split the deaf ear to let fall the inner word, speaking within speaking, are special powers of the Muses's office. Poetic conceit, illusory drama and passion, the chant of waves and sirens: these poetic functions came long after forgetfulness blunted the Muses's function, not until the time of Simonides. The original power of veracity—truth telling—arises in the double ("duplex") action of inducing false belief as true, then ripping away the blinders. There is desire and the far side of desire. There is seduction, luring thought toward an object of desire, beguiling the subject's autoeroticism. Then there is the sting of truth, awakening to the lie that the subject itself has grasped. For in order that the lie be believable, the subject must have snapped up the lure and swallowed it. Exploitation of credulousness permits the Muses to awaken the subject from the world dream and restore its vulnerability to the task of memory. Credulity is the preamble to the text of responsibility.

What is the full practice? As true daughters of *Mnemosyne,* the Muses specialize in deceptive or false memory, error disguised as a truly remembered time. Injected into thought and retained by the subject, deceits are designed to mislead the subject about the past, cultural and psychological. Thoughts, images, and narratives of unreal events enter into a self-concept and maintain the substitution of identicals for identicals. Since the subject *is* that with which it identifies, such memories—both personal and cultural—exert a huge influence on the automatism. They constitute nothing more nor less than a fallacious history, a narrative deftly distorted by the Muses. This one tells itself the story of a blissful childhood that contained no traumatic events—though it did. That one thinks of an influence as a young adult—but it was otherwise. The other one thinks of having had likes and dislikes—but other than what it had. And so on. Implantation of deceitful memories follows a hermetic strategy: lure the autoeroticism into belief until the time to undergo the ordeal of judgment and responsibility. The seeds ripen into a bitter fruit whose taste reminds one of that which has been held at arm's length, beyond the perimeter of life, of a procrastination, a delay. Therein resounds the summons of the heart and the suffering of subjectivity to respond.

Can the subject know the cause of its suffering? This is an ancient conundrum. The subject suffers from not knowing the cause, yet once known, cause and suffering both vanish. That desires of the represented self, the ego, the *ahamkhara,* must be suffered is given in a general way. The reason is that which speaks in proximity, through the flesh, can be heard only through the medium of suffering, just as sound requires a material medium. Inasmuch as deceptive memory helps maintain the automatism, the subject is cast into purgatory. Memories lull discernment and activate autoeroticism, fueling the subject's illusions of freedom. Deceptive memory, morbid or pleasurable, also serves an economy of the *cogito* by distracting awareness from the exertion of retention. Autoeroticism reduces expenditure otherwise given to anxiety over the relentless pace of production, its automatic character, and the lack of presence of a higher command. Reminiscence, daydream, reverie, fantasy, free association: are means to provide drama or tedium, spice or blandness, to distract from thought's apprehensive outlook. As we know, success is only partial since anxiety oozes through the cracks in time. Even with sublime deceit, subliminal pain arises—and grows purgative. This the Muses serve.

The Middle Voice of Guiding

What act is the reciprocal to being guided? It is a question that can help us arrive what subjectivity requires of itself. The reciprocal cannot be simply "guiding," as if the active voice can substitute for the passive one, and the page of guidance turned to its back side. This is not possible because guide and his Dante are secretly one, like cure and disease, and that in the dyad, the roles are interchangeable. To guide and to be guided are not opposites at all but mutually presuppose one another. Leading and following are twin manifestations of one and the same process, the movement to proximity. Hermes corresponds to an awakened aspect of the subject ready to respond to the task of memory. The dormant, resistant aspect, the follower, trudges behind, weighed down by machinations of the automatism. There is an analogy to truth-telling. Truth is not opposed to lying but includes believable lies that delude the subject in order that it may suffer their eventual implosion. The one who believes lies is being primed for the traumatic event. Such is the nature of compassion, in its ability to inflict pain for the sake of awakening the mind to remember.

The problem is clarified when we remember who follows whom. Eurydice, the laggard, actually leads the procession from her rearward position while Orpheus, who heads it, obeys her guidance. The alignment emphasizes the intrinsic vulnerability of the subject. Orpheus's guide is not visible, outside of his field of vision, and therefore not susceptible to his scrutiny. Guided from behind, Orpheus must place trust in proximity, in sensitivity, in whose flesh of his flesh is writ the summons of the heart. Such writing does not record an "event," nor the appearance of a phenomenon whose meaning can be determined in accordance with the regulatory principle of the understanding, nor the identity of an object that is identical with the identity of the subject, nor as a univocal or nonequivocal assignation. Such writing is akin to that which suddenly appears on the wall in a strange tongue, saying *Mene, mene, tekkel upharsin,* which leaves signification hanging in the air, a catch in one's throat. What is its source? What does it want? How am I to respond? Is it to be trusted? The guide wields an unremitting probe into the interior of the subject, a goad applied beyond limits of consciousness, not merely the subject's contemporary state of consciousness, but beyond all possible states of consciousness. The disposition to be guided is attacked from within, with the vehemence of a fanatic whose utterances for all their foreignness evoke a deep anxiety. The guide who decapitates the body of knowledge, severing brain from trunk and pumping the heart dry, leaves the capability of receiving guidance in such disrepair that only courage—beyond trust in thought—can return the subject to itself and permit one step toward following.

Torn between guiding and being guided, the middle voice of a forgotten inflection speaks of *seeking guidance.* Without hidden opposition, no exchange occurs between the one and the other. In Orpheus's case, the delusion that he is the guide, the other, precludes his seeking guidance. Orpheus is deaf to the middle voice. Only when a suspicion that Eurydice is lost grows unbearable does his pretension weaken. Then giving into his temptation and facing a forbidden direction, he is enlarged enough to beseech the guide. Invisible, a mere whisper, Eurydice again has become an indication. And Orpheus, who tragically cannot read, turns his back on that which he sought to regain—his way.

Chapter Nine
Resurrection of the Flesh

Irritability

Subjectivity is repetitive confinement and its attendant irritability. Forced into a skin too tight for itself, subjectivity bursts open through the seams and pores . . . to find itself encased in a new, larger skin still sizes too small. Fissure and containment are the restive phases of subjective life, an alternation between flesh and subtle body. Pulled out by the automatism and the world-idea, proximity retracts and becomes armored. Released by the automatism, the subject moves within as vital energy, an *elan vital,* that is as natural as the kinaesthetic flux. But irritability is much more than a biological reaction to stimulus, the way the skin when repeatedly rubbed becomes irritated and causes a painful sensation. If this aspect exhausted irritability's meaning, subjectivity would be a tropism. Although the root of irritability moves through the reactive emotion of anger (*ira,* Latin), it does not draw sustenance from there. Even if anger is stripped of its vicious connotations and given an epistemological function (as Achilles' anger provides a directive for his thought—and affects the tempo of the automatism in a fundamental way), still irritability's root goes deeper. Its source lies in that which is "suffused with the passion of the holy," in the Greek *hieros.* Irritability's passionate connection with the divine enables the subject to endure an inert, resistant, constrained condition of the epidermis and to work toward release. Irritability is at the point of being between, a sensation of the intermediary abraded on two sides and is always rubbed the wrong way. Irritability is the way two opposing impulses meet, irresolvably and without reconciliation, "being opposite, and nothing else, and always opposite."

Subjectivity presses against the skin from the inside. The subject, having been given skin too small, is irritability itself. It is the restlessness of the subject's trying to make room for itself; formication. The motility of irritability is desire, the autoerotic. The source of irritability is passionate concern with the whole, the holy—which is to say, nondesire. Irritability is the very tension of being pulled in two opposing directions, which results in too tight a cover for the body. Desire as restlessness, Locke notices.[1] Its outward form, motility, is aggressive. Thought in the service of desire is, therefore, aggression. The trope of cognition-as-wrath is given in the opening scene of the first Western epic text, the *Iliad,* in the character of Achilles, in the train of whose anger follows the military campaign of the entire Trojan War. Contrasted with desire is nondesire. Nondesire undoes the catharsis that desire finds in its object by retracing the irritability to its source. The source or mouth speaks in words of thorn. These lodge under the skin and prick from the inside, and after time become reminders of the debt owed by the very fact of breathing. Difficult, disconsolate speech is foreign to the *cogito* but understood immediately by the bruteness of body. The thorn of conundrum, the fester of pain that arises when not-wanting surfaces within desirous blood, summons the way that death does—not through thought but through an organic apprehension of embodied life.

The apprehension knows embodied life not only as limitation (the necrosis of animal tissue) but also as limitlessness. It is true that death delimits flesh and brings agony to ambition, the desire of desire. Death defines "the limit of everything known" and brings mourning to the possessor of knowledge. The far side of death, the vacant site that thought cannot occupy, is limitless but bounded, a noneuclidean space. And the act of mourning, which weeps and wails because of vacancy, stems from the selfsame root of remembrance as delay since *mourn* derives from the Sanskrit *smer,* as in the sacred texts the *smrti,* "that which is to be remembered." Tears of mourning at death's visit at the same time recall the heart's delay. They are both flood and rainbow, promise vouchsafed by the divine. Like a rainbow, the heart's utterance is late in coming and an occasion for sorrow, but its secret meaning is not. For the secret of the delay of the heart has to do not with death but with deathlessness. Just as death sings agony over the desire of desire, so too the heart's word is a song of joy over the death of death. "Death, thou canst not die" is, as a thought, exactly wrong. Initiation into the heart's secret, which concerns delay, brings liberation from death—in the fullest measure possible to a creature of an undying creation.

Pressure from the inside, irritability attacking not the object of desire but its objectification, attacking the tendency to "make something of" one's likes and dislikes through automatically striving "for the sake of"—that pressure is born from a source wholly different from its outward expression. If a vacuum exerts no pressure, it is nonetheless pressure. The negative source, the *hieros,* passionately attends to the summons of death, for the reason that death conveys unboundedness as well as limit. Pressing from inside, the hieratic "itch" releases an organism from its complicity with desire, but not without an act of the intervening subject. The robe of the initiate must be worn in order to respond to an impulse of passion. A compulsion to seek the object imbues the subject with a self-sense that clandestinely confirms the concept of self. A specific act of intervention on the part of the subject is needed to bring a moment of disconfirmation and intervene in the ongoing program of autoeroticism. Then, released from gravity of thought, an organism finds itself filled (the way an itch can fill) with the privation of desire. In the absence, the longing is for a stillness of the divine.

Could it be that the states of ire and desire point to a single source, parallactically? The restless eye of *desire* originates with the unsteady light of stars (from the Latin *sidus*) as it passes through the earth's atmosphere. There, a constant beam of radiation is broken by random movement into a on-off "twinkling." Analogously, the passionate longing that lies at the root of *ire* is broken by an atmosphere of the self so that its infinity now seeks out only limited, discrete objects. Anger's source in inward divinity is echoed in desire's sighting of "heavenly objects" that peoples have recognized as divine beings. But a lack of proximity leaves the organism unreceptive to a movement of return. A body armored for battle with the object is at a loss for sensitivity and is lost to the relation between desire and anger.

Death

No thought speaks to the body like the thought of death. Is this because death is termination of an alliance between thought and irritability? Thought at the disposal of irritability discerns the object, mobilizes the senses and the body, and sets out to obtain. When not actively engaged, thought at idle occupies itself with stories about desire: future attainments, reminiscences, reveries about conditional times. A thought of death severs the alliance and profoundly affects an instrumental use of the body. If the body is no longer a lever by which to move the world, is it anything in itself? The subject that defines itself autoerotically trembles at the empty plate passed before it. In the passage, anger changes to fear and fear to a paralysis that says, "Nothing to be done."

But thought of death, the death-thought, does more than paralyze the body with its Medusa eye. Stripped of irritability, the body collapses into a pool of dysfunctional tissue. In the grace note of the stop, the subject can work toward an intervening impulse. An iota of agreement or of nondisagreement vis a vis the arrest changes the effect of the thought, the way a mote of dust does the eye's vision. The instrument once demobilized is discarded, like a jammed rifle on the field of battle. What is left is the flesh not barren of agency but agent of a potentized irritability, that is, of a hieratic force. What is the agency of such flesh "purified of the sin" of desire, an illusory autonomy, and a faulty system of reference? What specifically is the meaning of *to act?* When a death-thought stops the body's restless hunger for the object, the inner body—flesh of the flesh—is able to respond to an admonition from above. Action in this context is *submission,* as the word says, going below in order to let go of. The subject musters a response in the flesh, for the summons requires utter specificity and complete individuality. On the outside, the body is as inert as death. On the inside, it has risen—not as the sun rises but as grapes do when they turn into wine.

The suspended animation of desire is precisely the flesh "given up for dead." When objects cease to rally thought for irritability to instrument the body, action is possible in a way that was before impossible. The act has subjectivity itself as subject. The act is *act* because it emerges from utter specificity, complete individuality, and unqualified identity of the one, subjectivity itself. That *solus* necessarily acts absolutely, ab-*sol*-utely, for the sake and solely for the sake of responding. The vague, enigmatic, and exceptional indication to which it responds in some measure invokes the act, but it is of the essence of action that the subject acts with absolution, freed from the compulsion of desire and its lure of the world production, "alone with the alone." It could be said that response is an end in itself and for that reason action takes place. We need only remember the primordial meaning of *response* to confirm what the death of desire has wrought. *Respond* (from *spend-*) pertains to making an offering, performing a rite, or engaging in a ritual act. To void the self and to avoid the self-sense of the flesh is to offer the one, the *solus,* for no purpose other than to respond absolutely. In observance of absolute response lie the means and the end of unqualified identity. In such an identity, no substitution of identicals for identicals is thinkable. For the absolute response joins a raw *thisness* of the subject to the immemorial, time to eternity, and their mutuality to the flesh that remains after desire dies.

That to act is to respond absolutely, for no purpose other than observance of the response, is the germ of Kant's thought in asking how "pure reason can be practical." Observance is an involvement richer than visually perceiving a phenomenon since it encompasses an obedience. The traffic sign "Observe speed limits," reminds us of that. In pure reason, Kant shows that all concepts of the self are empty and beyond the limits of experiential verification. The practicability of pure reason therefore depends on emptying the self-concept without deserting the field of action. Duty for duty's sake, an ethics of deontology, proposes an action based on responsibility alone and the ethical is directed to awaken responsiveness and nothing other. Could duty be said to be an impossible task, the fulfilling of which is an initiation of subjectivity?

In the impossibility of Kant's duty we find a clue concerning the dynamics of the act of submission. If one is summoned to do what is impossible, accomplishment of duty requires an intervention. Since intervention cannot come from outside (or else it would be imposed or coerced), the subject itself must be capable of intervening in such a way as to "do the impossible." If the intervention is voluntary—that is, a leap of faith (as Kierkegaard would say)—it is a leap backward, into an opaque obedience. The subject cannot discern what is to be obeyed, if it is a *what,* but responds absolutely in the flesh of the moment by affirming the directive from that which is in the background. One does not abandon the specifics of embodiment in favor of something more divine, but feels the flesh agonize over the absolute summons. In *agony,* understood in a fundamental way, we find a missing element of agency in that the Greek *agein* has a root in common with the Latin *agere.* Both point to a suffering over the relentless impossibility of an obligation born before one's heart starts beating and remaining unfulfilled until the pulse of thought ceases.

In an agony of struggle, as in an agony of death, impossibility becomes possible and an act ensues. For the act is always a limnal event. It takes place at a threshold or in a doorway, where agent is no longer bounded by the same conditions or under the same influences. In this way, an act belongs solely to a terminal situation: no exit. To act is to be *in extremis,* where flesh is dying and is perceived as dying. In the transfiguring of impossibility into possibility—the act per se—the enabling force is drawn to the agony in the same way prayer is drawn to the dying soul. If it seems absurd to say that the act arises only through anguish of an impossible duty, then life must also be so. For life is born in an anguish of contraction that expels the infant headlong through the birth canal, where there waits an obligation as well as a first breath. That an impossible duty, an absurdity, defines human subjectivity presents the ethos of the paradoxical summons. How can the subject encounter that which lies beyond thought? The selfsame paradox, which cannot be represented by any phenomenal assignation, describes terms of hope: the advent of a positive prospect in an impossible situation. The duty of dying to the flesh of desire, that "thorn in the side" of subjectivity, is beyond the subject's power (*posse*) since power is derived from autoeroticism and the self-willing constitutive of the automatism. Nonetheless, by its own intervention, the subject is able to cross the threshold and *act.*

An Intervening Cause

No doubt that having the flesh "given up for dead" is the result of the act. So is having the flesh of the flesh, the inner body, enlivened. It is not because they are tangible and felt that they are results, for to all appearances they precede the act. But they precede in the way that Orpheus precedes Eurydice: they precede by following. In a similar fashion, awakening the interior of flesh as well as sloughing the exterior follows the response to irritability whose intervening cause is the subject itself. The direction comes from behind, spatially and temporally. Phenomenally, the response is to an irritation spatially removed and temporally delayed from the given moment.

What is meant by saying that the subject is an intervening cause? The notion is a puzzle. Certainly the subject does not bring about a response that melts desire in the heat of a radiant body any more than light brings about vision. Nor does advent of the act take the subject as its agent, any more than a new sight just over the horizon is due to the eyes. By the same token, the subject is not a mere catalyst whose presence is needed for the act to take place but who *in ipso* is not changed. Intervention profoundly transforms the subject, so much so that intervention no longer is possible—whereas in catalysis, reaction is no longer possible but the catalyst remains the same. To meet the paradox of obligation, subjectivity must intervene in its own self-willing process, yet meeting the obligation paradoxically removes its possibility of intervention. Being an intervening cause, the subject "comes between," it is true, but between what and what and in what manner? Between a headlong rush of autoeroticism and the muffled appeal of the heart, the subject responds with a caress. The caress is an elemental gesture that welcomes the heart's utterance without rejecting desire's. In fact, the *ka-* of *caress* signifies *desire,* for instance, in the Sanskrit *kama.* A caress melts resistance by means of warmth, which relates it to irritability, which also generates warmth of a kind. The warmth of the caress, however, is not that of strategically directed thought (as is anger's) but that of charity (*carus*), a receptivity. The subject intervenes in its own automatism by stopping so to say to gesture caressingly toward heaven with outstretched arms.

The stop is ritual gesture of caress. It is a priestess' stroking the holy lamp to kindle a flame. A light, caring, nonviolent touch ends the irritability of the flesh and opens a door to the other. It smothers the gutting flame of compulsive desire while breathing warmth into the subtle body's veins. Any aggressive movement triggers an apprehension of discontinuity and freezes breath, blood, and pores, allowing no composure. That which is caressed to a stop is the self-sense, love of which constitutes autoeroticism. Everything else continues as before. In this fashion, irritability returns to its native form in the inner body, as a passion for the holy.

That the intervening act takes the form of a welcoming—most adequately expressed as a caress—may be obvious from the primal meaning of *intervention.* Strangely, the movement of "coming between" (*inter + venire*) to don the robe of the intermediary, shares the same root as that of *welcome,* namely, $g_w a$. Interventionary force has nothing to do with the goal-productive activity of the automatism. Related by the same thrust of signification, we find the meaning of *guest,* the one welcomed. The act of intervention per se is that of "welcoming the guest." The guest, necessarily other than the subject that welcomes, is let enter. In a mighty influx of fine energy, the guest arrives and comes "into the temple of the body." Its arrival heralds a full-scale reorganization of concern since now the needs of the other take precedence over those of the self-sense. In release and expansion, there is a principle of becoming. Such growth might be expected since *becoming* is another component of the primal meaning of *intervention.*

But how does welcoming, especially with a caress, bring the subject to "give up the flesh for dead?" Surely one aspect of the massive reorganization of attentive concern is withdrawal from objects of sense. Retraction of "the limbs of the tortoise" is the phenomenal face of a fractured identification. When signification is no longer assigned by substituting identicals for identicals, word for object and object for word, the paradox of meaning is again spoken. The quest for meaning, whose restlessness is subjectivity itself, abandons the feckless pursuit of noncontradiction, exclusion, and rigidification and submits to a concern for the other. The speech of the other, "vague, enigmatic, exceptional," fraught with peril, is again spoken. To heed the speaking is the essence of welcoming. To welcome the other's word sweeps the subject away from the phenomenal world that belongs to flesh and toward concerns that annihilate the self-sense. This is death by the left hand and life by the right. As intermediary and host, the subject undergoes the joy of the latter simultaneously with the sorrow of the former.

Resurrection

As no other action can, a caress delays the automatic production of a phenomenal self-sense. True to its time, it detains the *andante* tempo of thought. Projection, assignation, and autonomy are stayed by the sensation of caress—a warlord about to rush to battle detailed by his beloved—and the subject has played its part in the act of intervention. The flesh melts. This is death to stratagems of the automatism that deny the flesh of the flesh and its life. The sensation of caress draws a consciousness to it of the inner flesh and, although the act is already behind, a movement of the inner body surges. This is the resurrection of the flesh.

Look at Luca Signorelli's *The Resurrection of the Flesh*. From under a flat gray ground, people pull themselves up. Just below, they are a skeleton, bare structure, the calcified remains of life. The skull is first to wear flesh over a familiar, aged-bone color. The human skull: universal symbol of death. Then neck and shoulders, upper torso, abdomen, pelvis and thighs, legs, and at last, feet. There are the many stages of embodiment. This one lacks the lower half, that one, one leg, still others, only an ankle before they are able to move about, speak in groups, dance, or embrace one another. Ones nearest to complete restoration are conscious of responding to "the blow to wake the dead." Their eyes are turned toward overhead where two huge angels are sounding long, valveless trumpets. Some stretch their arms upward in thanksgiving toward the source of sound. None is able to reach through the intervening space and touch the heavenly host.

Signorelli's careful depiction of resurrection, like a camera's lens, inverts the image. More precisely, his use of traditional symbolism, figure, and design objectifies a subjective process. The effect of inversion is to project from inside out and from the end back to the beginning: a double inversion. Viewed with this fact in mind, the painting illustrates the caress of life as a putting on of outer skin, wearing fleshy tones over an ashen skeleton. The body of desire then engages speaking, dancing, and socializing. For the subject, however, the caress opens a way to the soma, flesh of the flesh or true flesh, through adverting the mind from the body of desire. Objectifications of the desirous flesh become progressively empty as somatic awareness intensifies and the "invisible becomes visible." Movement is toward a form internal to the flesh-colored flesh, and so properly the unregenerated skeletons symbolize an end point rather than a beginning. Recall also that *Hades* originally refers to the realm of invisibility and you see that the flesh's progressive resumption of life is more like a descent into the underworld than a rising into the visible, catabasis rather than anabasis (and note that *basis* shares the same stem as *guest* and *welcome*). The skin too tight to fit is not fit for regeneration and to discard the epidermis for the soma brings the tree of life.

Signorelli also gives a literal illustration of the summon's emanation from a higher level. The angels who blow the horns are shown spatially above the resurrected throng. A clear separation of levels is provided by a strip of blue-gray firmament so that no higher form is contiguous with a lower one. Placement of the call outside and above the one summoned is the painting's second inversion. In reality, the triggering event that emanates from what is a higher, more dynamic, and stronger influence takes place within the subject's flesh. It is higher in the sense that wine is higher than grapes. In a place not definable in terms of the spatiotemporal continuum, a word-sound comes to caress the subject and at once dissolve flesh and awaken the soma. The subject needs to intervene to neutralize disdain and refusal and if successful follow the process of response. But the event itself comes from within and below to direct subjectivity to welcome the caress. This is to say, Signorelli's representation is a cipher that requires a key. The key is an observant obedience that distinguishes life from death, dead skin from vital somatic force, and a literal interpretation from a usable symbol. Once held in hand, the key can unlock the secret encoded in *Resurrection of the Flesh.*

Nonassignation of the Caress

Like a wave lapping the shore, an emanation from a place undefined by definite location caresses the inner surface of flesh and quickens the pulse of the flesh beneath flesh. Because the impulse comes from beyond the time-space grid, it is neither phenomenal nor epiphenomenal. Nor is it amenable to assignation by substitution. The flesh of my flesh is touched in its vulnerable spot (like a bruise) by the enigma of life and is left tender as a result. In the rising warmth of hieratic passion—warmer-than-blood warm—is proof of exchange as well as promise of intimacy and proximity. This is as much an intimation of origin as is given, but it suffices to arouse an interest in that which is not subject to decay, as things in time are. In welcoming the caressing gesture, the subject finds means to open to the immemorial.

That all things in time decay is the aphorism around which Husserl constructs the internal time-sense, following Kant in this regard.[2] That time is in actuality a derivative of the function of thought, the tempo of which is template for Husserl's analysis of temporal structure. But the *cogito* involuntarily sets itself over and against things' falling into ruin. It invents memory that makes as if to hold on to that which is passing away and reach forward to deposit the pattern of things to come. Retention and protention are agents retained against decay. Objectification and assignation by substitution of identicals provide a stable currency with which thought can purchase notions of permanence, constancy, and durability. In this fashion, the subject is provided for against the ravages of decay and degeneration and so, falls into a false belief in its own immortality.

But the illusion of eternity—eternalism—is brought to an abrupt end as soon as the caress summons the subject from dreams. It is like a kiss of death. Then, desire goes flat. So does the particular construal of irritability that posits "flesh" as a thought, be it with geometric implications (as Descartes thinks) or carnal ones (as Paul does). As if warmed by cupped hands, the flesh within the flesh stirs to life. But how could it ever have been other than alive? Thus does the passion for the whole, the *hieros,* convey an enigma of meaning not readily translated into unequivocal speaking. One could say that in the warmth of passion, the soma is brought back to a life that seems always to have been alive—as if Lazarus had merely been comatose when called back from the grave. By a kind of "misplaced emphasis," the soma had been given up for dead and buried in the potters' field of memory. But then, the strong impression of death and the return to life is left unexplained. Why say "life returns" when it is not the case that warmth causes the sensation of life peculiar to the soma?

Subjectivity is summoned by a caress back to a sensation of life. At the extreme lip of the phenomenal, it meets through the language of sensation an identity that has awaited it since time immemorial. Incommensurate as the phenomenal is with the far side of being, subjectivity occupies the interface. The identity cannot be substituted for any identical and even though it wears the face of phenomena, its original face is other. The subject is summoned to speak and exchange with the nonreplaceable identity so that each takes on aspects of the other's face. Through undergoing the meeting, subjectivity comes into its responsibility. Ceasing to be a self-will, it becomes the one-in-the-other.

"A single caress wakes the dreamer's heart." That which arises, a sensation of life, is indicative of an immemorial identity of which the heart constantly speaks. One might say that sensation is *sui generis,* that it is self-caused, if by that one acknowledges that although the sensation persists *in carno* without the intervening act of the subject, the caress opens the subject to both the sensation of life and the fact that the sensation is undying. Or, one might say that the heart speaks through a soft, caressing touch in a language that conveys the sensation of life. In either case, subjectivity is informed that it is not responsible for the origin of its life but is indebted to an origin other than itself for bringing its inner body to life. Signorelli is true to the idea in that, the summons is given by angels, beings alien to subjects whose flesh is thereby resurrected.

One can ask, what part does resurrection of the flesh play in a seizing of responsibility? The ancient question predates that of whether resurrection is necessary to the postmortum survival of the individual, a manner to which dogmatics and theology have devoted thought. Interest in immortality and life after death arose only after great awe regarding the indebtedness of subjectivity faded—and that with the death of conscience. In the era of conscience, it was recognized that—unless the flesh is brought back to life from the death of sensation—desire, autoeroticism, and dreams of eternity continue unabated. A fantastic freedom that derives from a transcendental idealism will carry the conviction of belief. Resuscitation of the inner flesh alone, the argument continued, provides a response to the caressing summons of the heart. Resurrection, the rebirth of corporeal agency, alone sensitizes the subject to a charity of the immemorial whose caring is incommensurably more enduring and more surpassing than any fine thing of time.

The inner flesh restored to life: it is an exact proof of the other, beyond the globe of phenomena and the time-space warp. Incommensurate in relation to any measure, the other speaks the heart-word *I* and caressingly summons the distracted subject to responsibility. From a position having no coordinates and a time that reaches things through interminable delay, the other abides in an "always and everywhere" both vulnerable and perilous. Relative to the other, visions of God as impregnable, invulnerable, and without weakness are a result of intoxication. Attacked from all sides, almost without allies, having limited resources to overcome a boundless necessity, the other issues an eternal cry for help—is just this cry. Unresponsiveness brings about great sorrow. With a caressing summons, the other reaches across, in hope and in anguish, eternally striving to stroke an awareness of need in subjects. The reach, from beyond the matter of objects, finally finds contact with the sheath of life, the inner flesh, the abode of the other-in-the-one. There from the heart does the caress speak. Does the word sound in the desert of the subject or does the subject make a solemn pledge of aid?

Vulnerability and Paralysis

That the other in weakness cries out a summons is an affront to our thought. Is not the other a bastion of strength, mighty and awesome, "doing wonders"? How could the other suffer and lack in qualities that we as subjects do? The notion deepens our solitude and deprives us of the consolation of living under an omnipotent absolute. Can we bear the aloneness?

In weakness the other speaks a silent word to the heart, and that suffices to summon absolutely—though I can dismiss the caressing plea and curse my fate. Because an aura of weakness rouses my apprehensions of exposure, I am guilty of misunderstanding. *Weakness* has roots in being pliant, the way a branch bends in the wind. Since weakness is defective in rigid structure, it is assailable by forces that have the potential of overcoming it. Weakness in the other—the vulnerable absolute that has absolute vulnerability—weighs on the very suffering that I dream being free of and armors me against response. How can it be that the work of the other is unfinished and lacks perfection? A need to be remembered and rejoined to the whole cries out and deafens me, but I am helpless. The paradox that *I* am needed paralyzes me, even though the need takes precedence over all needs. The image of God weeping alone in the desert follows from my ineptitude.

Yet, is not weakness another name for the susceptibility of the subject? The subject's effort is necessarily weak because it is susceptible to attenuating, distracting influences that govern the automatism. Its weakness is pliancy, a thread that bends, twists, thins, but does not break. In that sense, weakness is the subject's special virtue because, compared to the rigid strength of the automatism, disruption is not an alternative. In fact, in its extreme dilution, susceptibility increases homeopathically in potency. The more assailed subjective awareness is and the more wary it becomes, the greater is its mutability. As the awareness becomes more subjected to thought's assignations, susceptibility to disguise, guile, and surprise (degrees of mutation) proportionately increases. A sudden slip, a pratfall, an unexpected message, an untoward event, luck or misfortune: the summons of enigma, its miracle and wonder, breaks into the automatism and disrupts production of the world-picture. Whether the enhanced susceptibility is recognized as such is beside the point. Like draws like. Weakened, held captive, the subject draws to itself an anguished caress of the other. A tangibility that exposes proximity sends tremors throughout the organism that shake the dreamer from sleep. The weakness whose symptoms include a submerged awareness and domination by the self-will awakens the subject to the need to hear the heart's word. The unfinished condition of subjectivity is in the very likeness of the other.

Is it weakness to summon with a caress? Would a whip or a gun signify strength? The other in its pain submits to its weakness and therefore assumes no fixed form or holds no dogmatic attitude. Its utter fluidity is submission. Its utterance is fluency without content. A caress evokes the need to respond, but how? Even dismissal is a response. In ambiguity and provocation, the caress is peerless. Not minimizing its suffering, the caress of the other exposes a proximal source of anguish—its thirst, hunger, abrasions, injuries—and enjoins the subject to remember itself. Only through the task of memory can a work of completing the incomplete, the other's and the subject's own, be engaged, fructified, and accomplished.

Chapter Ten
Conscience

> A perfect animal, which is self-moving, most approaches unto a likeness of the whole universe: whence man, who is the most perfect animal, is called in a manner a small world [*minor mundus*] . . . but the noblest form in inferior bodies is the soul, which most approaches unto likeness with the principles of motion of the heavens; thus the motion of the heart in the animal is like the motion of the heavens in the universe. . . . Whence it is for this reason that the heart is the principle and end of all motions.
>
> —Aquinas[1]

Approximation

Against the manifold products of thought, the heart speaks from behind. *Behind* in this sense is behind the curtain. The confessor sits on the other side of the veil. The subject brings forth many things. When the confessor replies, the words are not direct. Expression vibrates with enigma. Assignation fails to obey the law of substitution and, therefore, threatens the cognitively established order. Obsession with commodity is gnawed away from the inside—as by a pang—and the door opened to proximity and the quest for proximal reason. Awareness melts at the fringes, giving rise to interrogation and prosecution. The subject, accused, on trial, does not understand the charges. The subject is summoned "to watch and to pray" but by whom and for what? In the hinterland of anxiety, a caress on the nape of the neck is an indication of that which is to come, but what? The sensation, a deeply ambiguous one mixed with desire, returns the subject to at-oneness, that which is passionately sought. The subject again is able to listen from *behind.*

In listening, the subject nears the utterance of the heart. But the approach does not alter the fact that the heart speaks from *behind.* If anything, the nearing increases the retrograde motion, just like zooming in on a receding star reveals how quickly it moves away. The phenomenon of approximation shows how an apparent minor gap in actuality is a yawning abyss. Or rather, only in proximity does respect manifest. At a distance, thought construction can project disrespectful images onto another. The soma's sensitivity, by contrast, communicates by contact and allows the other to be seen for what it is: one of the two primary meanings of *respect.* The language of proximal reason is nondistorting. The second meaning is that of looking *back,* preserved in the fact that nearing the other is achieved by a return to the source of the glance rather than through a dedication to its target. It is in a return of *respect* that the subject perceives a gulf widening between its position and that of the source. For the heart's speech is of another tempo and the subject up to now has identified with the tempo of thought and has founded its identity in the time of the *cogito.*

That from where the heart speaks is other than thought and by a trick of perspective appears as *behind.* Like sound in a grotto that originates at a great distance but is an intimate whisper in one's ear, the word is proximal and takes no time to deliver its message. If *here* does not designate a place but a lack of placement or "placeability," then *behind* likewise is not a place. In fact, *behind* and *here* share a common root *ko-,* a pure demonstrative "this"—the direct pointing of bare attention. Perspective is a product of thought while that from where the heart speaks is aperspectival. Inasmuch as appearances and phenomena belong to a world of perspective, the heart's utterances never appear and are not experienced as phenomena. Yet it would be incorrect to conclude that they cannot be heard. As precessional movement, the backward movement of the constellations over time, registers the invisible axis of the earth, so too does a speaking from *behind* indicate the heart's movement. In both cases, a widened perception of time is both a fruit and a requisite.

Speaking from behind, the heart is "what is missing." It speaks in absence, *in absentia,* because its tempo is not of presence. If it were, the heart's utterances would appear among phenomena and be understood by means of substitution and identification. But one can never identify with the word of the heart because of how it shatters the vehicle of identification. The paradox is that a fuller embodiment of presence is the way to hearing what is spoken and that disintegration of presence through inattentiveness "stoppers the ears." Absent, speaking from afar, the heart can never appear in an inventory and is known only by a gap—the way one knows a missing item in the parlor game. The datum *that it is missing* is not given. Because it is never given and is missing, the heart can be inferred. Or rather, it can be felt by a kind of *Urfuhl,* a forefeeling that is a forward shadow of a feeling that forever remains in the background. A forefeeling has nothing to do with a catalog of the emotions, such as a Descartes or a Spinoza might provide in *The Passions of the Soul* or *The Ethics.* Adumbration or prefiguration, perception of absence does not gain clarity or distinctness, important features of identification. It hangs back, looms, clouds, obscures, or threatens, but does not enter into a discourse of presence. Even its trail as though in a bubble chamber reveals where it passed, not where it is. Where it is never coincides with where it is or else could it not substitute for itself? Where it is, is perpetually *behind* where it is.

the free animal
has its decrease perpetually behind it
and God in front[2]

Inalterability

What is missing, when found, does not thereby cease to be missing. So what is missing is not, as Kierkegaard thinks, passion, for when passion is uncovered, it no longer is missing. What is missing is more passive than passion, whether it flares up, vents, or purely and without mitigation suffers. It is true that one yearns for what is missing. But what is missing is not thereby the cause of longing. Nor does the yearning dissipate when what is missing is uncovered, but rather the opposite. Yearning actually increases as the subject nears what is missing. Furthermore, what is missing abides absolutely without feeling even though one's tears run like rain down one's cheeks and one's chest aches from sobbing. The subject may be strongly, violently, or passionately affected by the approach of what is missing, but nonetheless to maintain the converse, that what is missing is affected, is pure projection.

What one finds when one finds what is missing is that it is meant to be missing. The missing "something" is necessarily missing. Its property of being missing is essential to its identity since its identity is precisely what is missing. Furthermore, its identity is necessary, unlike the subject's contingent identity. But if its identity were not missing but instead available, then that identity would be subject to the law of substitution, which it is not. Then the subject would be able to identify with it, and affirm, "I am the same as this one." Because identification is not possible, the subject remains in question, unattached, at bay, lost, and crying alone in the woods. When first found, what is missing turns out to be missing still. Like with a missing person, one wishes to rescue what its missing from the condition of privation. Only later does the mistake become apparent. Unlike a missing person who is lost, stolen, or strayed, what is missing lacks nothing. Its absence is not a lack but the very condition of plenitude. It is not altered, neither emptied nor filled, by "making good" on what is missing. Thus, on later finding, the fact that what is missing abides so to speak missingly is an increasing source of comfort. Its elusiveness to and negation of presence is a beacon of hope.

The inalterability of what is missing, its rocklike quality, is as close an affirmation of its otherness as humanly possible. On to the screen of being more passive than passion, the subject projects fear, anxiety, shame, doubt, and delusion. The value of an act of projection is that it demonstrates the limits of the visible. On the far side, what is missing remains missing, undisclosed, unillumined. On the near side, "within the limits of pure reason alone," the dynamics of disclosure occupy and preoccupy consciousness. The world and the self as produced by thought are revealed prismatically, as the colorful gleaming of a partially reflective glass—mesmerizingly beautiful. Fascination with individual and collective objects is momentarily put aside and a haunting sense of limit felt. What is missing waits and in its waiting allows the light of consciousness to make its disclosures. Only when the subject believes disclosure to be limitless does consciousness go awry. For the chief and foremost discovery is that of the limit of disclosure and of the inalterability of what is missing from disclosure. Without the discovery, the subject suffers from inflation and a deluded egocentricity. The delusion is that all is available to consciousness.

Longing and Passivity

Though what is missing lies on the far side of awareness and is in itself more passive than passion, still one continues to long for its disclosure. Are we not born to an obsession with light, one that has given birth to philosophy in the West? This longing constitutes a passionate knowledge of the other. Inasmuch as knowledge is constituted, it contains two different "optical" errors. First, because of the reflective qualities at the limit of consciousness, it places the other outside of subjectivity. Second, the knowledge, being knowledge, avers disclosure whereas in fact, the other remains opaque to consciousness. Nonetheless, just as the astronomer uncloaks a black hole by the absence of light, so too the other is inferred as an unrevealed absence. The absence, however, does not lie beyond the circumference but at the hub. What is missing belongs passionately to subjectivity and always will be a passion of subjectivity—without being a part of subjectivity. The "gap" in subjectivity induces a kind of weeping on the part of the subject, the tears of which, through accretion, yield a growth of responsibility. Rising to the surface, irritability provides a source of weeping that nourishes the growing pearl. Without tears, there would be no coin with which to repay the debt of contingency.

Though to miss what is missing is different from missing what is kept from sight, metaphorical or actual, one experience points toward the other. One's distress over a missing article, especially one irretrievably lost, is a mourning, and like all mourning, is a ferment from the seed of delay, *mora.* To suffer the lack is to be gnawed away from the inside as if by a thorn under the skin. Is not irritability or susceptibility what it means to wear the epidermis of a human? The shedding of skin from the inside (like chewing away at the inside of one's cheek) is the very weeping that causes an accretion by hollowing out. Stabbed from the side of proximity, as if betrayed by what is nearest to one, the subject yields longingly to a memory of that which traces a path backward through the sands of time. Filling the emptied-out cells of the soma, that which is other than the productive ego engenders new life. The soma is dead. The soma has risen again.

Strangely, what one misses and has gotten "under one's skin" is not there by special dispensation, like a private coach for one's person, but is common to all.

Perhaps Heraclitus's *logos* refers to the ultimate degree of passivity, but then his thought has usually been taken to deal with the *epiphanious,* the Apollonian light-giving function, rather than what waits to offer response in the central darkness. Heidegger alludes to much of the former in his *Lectures on Heraclitus.* The temptation to attribute consciousness to the common element ignores the root (*mei-*) that *miss* and *common* share and overemphasizes what might be only a chance direction followed by Western thought. To feel longing for what one misses commonly gives rise to the inner weeping of subjectivity. This is no isolated expression. On the contrary, the weeping is an expression of a community of weepers whose two eyes are "wet with weeping." The absolute solitude (*solus*) of responsibility takes place only in meeting proximally with the other who also weeps. To share in a common suffering is the oneness that the subject and the other enjoy. Taking place in light's absence, prior to thought and feeling, the common suffering—the ultimate degree of passivity—calls out, as does any suffering, for help. In one's response is subjectivity born.

To respond to the other's cry for help and thereby forfeit dreams of autonomous freedom reaffirms the total separation between address and response. The nonsubstitution of one for the other again comes to the fore. The subject does not identify itself with the suffering other as though emphatically to suck an identity from the other's tears or sympathetically to resonate with the weeping cries. Both involve an "anthropomorphic fallacy" that discloses the other *like* oneself and so substitutes likeness for unlikeness. The help needed, by contrast, involves respecting the other's unrevealed nature, its nonluminous halo, and the action of its emptiness. In responding to a cry for help, the subject is unable to take the other's place (since there is none) and gains nothing from the interaction but intensified longing. Alleviation of suffering incurs greater suffering and for this reason the caressing summons of the heart is all the more welcome. It goes without saying that greatness of suffering has to do with a quality entirely absent from ordinary suffering, for in taking on the other's suffering, one inherits one's birthright of subjectivity.

Daimonion

Could one say that what is missing has a specific embodiment? Not that the unmanifest is able to appear but that appearance itself provides a record—a record of being unmanifest! The *daimon* seems that sort, an enigmatic apparition barely within but never of consciousness, "that slight movement seen out of the corner of the eye that is never there." Leaping from behind a veil, the *daimon* can be objectified as a source of guidance, but then, only strangely. For as it comes and goes on its own will, the *daimon* speaks darkly, like a caress, and sparingly indicates discrepancies. The form of its speaking is: If the subject would do this, the other's absence would not be respected. There would be no help offered to the Alone crying in the desert. There would be no tears for the other's weeping and no coin to amortize one's debt of responsibility. The immemorable task would be expunged from the book of memory. In the words of Plato's figure of Socrates, the *daimon* speaks in the voice of omission, of how to go about absenting oneself from doing. If the background of a canvas represents a hollowing out of the foreground, the *daimon*'s hollowed out words scoop a surfeit of meaning from the subject's thoughts, and leave a residuum of awe at the sudden, vast, empty domain. They also preserve a gap in the only way that speaking can respect the other's absence, by apophasis.

In many ways the *daimon* embodies apophasis, whose meaning is described by Plotinus in terms of a luminous globe: "If someone should take out the corporeal mass but preserve the power of the light, would you then speak of where the light was? Or would it not be everywhere, distributed in and over the entire sphere? No longer can you say through *dianoia* where it was first located, and so no longer can you say whence and how it came. You will be brought into perplexity and wonderment."[3] In speaking, the *daimon* sculpts out assignated meanings, deletes identifications, and leaves the subject agog. In the eye of Plotinus, the *daimon* removes the glowing mass of light—consciousness—and leaves the power of the light to operate intrinsically. If this is direction, it is direction by stupefaction, for the subject is stopped in its tracks by the deep excavation of bedrock by the *daimon.* Witness Socrates' trance, as Plato portrays him, on a stoop near to Agathon's gate. In an abyss opened in the depths of the world-picture, he meets a force that annihilates assignations, an antiforce, a force that antedates the productivity of thought. Clarity dissolves to opaqueness, definition to discrepancy, and retention to a dropping of all reserve. Thought's tongue is severed at the root. The merciless destruction of intentionality, leaving him with "nothing to do," proceeds to such an extent that he is left solely with the task of the immemorial. In the space illuminated by language, a brain lobotomized of consciousness-for-itself then glows with a different, subdued radiation. It speaks but only in the riddance of meaning. It designates but only in the collapse of designation. It utters but only in the frequency of silence.

Saying by unsaying, the *daimon* presages contradiction, or rather, subjectivity as self-contradiction. By an inversion of logic, the subject is demonstrated to be inconsistent with itself, affirming and denying one and the same, a mire of self-negation. In its way, this is a logical consequence of the subject's exemption from the law of identicals since nothing can be substituted for a contradictory proposition. For each representation, the opposite also is represented, but in a hidden, secreted, *sub rosa* fashion. Daimonic speech dramatizes the "not this, not that" by a play of opposites in every position that results in self-destruction and annihilation. Unsaying, apophasis, eats away at the yolk of meaning, leaving a hollow shell to crumble around the subject's pretensions. The acidic trace of a missing agent is given by the trail of debris, if that is possible to follow. Since disorientation is the specter of the utterance, that which can glean the evidence is strangely unavailable to pursue the trail. Instead, as Socrates tells, the ear is differently opened and one hears the voice of admonition, mourning, and delay caress the subject in proximity. If there is a name for the event, call it "conscience."

Division by Nonsubstitution

Daimon is in its original meaning "the divider." From that sense, it degenerated to the notion of a resident or personal divinity, though Plato plainly assigns the *daimon* to the intermediate world, neither mortal nor immortal. In fact, the *daimon* is a response to an important question: How does what is common to all relate to subjectivity? The common element—ether, or the quintessence—is, as was said, what is missing. The subject is in search of, and replete with, what is missing. Its longing engenders that which speaks for what is missing and in speaking utters the heart's deepest desire. In its total absence of objective content, the word is devoid of what can be spoken of, one with the other, since that speaking refers to substitution. Yet in wringing the last drop out of objectivity and thereby becoming "uniquely subjective," the word is what alone can be spoken of, one with the other. For then, it is the single real token that can be shared, one soul to the next. It is "the one needful thing."

The question of division that the *daimon* poses is not quite the venerable problem of universals, namely, how many divisions of a universal thing are needed to derive a particular. The incommensurability of the latter is well known. Countless divisions of a universal do not yield the suchness of an actual identity whose essence escapes the finest net of categories. Instead, the question of division refers to the separation of "self from self," that is, the automatism and autoerotic aspect from somatic intelligence and proximity. In sifting the fine from the coarse, the *daimon's* admonition is that sieve. Its caress warns the subject as it brushes against the sensitivity: "not this." As caress and not blow, however, its fracture of self-will and the productivity of thought can be variously perceived. Hearing the delay directly, Socrates stood stock-still for hours, retracing pathways back to immemorial time. More often, the delay is echoed or reflected off of thought's projects in which case it is perceived "as an inexorable outer coercion, preparing and controlling what, though it cannot be revealed to the individual, he must never get wrong."[4] Through opacity, through a dialect of nondisclosure, the *daimon*'s speech divides the subject into its native duality and through the division summons it to trod the way to nonduality. In the conflict between habitual preference and the perception of the inner ear, choice becomes the trial and the judgment. Although "to choose oneself" has nothing to do with conventional moral decision, a new disposition emerges. It is able to endure the ordeal of longing in the face of unsatisfying options. Its suffering for what is missing gradually engenders an enigmatic attentiveness that goes by a prescriptive name, conscience.

Although not obvious, dividing self from self and choosing subjectivity necessarily invokes a temporal dimension. A connection is apparent when one is mindful that *da-*, the root of *daimon,* also yields the word *time,* whose divisions in an unrestricted temporal flow mark inner or outer periodicities. The *daimon* represents a certain stand with respect to Kant's first antinomy of reason, which asks whether we can decide if the markings predate the flux.[5] In its very utterance, the *daimon* recalls the subject to the fact of division and thus to uninterrupted time. Can the subject remember a time not so divided against itself? Is the subject prepared to respond wholeheartedly to an obligation already in force prior to time's divisions, an obligation that pertains to an absolute identity of the subject vis a vis the other, that is to say, a necessary identity of the subject? If there is such a responsibility, the antinomy tells us that it cannot be met by productive thought. Pure practical reason owes its intelligence to a relation with a tempo prior to thought-created divisions. One could say that the *daimon* is an "immanent spirit" of a priori time whose charge to the subject is to actualize the specific identity allotted to it. Its specific reason (daimonic intelligence) lies in knowing a form anterior to choice's embodiment of it. To be visited by the *daimon* is to be visited by a future that has already happened, the déjà vu. It is to be confronted while still a subject in embryo by a fully completed subjectivity that implores, "Remember who I by necessity am!"

The Mercy of Secrecy

Through a voice of nondisclosure, through an undisclosed voice, though a voice that closes the door to substitution, what is missing returns to the conversation initiated by the subject's yearning. If the oracle of conscience speaks, a key to its code lies elsewhere than in the speaking. In speaking by cipher, utterance is of no value unless the subject has broken through. Or rather, the breakthrough is precisely what is of value. Otherwise, utterance is meaningless gibberish. Valuation derives from repeatedly decoding the mercy of secrecy. Without the secret, there would be no value. Without the promise of value, the subject would not be impelled to decipher the secret.

The speech of conscience is ciphered because the organ lies so far back, in the region behind. The cipher is zero, a null point which, when divided into any digit, yields infinity. Displaced and from no place in particular, the speaking enters the vale of place and takes its place. It is an inherent lack of place that brings an aura of discrepancy to any meaning assigned to the speaking. No assignation sticks to the naught. Like an uninvited guest that does not fit with a wedding party, the utterance sets thought aquiver that wants to know the identity by its difference. At the same time, an uncanny familiarity gives the guest a certain force. He knows that the groom has concealed an aspect of himself but tells no one. Yet every word he utters exudes the knowledge. That he speaks in code is apparent to an attentive ear, but how to understand that he states nothing?

The value of conscience's voice is precisely by force of nondisclosure eating away from inside of the crust of identification. Hollowed internally and made more womblike, the subject is more fully available to another influx. In fact, *availability* and *value* derive from the same Latin root for strength. The strength of availability, as Marcel shows, lies in the empty place-holder. If a place is occupied, it is to no avail to try to take it. The subject's responsiveness to nondisclosure is the way of subjectivity. It is to choose the cipher of self over the wealth of substitution.

If one could say that a science of conscience teaches cutting away at the body of knowledge, then this would accord well with the Latin root *scire* (from the basic root *skei-*), which has the sense of cutting. The scheme of substitutions, infrastructure of the world-picture, is pared from . . . nothing. When conscience speaks, it does not reveal a thing, object, principle, or way—all of which constitute another but deeper layer of the same product of mind. Instead, the utterance delineates by a dark admonition, a guilt, a shadow that floats free of objects, inner and outer, to summon the *solus* absolutely. To cut into the flesh and separate the proximal sensitivity from the mind-regulated habits causes pain, whether or not of the body. Thus, one could also say that the science of conscience teaches suffering, if self-naughting is that. In any case, the cipher that is the mouth of conscience threatens infinite divisibility of thought's univocity, infinitely endangering the subject identified with thought. The peril alerts one to the need to respond without delay to a task that cannot be borne in memory, and to respond to a summons delayed since before mortal time's beginning. In the response, nothing is disclosed, thus sealing the tongue of conscience.

Why speak at all of conscience if there is nothing to tell?

Destiny of Subjectivity

In the subsidence of telling, the desire to tell, and the autoerotic urge, conscience speaks, obligating proximally. Of course its speech gives indication of the destiny of subjectivity, that is (if it could be said), how the subject needs to act if to complete the given terms of its responsibility. But this expression makes it sound as though subjectivity is a precast awaiting a content to be poured in instead of a material in need of transformation. The subject of knowledge needs to become incandescent as it bows its light to responsibility. Deformed by productivity of thought and in need of being unmade, melted down, and struck again in the "dark light" of beneficence, the subject gives ear to what is missing. Simultaneously, the freeing of old form and the arising of the new *I* follow an unknown, nonlinear course—that retraces the course of delay. It is true that one might tell the story of human destiny, but conscience speaks more than the destiny of subjectivity, or else the many volumes already written on the destiny of humankind could constitute an encyclopedia of the subject and tell all. There is more. Conscience repeats the secret cipher of delay.

To decipher the secret delay of the heart requires other than a fulfilled destiny of subjectivity, but it requires that also. If the latter is the first liberation, the former is the second. Or, could it be put that the first is one's mortal birthright, the second, one's immortal earning? To decipher delay and understand the reason that Euridyce lags behind Orpheus unlocks the meaning of *mortality*, its root *mors*, and its inner contents, *mora-*. To decode any of the related meanings opens the others. Take the classic image of pure justice alluded to earlier, the weighing of the heart at death. At death, according to tradition, the heart is weighed. It is placed in one pan and a falcon's feather in the other. In some accounts, the hand of Horus holds the balance by a golden thread. If the scale shows that the heart is wanting—that it is heavier than a featherweight—the soul is rejected as unworthy. It has not yet penetrated the cipher of delay and cannot be responsible for its immortality. But if it is and weighs equal or less than a feather, its understanding has grasped the fact that its weight *in delay* has been determined. It knows a definite and fundamental interval: that from when life goes out and is existentially extinguished to the mounting of an effort to return. The interval is that of death. The measurement is of the striving to renew life through an awareness of death and life, and of what is beyond the two. The scales show that the weight of the heart is in terms, not of gravity, but of time. The heart's weight, which is its delay, is homonymously a waiting.

Can one say that inasmuch as the source of utterance cannot be uttered, the heart is no thing but a tempo? *Heart* pertains to a temporality more passive than passivity, *the basis rhythm,* onto which the tempos of all action takes place by projection. To strive to return to the original timing from the tempo of automatism and thought lightens the heart. It lessens its wait. In the cavity of the chest hang the pans of pure justice, the justice of death. To strive to relate to heart-time is put effort on the scale in place of the heart. It is not the heart but longing for it that is then measured. In suspended time, the heart waits, wanting or in balance, until the time to be restored to life. That time is given only by the subject's initiative. The heart awaits the *I*'s response during a delay. Delay may be long or short, forever or almost never. Death is a weight that tugs at the heart, pulling its tempo down. Slowed by death, the heart weighs more and waits longer. The larger the death, the greater the striving must be, if the delay is to be answered. Is it final or inevitable that death will win out?

The secret of the heart's delay, which is the secret of death, cannot be disclosed. Disclosure belongs to a temporality sympathetic with thought's functional beat. Disclosure issues utterances that obscure a time more passive than passivity and undermines the task of remembering the immemorial. Yet, not to be disclosed, the heart's delay uniquely obligates—or rather, by its obligation invokes the unique subjectivity to respond. In effort born and yearning suffered, death is met and repelled. A force of responsibility is repellant in direct proportion to its strength. Repelled, death does not diminish but forever retreats as long as subjectivity relates to the undying. If there is a "victory over death," it lies in the memory of the immemorial and the subject's success in meeting Death's sister *Lethe.* To remember oneself even unto death is to immunize a portion of one's life against that final sickness. In this regard, we can recall Horace's claim:

> Some part of me will live and not be given
> Over into the hands of the death goddess.[6]

Chapter Eleven
Hope

> For whatever the particular features of the experience may have been, I have wanted to commit them to memory, so that I could in a way go back to it and take it to myself again whenever I was so minded and so submit this power to my will whenever I chose. But every time this happens I hear the Lord say to me: "The Spirit blows whither he will."[1]

Specificity

Knowledge of the heart is a phoenix that rises from a collapse of cognition in the form of a "concrete specification" wrenched from the world, from horizons and conditions, from the emptiness of space, from space signifying emptiness, from the desert, from beyond the pale, from uninhabitability, exile, and rejection. It is raw, unprocessed by concept, category, representation; a heart unreconstructed and therefore not at peace with falsehood, strange to itself, not knowing its own protective shell, exposed and prevented from slipping away. The ego perceives itself as universal and is always already elusive, whereas the heart cannot ask for replacements—as if there were an army of volunteers ready to assign. There is no other who could stand ready to face such accusation. The ego, a consciousness reflecting on and for itself, escapes its own critical eye by its spontaneity (as Kant notices), which permits it to take refuge in the very eye that judges it. Is this not another way of speaking of autoeroticism or the source of autoeroticism? The negation of detachment—the eye detached from itself—is, from all points of view, the pain of responsibility. The negation of detachment is not liberation but necessitation, an obedience.

Lamentation

The collapse of cognition, the aneurysm of thought's functional beat, is, however, not self-willed, not automatic (*auto-* + *matos,* willing), any more than a cardiac arrest is. The upsurge of the heart's delay—the absurd itself—on the plane of assignation is no event of meaning but of the annihilation of event and meaning together. Delay is a crater in the plane of phenomena, an illogical grate, a vent to chaos. Though longed for, it cannot be courted or counted on as ally, accomplice, partner, lover, or spouse. The nonevent speaks for itself and in fact speaks before itself since it takes away what is said before the saying. That it cannot be bespoken for follows from the fact that delay is summoner, not the summoned. Delay summons in a summary fashion. Although its advent is delayed, it does not brook a delayed response. It has no time for that. Because the time that it keeps is not memorable time, that time cannot be kept. Yet, to respond to a delayed summons to bear an immemorial time in memory is more than a subject can bear. To lament the impossibility of the task to remember immemorial time is a way of longing. In longing is a "cognition" of what is missing, though one that escapes definition.

But is the subject not so constructed so as forever to hope for an outcome of striving? Are not thoughts of causality and considerations of consequences so intrinsic that life would be an embarrassment without them? Is "duty for duty's sake" even possible? Such global questions need to be set aside first. The fact is that only with phenomena is the expectant attitude fostered by thought's functional rhythm helpful. Then, certain "analogies of experience" permit meaning to be assigned to the emerging new order. It is otherwise when the phenomenal field is ruptured. There, retentive and protentive phases of thought produce a gaze that forever looks off expectantly. *Expectation* involves a seeing that spies on the future. Like a good espionage agent, it makes things up on the basis of incomplete and outdated data. Such a gaze overlooks the break in the field much as the perceived field of vision overlooks the optical blind spot. If data for the present task of memory are to be apprehended, an anticipatory attitude is detrimental. Hope as we know it is an obstacle.

The matter, however, does not come to an end here. The arrest of thought's rhythm, attended by a death-tremor, simultaneously strikes down the subject's upright posture and pride. The skull-face of mortality brings a terror to strip away the illusion of freedom, self-willing, and autoeroticism as its empty eye sockets "see" past the time of thinking. Their "gaze" symbolizes patience of responsibility—that which waits because it has been waiting since before the subject was conceived, much less born. Bereft of habitual support, one bows down to a patience before which "every knee must bend, every tongue give homage." It is with an inner gesture of prostration that a hope beyond hope is found. Yielding to a patience more passive than passivity, the subject momentarily abandons an impulse to identify with products of mind and substitute an object for itself. In the effort of yielding lies a hope beyond hope. Without the gesture, the subject is inclined to a false hope, hopelessly unaware of the connection between *hope* and the Latin *cubare,* to bend down.

Prostration as a physical act retraces the inner circuit of hope, the return to the fold of the soma. Relinquishing an upright stance in acknowledgment of a height greater than one's own, the subject prostrates itself in order to give the most human of responses. Lowering oneself, one raises oneself. In *humble* and in *humus* (the soil one touches), *human* finds its origin, *dhghem-,* earth. In prostration is the somatic memory of the human aspect of subjectivity's original place—though we should not find it the only aspect. Prostration commemorates the earth as a source of *life,* the signification of *soma.* Although prostration, the physical act of bending down, serves to return mind to the soma, to recoup somatic awareness by any means is to prostrate oneself. The visible signifies the yielding inward. The act of reentering proximal awareness is the basic act of prostration. In a sensation of proximity, a hope "worth hoping for" is born.

To come to proximity is to come *down. Down* designates the direction of the somatic body relative to thought's aloofness, flightiness, and rarefaction. *Down* denotes both a process of condensation that is opposed to vaporization, and that of a slowed tempo, abandoning the acceleration of thinking. *Down* is also the fifth direction hidden in the four directions on the compass of thought. Indicating depth, it belongs to an axis that simultaneously points to height. The kinship of *hope* and *height* is brought by their common root, *keu-,* which binds the act of hope to the recovery of the axis of proximity. Condensing itself from a dispersed condition, the attention lightly falls to touch the body. The time it takes to light gives the response time to the delayed summons of the heart.

The Vertical Column

That hope is born in a *rapprochement* with somatic intelligence differentiates it from mere expectancy. Unfortunately, the English *to hope* does not clearly distinguish itself from the expression *to hope for.* The second takes a particular result as its object (one hopes for wealth or rain or victory) while the first is intransitive and takes no object. *Hope* refers to the act whereby the attention surrenders thought's authority to assignate meaning and prostrates itself before the inner sensation (*phantasia*). The act constitutes a recovery of the vertical column, that which corresponds to the spine or backbone of the physical body. The vertical column supplies the condition necessary for the subject's orientation with respect to levels. It is the subject's "east" or polestar. It is the recovery of the compass-point of subjectivity that specifically engenders the hopeful quality of a moment and without which one wanders aimlessly in the circuit of *samsara.*

No mere affective process, hope conveys an incomparable superior intelligence. Spinoza entirely misconstrues hope when he describes it as "inconstant pleasure, arising from the idea of something past or future, whereof we to a certain extent doubt the issue."[2] His confusion of hope with a diffuse kind of expectancy overlooks how the reembodiment of the vertical column bridges the two levels of the subject and permits subjectivity itself to respond. Without an actual (and not virtual) verticality, the circuit of inner sensation and the higher background energy of what is missing fail to communicate. They remain on different frequencies, operating at noncorresponding tempos. An interaction is precluded. The vertical column functions as a voice box. The finer utterances of background frequencies can then speak to the lower somatic frequencies, and conversely. Hope is that which facilitates the exchange. Without hope, heaven and earth cannot understand one another. With hope, subjectivity, born of their mingling, cannot see out its unique responsibility of the moment, its response to its own uniqueness.

Hope, prostration at the feet of proximity, is an act of renewal, as opposed to what is hoped for, which is an act of futility. Staging a reentry into the somatic mass for the sake of opening to the missing element, hope informs the subject from above the incarnation of the moment. Restoring the subject to an inner circulation of sensation, while prostrate on the vertical bridge, hope entices even the surpassing to enter into focus. Such is the overwhelming power of hope's caress, that it is bold enough to perform the impossible act—of relating to that which surpasses both possibility and impossibility. Thus, actuality enters the subject, and subjectivity is thereby rendered actual. Restoration of verticality is precisely the attainment of which hope actively is capable. For the vertical gives the subject hope of responding (in a literal fashion) to Epictetus's ancient riddle, "What is up to me?" The oracle again poses the enigma of responsibility. Only on this occasion, the subject's reply coalesces along the very axis that hope brings. Emboldened by its own prostration, the vertical column introduces the new element that commands the subject's response. It is here—between a life inside, the soma, and a life that enters from above, surpassingly—that the subject encounters that which takes precedence. It is in the meeting, of higher and lower life, that subjectivity prospers and is born.

The great knowledge that belongs to a gesture of bending down interiorly is of height. By decoding the meaning of directionality, hope thoroughly plumbs somatic depth and thereby relates the subject to a vertical axis. Because it knows the meaning of *up,* the subject is no longer mute in the face of the heart's summons. Knowledge of the "third dimension" gives the subject new suppleness (a word that shares the same root as *up*), an ability to move within and accompany the circulating sensitivity. Could this movement be the inner meaning of supplication?

Prostration

As the vertical column lies between above and below, so verticality denotes the space between, *der Zwischen.* Hope, the occupation of verticality, also denotes the medium in which growth of subjectivity occurs. Conversely, the absence of hope, meaning, the vacantness of effort, leave subjectivity without the culture of its growth. "Hope deferred maketh the heart sick." It is by relating the possible with the impossible—thought's function to the memory of the immemorial—that actuality is seized, and subjectivity brought to bloom. It may be that in the Elysian fields of the immemorial, hope is as constant as breath. Temporally, however, hope is short-lived, as if the position of prostration were exceedingly difficult to maintain like a yogic *asana.* Wrenched again and again from actual subjectivity, the subject then dwells in a mix of thought and the immemorial background, awaiting hope's return. In a hopeless, despairing condition, the hope lies in proximity and in the resurrection of the inner circulatory body. Indeed, to seek an avenue to somatic awareness is to turn to hope before hope.

If, however, the act of prostration is conceived in too insular a fashion, we fail to recognize its intersubjective dimension. To hope is also to bow down before the other's need to be remembered. Hopefulness at meeting one's task of memory, in addition to penetrating the integument of one's own body, involves entering the skin of the other. The fact can be put more strongly. Unless one puts oneself in the other's skin and prostrates oneself before the other, hope quickly becomes deficient and gives way to identification and the law of identicals. Unless one's hope puts bread on the other's plate and a shirt on the other's back, it is chimerical. It merely serves the self and fails to resurrect the body of subjectivity.

How can one be responsible for the other's task to remember the immemorial? Does this additional increment of responsibility not bring the total to beyond human striving? Does not the meaning of the nonsubstitutivity of the subject mean that I am not my brother's keeper? But to continue to think along these lines is to misunderstand the recovery of the vertical column. In one sense, the matter is straightforward. There, having approached the sensitivity of the inner body, the subject abandons the whole assembly of assignations of identification. When the law of identicals and its logic of exclusion cease to regulate the subject's attention, the subject need not posit itself "over and against" (*trans-* and *contra-*) the other as though a moat and walls lay between the two. Discontinuing the regulatory principle, the subject rejoins the somatic circulation in a gesture of prostration and *rapprochement.* Ending attachment to divisive thoughts, the subject is momentarily informed by an indivisible force that descends the vertical column. This foretaste of individuality effaces the skin that separates one from the other—like the effacement of the cervix—so that a union can be born. The basis of help found in the act of effacement proves that the subject's act of intervention in the other's affairs is less the erection of a barrier and more the offering of a caress.

The intervening subject bows down before the kinaesthetic flow and in so doing unstoppers an ear to the mouth of it. An influx of energy descending the vertical column is the source's utterance. Kinship between the higher source and the inner word is preserved for us by the root of *utter,* which also designates the direction *up.* Prostration, the intervening act, places one under the auspices of a proximal speech that is common to all, even if understood by none. It is the speech of a "common presence" that speaks to me in my absence. In prostration, hope moves beyond hope, and the fluency of that hope is that all—subject *and* other—understand the utterance of indivisibility. This hope is utterly different from wishing that both subject and other be the same. The wish to be absorbed into the Godhead or into the hodge-podge of the *polis* is a temptation and an abnegation. It is a misunderstanding, stemming from a disguised nihilism, of the process of effacement. The hope of understanding the utterance of individuality, by contrast, hopes that the other be lifted up to an effort to listen to the heart's delay. The region of hope is located in the other's weakness. In hope, the subject supports the other's ability to seek proximity and the near speech of common presence—that the exchange within may include the other's participation. In such a way, the subject hopes to communicate the act of intervention to the other, in need, in the misery of need, in the poverty of misery, oppressed and without heart.

One is obliged to put oneself in the other's skin in and through the same act that one is obliged to put oneself in one's own skin. Caressingly, one disrupts the functional rhythm of thought and enters proximally into sensitivity. Through the selfsame act of intervention, the other's despairing thought is disrupted and effort renewed. By a sympathetic vibration, the other who was downtrodden, oppressed, numbed by suffering, wretched, and lost, is suddenly able. Bread that was meant only for one is enigmatically sufficient also to feed the other. The act of intervention that was initiated by the one, by courage, clarity, and purpose, equally serves the other in its dissipated, confused, and rudderless state. Such is the force of hope, that it communicates through darkness, distance, and dread, even to the other who has nearly forfeited a human responsibility. Yet its power to "raise from the dead" is as gentle and no heavier than a feather.

Does the sympathetic action of returning oneself to the somatic fold absolve a subject from physically holding a hand out, giving the shirt off one's back, or binding the other's wounds? Who would think that? One who believes there is absolution in performing the outer act without the inner is legalistic and hypocritical. One who believes there is absolution in performing the inner act alone is an idealist. Both misconstrue the form of inclusiveness that is obligatory. For, even the superlative act of prostrating myself before the interior sensitivity while taking bread off my own plate and feeding it to the other does not absolve me of my responsibility. Responsibility remains unmet until one becomes absolute. Stern yet caressing, it bears witness to one's groping toward effort, that which comes from strength. Effort, however, does not diminish responsibility. Until the advent of individuality, there is no remission of indebtedness, no lessening of the task to remember. Perhaps the desire for absolution is itself chimerical and requires an absolution made possible only by responding to a need to be remembered.

Localization and Vocalization

The object of responsibility cannot be the self since that concept does not allow for maturation of hope. "Work on oneself," if it refers to an inner act of prostration, is not *for* one self, as opposed to an other. Or, if it is, then the conceptual grasping that is reflex to thought's functional beat has not yet been relaxed and made to yield to a proximal awareness. Much can be made of the conceptual self, even to the point of construing an ethics of "responsibility." But injunctions and precepts of such an ethics will of necessity be imposed, meaning that since one *ought* to treat the other in a certain way, one is in need of imposing one's will on the other in this way. The approach (if it is that) to the other is through an external coercion, as an outsider, as if it were an afterthought. Only in this fashion is one's autonomy—the automatism and its illusory freedom—preserved. The terrible offense of autonomy is defense of the ego. In this regard, it contrasts sharply with an act of hope that opens the other from inside and from the beginning includes the other in its yielding to sensitivity and relating to verticality. Hope knows the other as a quality, without the consideration of which the advent of individuality is a mere dream.

The maturation of hope coincides with an understanding of the pronominal nature of a need to be remembered. The subject that is summoned to that need and commanded to respond to an authority whose memory is infallible and who, therefore, keeps the forgetting in mind, is bound to raise questions. Why should such a one from whom "there is no place to hide" need be remembered? Does the need not add superfluity to superfluity? Yet, the deficiency in a subject's memory lies precisely in its "localizing" the need. Thinking that it is the subject itself that needs to be remembered, one is not yet ready to yield to an encompassing sensitivity. When vestiges of self-willing, the automatism and autoeroticism prevent an effacement of exclusiveness, the subject fails to participate in a circulating sensation and its logic. In the compass of the circumnavigation, the meaning of *my* and *mine* shifts from assignation to a particular entity or self to attribution to the primordial word *I*. Then, the *myself* in need of being borne in mind does not refer to the subject itself but to a quality of the circulating flow that passes through the subject's own interior without ceasing to stop. The error of localization or "misplaced concreteness" (as Whitehead calls it) mistakes the possessive for the nonpossessive pronoun because it stop-frames a small segment of the flux and identifies it with its encompassing nature. The *I* that I am in need of remembering is not myself but an unknown *I* that caressingly reminds me of my forgotten obligation.

Hope matures with the thawing of reification, the "thinging" of the automatism. Circulating kinesthesia no longer follows Husserl's scheme of foreshadowing a noetic act that belongs to a subject but rather performs a minor arc of an exchanging flow. It becomes a conscious link between the source and the mouth; in other words, a windpipe of utterance. The voicing of sensation, its modulation within the specific metabolism of a subject, surely differs from one to the other. What does not change, however, is the need to complete the communication of an inner resonance, from one to the other. Inasmuch as the movement within the soma, a kinesthetic frequency, is lifeblood of memory, its actualization satisfies the need to be remembered. To prostrate oneself, to bow to the circulation, matures hope and quickens a memory that encompasses the other as oneself.

Put in this way, one can say that hope provides an authentic voicing of the primordial word *I*. Its articulation is providential. Its inward audition, experienced through an induction into the soma—that cave—permits a subsequent relation to the vertical axis of life. It becomes obvious that the reverberation of the word extends hope to the other in the same act as to the subject. Hope consumes the barriers between each other without consuming the differences. Just as it imbues the subject with the intelligence to pursue its responsibility, so too for the other. We should not, however, conceive of hope's communication as that between windowless monads, one of a "preestablished harmony." That would be to misconstrue the action of sympathy that underlies the shared communication. The power of sympathy is to bring about a harmonious condition in the other by means of the inner sensitivity of the sympathetic subject—even to wrench it from disequilibrium. Transmission from one to the other is unmediated and without conceptual content, but is transmission of the highest degree.

Heteronomy

"Hope is an earning, not a given." From the standpoint of the autonomous subject, the opposition of grace and will is important since it demarcates boundaries of an ethics "within the limits of reason alone." Is obligation not defined in terms of a conflict of will, that between desire and the Ought (*Wilkur* and *Will*)? Or perhaps a conflict between autoeroticism and an indebtedness to a transcendent principle, a categorical imperative? Within this frame, the problem is how to mount an attack on the subject's nature, the stronghold of which lies in its natural preferences and inclinations. Until weakened or overcome momentarily, the subject will be unable to act as a self-legislating being (*auto-nomos*) but only as an outlaw. Effort is experienced as a conflict within the heteronomous will, the subject's attempt to subjugate its nature to a supranatural authority. The self-containment or self-constraint of desire is necessarily a contraction, a clenching of the will. If and when hope appears, it is a causal result of the sacrifice of preference and inclination on the altar of principle. It is a well-earned outcome of an arduous exercise of restraint.

Not only from the standpoint of autonomy is hope the subject's wage for energy well spent. Disrupting the functional rhythm of thought by an act of intervention, the subject yields to a sensitivity that conveys a summons to remember the delayed word of the heart. That yielding requires an inner audition in order to flower into the responsibility of subjectivity, namely, to bear the memory of the immemorial. Effort is needed as an effacement of itself, as *ef-fort,* that which flows from a higher strength, as the root *bhergh-* shows. Where dissolution of blockages and constrictions is the keynote of an effort practiced from a viewpoint of somatic awareness, submission mints the coin of the realm. For matters dear to the subject stand in its way of being penetrated by the pulse of the soma. To pay for opening the channel to clear communication, the subject is asked to violate the law of identicals and break with certain identifications of itself. Thus, in this case also, the advent of hope is perceived as a rightful result of a subjective undertaking, earned and won.

But from the standpoint of hope itself, its gracious arising, as an impulse, is not different from the subject's winning of it through effort. While hope before hope involves the cultivation of an inner prostration that is dry and unforthcoming, hope beyond hope is simply an uninhibited flow of energy through the very same posture. Whether a trickle or a gushing, hope navigates the identical channel, the only difference being that of the tide. The periodicity of hope, its cresting and shallowing, depends on the heart-word's systole and diastole. It annunciation brings the tidings of hope forth in its own time, whether or not it coordinates in time with the subject's effort. When it does, hope has a supervenient quality. When it does not, it seems adventitious note that graces a preoccupied and brooding canvas, a cause of renewed strength rather than the result thereof.

Resonation

Hope names the language of intersubjectivity. Its proper milieu is that of the group. Hope addresses the basic need of the group, and indicates the fruit of responding to the need. In the way that it mobilizes *phantasia,* repeatedly disrupting the cognitive rhythm, the group inwardly bows down before this altar—the other's need to be remembered. The inner prostration can be visualized as a way of the group's accommodating itself so as to serve as a circulatory system for the lifeblood of sensitivity. Sensitivity, when made available to the task, summons each subject to allow passage of a finer energy that makes whole. Each subject, in varying degrees, is enabled to open to its full, integral subjectivity. Through the prostration of the many, each one is returned to the task of memory and weighed vis a vis the responsibility of subjectivity. But further, through the promise and the fruit of hope—the group's resensitization—the other itself recollects the need to be whole. The recollection constitutes an acknowledgment on the part of the other itself that it is not yet whole and for that end it is in need of help. The group's impression of the lack forms the basic datum of the lack within each of a wholeness that is analogously lacking in the other itself. Somatic awareness of the datum is awareness of that through which the heart caressingly utters its call, its longing.

One could also say that to speak the language of hope is the group's work. To bracket substitution, which is the logic of identification, the group "bends down" in a gesture of prostration. This is a homeopathic action inasmuch as a bracket is similar to a bend. When like meets like, the assignation of objects is neutralized, and with it the subsequent equation of self with object. Intensification of inner sensation, *phantasia,* is reversion to the speaking in which the primordial word *I* is uttered to be heard. As said earlier, whenever language reverts to the primordial, it is the work of a group—whether in physical contiguity, as a diaspora, or even as a diachronic entity. Resonation of *I* (and the conditions that make it possible) is never the work of a single individual, although the word refers to the individuality of subjectivity. The *I* resounds in the voicing of an implicate whole. It cannot be spoken by a part without its whole. Although uttering *I*, moreover, is the final end of hope, hope is undiminished in quality if the *I* is not attained.

The special creative action of hope—"one word can release a soul from despair"—in the intersubjective realm is obscured when hope is referred back to the autoerotic. Descartes in *The Passions of the Soul*, for one, is guilty of ignoring the origins of hope. "But when," he says, "besides that we consider whether there is much or little prospect that we shall obtain what we desire, that which represents to us that there is much probability of this excites in us hope, and that which represents to us that there is little, excites fear, of which jealousy is a species."[3] To derive hope from assignation and render it a twin of fear is to subscribe to an ethics of despair, for then any incursion of the infinite into the subject is precluded. Descartes's infinite God who casts out the evil demon of doubt wants nothing to do with subjectivity other than to furnish proofs. He is of such supernal purity that he never ventures into human thought, save geometrically. He has receded to such a degree of abstraction that no point, no intermediary, can approach him, and apparently is wholly uninterested in communication with humanity. There are, therefore, no holy passions and all passions are, therefore, degenerately human, "excited in us by the objects which move our nerves." There are no emotions that summon, admonish, or muster the subject to a responsibility that stands in contradiction to thought and calls for the *cogito's* effacement. Like a God who casts proofs alone, thought is god of the subjective realm and subjugates the subject to the order of demonstration and evidence. Such protocol advocates avoidance of the inescapable gap in thought, In other words, it contradicts itself and throws the subject into despair.

That desire has a hopeless nature in itself ("Abandon all hope ye who enter here") means that a hedonic ethics keeps the subject from initiating an inquiry into the heart's delay. Whether the fact of desire implies a sacrifice of the autoerotic or only its integration into a fuller whole is a large question. Leaving it aside, we can say that thought is for the most part in the service of desire and plots out causal schemes by which to satisfy the subject's wants. This is true not only for appetite and feeling but more especially for deeper proclivities like desiring a uniformity of time, conditions, and experience. Breaking the linkage of one thought to the next provokes despair and anxiety, and not only because of failed ends but more primarily because of the threat to the causal order itself. The *cogito* resists hope because hope undermines belief in causality and is not hoped for by the desiring subject. Hope is a representative of an acausal order whose advent can never be adequately represented or predicted and therefore must be guarded against. A form of cognition more docile to the acausal incursion of hope, if it were possible, would be cognition in service of what is other than desire. If it were thought at all, it would be sensitive to the summons and knowledgeable concerning the delay of the heart.

As a result of its protentive nature, thought is hopeless, despairing of ruin and decay. Indeed, thought has just enough attentiveness to witness its degeneration over time. To a certain extent, its pessimism or subtle nihilism is warranted. Since it bars the advent of hope, the automatism dwells on transcendence. Transcendence posits the possibility of the subject moving beyond itself, shedding its skin and, like a caterpillar, becoming another species of being altogether. The possibility is imbedded in a more pervasive approach in the history of Western metaphysics of regarding being and consciousness as the touchstones of subjectivity. An progressive negation of determinants to (meaning, constrictions of) consciousness, on this theory, leads to an enlargement of the subject's being (as Hegel proposes), or an incremental relaxation of control over consciousness leads to a widened horizon of being (as Heidegger suggests). The strenuous concentration on thought, as favored by the tradition, intensifies thought's concern over the means of production while it masks the hopeless tenor of the approach. One is forced to adopt either a messianic vision (that transcendence will come with the proper emissary) or an idealism (that one is already transcendent).

Chapter Twelve
Atonement

Exile

In exile, the only real problem is atonement. For the one who has separated from the other, expiation is the only real matter of concern. Whether the separation has come about by will (one's own or one imposed) or by happenstance is irrelevant. Whether one wants to attribute the separation to fate, miscalculation, or ignorance, the only concern is getting back. Attribution or assignation is not an issue. In order to return, atonement is requisite. Without atonement, the exiled state establishes itself all the more firmly, like a splinter setting in under the skin, getting ready to fester. Without atonement, exile grows bitter and instead of being localized as a singular theme becomes *the* thematic of thought, becomes thought itself. The *cogito* enters an exilic condition and grows oblivious both of its fragmentariness and its master. Atonement then is the special salt that the exile needs to soak its skin in, so that the bitterness will be leeched from the pulp and the fruit will again be palpable and delicious.

Any separation brings a need for atonement. Death is one such separation. Separated by death, Orpheus is compelled by need to seek Eurydice in the underworld. To be reunited with her in the other realm, he must exercise his musical enchantments to the utmost in order to calm the restless, malevolent souls. When he is finally granted his heart's desire and leads his beloved back to this world, each step is an act of atonement. Each step stops thought and its mechanism of production. Each step reunites him with a sensitivity equal to the task of remembering a time before this or any present time, a time before presence, an anarchaic time. Each step absolves him of his love of manipulating things, singing and playing his lyre until flowers weep and the wind stands stock still. Each challenges his willingness to continue. The account gives no mention of the actual limit to his atonement, only that expiation was broken off at the time that an irresistible grasping for his beloved sapped his resolve. It is also clear that in losing Eurydice forever, Orpheus lived the rest of his life in atonement, doubly remorseful because he lost his love *and* his resolve for atonement.

Death is not the only separation that brings a need for atonement. If it were, our life would be one of belonging and our mortality, the sole cause of exile. But it is not and death is actually a derivative cause, springing from the primordial separation that delay entails—the way that *mortality* springs from *mora.* The word *I* uttered in the heart takes its own time to light in the assemblage of thought, and the difference is registered as a temporal interval, the number of minutes, hours, or years that it takes for the heart to be heard. If the gulf did not separate speaking from comprehension, if one had an understanding heart, there would be no need for expiation. The very depth to which one feels exiled then is a foreshadowing of the judgment of the pans of justice, of the weighing of the heart. A quiet or poignant longing to be remembered by a memory of the whole is the very hunger of expiation. When longing is so sharp that the exile wants to rub the skin off one's body to end the separation, then one is ready for atonement—though through death there is no atonement. Atonement lies in perceiving the heart's delay and exerting oneself to catch the strains of the faint utterance *I*.

Because of a cleavage internal to subjectivity, one needs to atone. Even though the cleavage is not due to anything the subject has committed or omitted, even though the cleavage predated the subject and lay in wait for subjectivity to coalesce around it—as a raindrop around a dust mote—one needs to atone. The inner separation is the statement of delay summoning one from across a divide . . . to leap. It is a statement of debt, of payment owed, an accounting kept from the very first breath, and before. Comprehending the command, and leaping, one is free from the gnawing of atonement. One is then no longer so fully indebted, under obligation vis a vis a possession borrowed, and a little more free from owing. But having leapt and finding oneself on the ground of expiation once again, the inner irritation starts anew—as if the condition of subjectivity were resolvable only in its irresolution. The leap changes nothing for the subject, least of all the need for atonement. Yet without leaping, nothing changes for the subject, and this fact bodes ill. For unless one responds to the need to be remembered, one's indebtedness is not amortized but actually increases. Unless the moment of leaping over the chasm near the heart of subjectivity is seized, the subject has not responded and atonement not served.

Exile means isolation. The *solus* is made more solitary by being cut off from the community of consolation. As I said, the community, actual or virtual, comprises a condition necessary to the subject's entry into proximity. Strangely, without the consolation of the community, one is unable to approach somatic awareness, as if the soma itself were a dominion of the community, concealed and wrapped in obscurity, as if a password were required. Offered by the group, con-*solation* directs the subject toward inner sense by a double means: by effacing its cognitive concerns and by mobilizing a sensitivity to *phantasia*. When in exile, "when in disgrace with fortune and men's eyes," no guidance is given and the exile becomes a wanderer in thought, one held captive by wandering thoughts and the staccato rhythm of the *cogito*'s function. When in isolation, one is not, however, without means to unplug the ears and listen to the embodiment of the heart's word. Perhaps the exertion is more arduous; perhaps not. In any event, the means are given through atonement.

To devote oneself to enduring the unendurable articulations of thought is the form of expiation. To guard against agreement with the law of identicals that would substitute an identity for oneself is the form of expiation. To reject the assignations to objects is expiation. To dispel the story of self, its autobiographical commentary, and its autoeroticism, is expiation. Yet the self-ending of thought, its discontinuity, is not the outcome of expiation. The heart-word, delayed an incalculable length of time, rises to and stills thought momentarily, but its advent is not caused by the expiating subject. The gap in thinking, in a kind of symmetry with the cleavage of subjectivity, manifests out of respect to the speaking of the heart. Through the keyhole, the subject who seeks a finer inner audition may listen to the summons, and though distant, respond. Through expiation, disruption is lent value. Through expiation, the subject meets value in the moment of responsibility.

The approach to proximity is not causally indicated, yet the causal approach is the only one known to the subject. The *cogito* is like a spider that has spun the web of causality. The subject's attempts to disrupt the functional rhythm of thought derive from such knowledge. The battery of techniques that it deploys to the objective of arrest each has the signature of the causal order, the order of control: thought used to stop thought, the wind used to stop the tide. Through the frustration, irritability—the ire of subjectivity itself—can be felt, and with it, sensitivity to an order of submission. A deft vigilance to the automatism, a withdrawal into the desert of it, seems more a reproach than a nearing to the soma. Yet the backward movement, and the entailed suffering, awakens the epidermis to the caress of the other, the gentle summons, implacably spoken, giving no quarter. In the intelligence of response that does not involve cognition, the subject finds a solitary communication with the other that answers the heart-word *I*.

The Community of Consolation

In exile, when one suffers loss of the community of consolation, what precisely is lost? Is not what is taken from the subject, as if nerve endings had been cauterized, its somatic awareness? For, to put oneself in one's own skin, to wear it, is to leave behind the desensitized hide of epidermis that protects one from the other's interrogation—a summoning that summons one to the task of memory. To live in one's skin, in the somatic flux, is, strangely, to join a communal life whose primary concern is to dig under the dermis and expose what is missing. The community bears the task on its shoulders like a rasp that scratches the surface and wakens the subject's irritability. Loss of consolation is also loss of pain since one no longer undergoes hardship of exposure. It is a deadening that obviates the need for consolation, community, and the summons of memory itself. It is a death that the sufferer suffers when stripped of consolation. Thus, consolation is more than a hand at one's elbow. It is a brush with mortality that raises responsibility from its grave.

It is the community that is charged with memory of the heart's delay. But is it not strange to speak of community in this way, as the soma? Does not *community* imply number, separation, and individuality? If we look carefully at what takes place in the soma, by virtue of its sheer fluidity, the dynamism forbids attachment of pronomial possessives or assignations. The attempt to determine the flux derives from thought whose project is production of determinate form. The escape from assignation is highly significant. It lends the soma a quality "common to all"—a raw material that is subsequently processed by cognition in myriad ways. However confined to one specific embodiment or subject that it is, it is the medium of exchange. Shared in the original sense of *koinomia* (the Greek root of *community*), the inner sensation is communal by virtue of being exchanged, one to the other, in mutuality. In an act of linking different subjects, it is the force of relation. Or perhaps it is the relating force itself, in manifestation.

The particular suffering of the exile, the "coin" of atonement, is dysrelation—most immediately, somatic dysrelation. The *cogito's* isolation gives an appearance of individuality but at best leaves, as Descartes sees, the question of the body obscure and the relation itself, contingent. A whole history of disease is implied by the condition. The fact that such a history is implied explains the close connection that philosophy has traditionally enjoyed with medicine. Without consolation, the subject's hope is reduced to a frontal attack on cognitive productivity, a deployment of the scant resource of awareness to stage a determined arrest of thought's functional beat. One accidental product is physical strain. Without consolation, the subject is ignorant of its distance from the *initium,* the beginning of effort, and proceeds without direction and under duress. The stressful, solitary blindness of its undertaking constitutes the subject's initial expiation.

If rejoining the community is sought to end atonement, the subject is misguided. Consolation ends exile but not expiation. Not only is it not the end of suffering but rather its beginning, its *principium.* By exposing the soma, consolation reawakens the subject to what is missing, the festering sore of the immemorial to be borne in memory. Hope mitigates since in hope there is never exile. In hope, one is never in isolation. To a certain extent, hope removes the sting of atonement without annulling its action. For the subject is asked to atone for the discrepancy between its identifications (as retained by thought) and its responsibility to subjectivity, and the discrepancy is heightened, not diminished, by the effect of community. One could rightly say that the community is one of atonement. To be more accurate, it is a community whose continuous present is that of preparing for atonement. Welcomed by its gesture of bowing inwardly, the subject is received by a caress in the communal effort of being ready for atonement. The welcome makes the subject ready to be fit to atone. Without acceptance into the community, one is not fit for atonement and suffers being a misfit.

An Embittered Cognition

Preponderance of wandering thought is the bitter herb of exile. An *exul* in Latin is a wanderer. An overstressed cognitive function with its retentive and protentive traits—the *cogito*—is the shadow of the exile. A strategic emphasis on productivity and avoidance of nonproductive discontinuity keeps awareness of hardship at bay. The *cogito* embraces and wraps itself in the cloak of transparency in the absence of consolation from the somatic community. It makes itself invisible since one who wears the ring of Gyges is the ultimate exile. In absence of a medium of exchange, thought speaks incessantly to itself. An autoerotic history is thereby composed, embellished, and rehearsed. An automatism is confirmed by a script of its own composition.

What makes these words that I now use different? The bitter herb, dipped in the salt water of atonement, is eaten to signify the subject's passage to responsibility. Similarly, the wandering thought, its occasional consoling clarity and its twisting, circuitous itinerary, is here to be consumed. Why? The taste of the *cogito's* imbalance is unpalatable and that very unpalatability nourishes my hope to become responsible. However briefly, the taste recalls both my exile and the momentary end of it. Thoughts stop, proximity is regained, and there resounds a barely audible echo of the heart's word, delayed in time along its immemorial passage. The need to be remembered is tended and met by the utterance of *I*.

This speech having been said, what more is there? But these are words at the disposal of thought and ignore *mora,* the delay. Its dynamism in time is the *mo*ment, whose signifier carries the impress of the imme*mo*rial in the *mo-* particle. The impression is specific to a specific moment and rises, flourishes, and perishes with it. The words uttered concerning thought's exile were consumed, played a part in responding to the summons, and are no longer. These words, of a new moment, serve the heart's delay in a like manner, but are different servants of the same.

For the subject, the bitter taste of thought is both disease and cure. Signifying the split internal to subjectivity, bitterness speaks through the root that provides the word's origin, *bheid-*. *Fissure* comes from the same stem. Thought's dream of freedom, the automatism, and autoeroticism, all derive from the bitterness that meandering, desultory cognition expresses. The embittered attitude of the cogito comes from its rejection of hope, that would require thought to kneel before the soma. Yet a hopelessness turned bitter—that biting truth—can arrest the mind and allow the subject to separate itself from the cognitive function. In the break with the law of identicals, the subject is momentarily cured of identification. In bitterness is the command to prostrate oneself before inner sensation, and thus the bitter taste serves as an eloquent mouthpiece for the community of consolation.

Accusative

The Diaspora in its exilic condition wanders restlessly from place to place. Is there a safe haven? The very act of settling leaves the mind unsettled, with the re-establishment of the functional beat and its retentive urge. The alternation between bitterness and sacrifice ultimately fails to satisfy a need for quiet recollection. The subject is diasporic. Its search for responsibility mirrors its search for relief—save in one regard. Relief, an analgesic for the irritability of existence, is unattainable. The subject, however, can attain unto its responsibility. There too will it be relieved of its suffering, or rather of making suffering its primary possession. If there be suffering for subjectivity, it is holy suffering and not owned by one or the other subject. Its owner is the suffering community of consolation.

Unsettled and running from bitterness, one is arrested time and again by . . . what? The variable set of signifiers for the arresting force is a further expression of the subject's unsettled, irritable condition. An impulse to objectify and identify meets a force that annihilates any result thereof. The further one suspends assignation, the more one is quickened in and impregnated by the delay. Withholding *that,* the articulate circuit of sensitivity is rendered audible. As its utterance becomes the utter focus of audition, the *arche*-word *I* is pronounced—as a vacuum draws a primal sound into it. Yet the speaking does not cause arrest, nor the converse. The arresting force, more passive than passivity, has overtaken the subject like one who knew the subject in another life, another place, another story, and now bears the recriminations of that time. In the delay is accusation. In the accusation is expiation. In the expiation is hope.

The exiled subject has left its community. Abandoned also is proximity whose vessel contains the memory of the immemorial. The subject has wandered through foreign lands, resettling many times, adopting different roles. It has, finally, established a stable version of itself, of the itself per se. Then, into that life comes someone from a former time. That other remembers the wanderer before its present alias. Would not the subject tremble in the sight of the other, at the memory awakened? Would not the other's presence suffice to accuse and call up an indebtedness, even a fear that the need to be remembered had been neglected? Would not the subject seize on the task of memory and reclaim the heart's delay with renewed alacrity? Such is the force that in midflight arrests the fleeing subject, the one susceptible to autoeroticism and fantasies of freedom, the one who believes the story of its identity as told by the law of identicals. In that moment, the subject is moved by its responsibility.

The Fit of Longing

Expiation is never complete because for the most part it never begins. At best, one prepares to expiate. At worst (which is usual), the subject confuses expiation with the reparation for a tragic event, like paying insurance to the family of an innocent victim of a traffic fatality. On closer examination, no payment can replace the life lost, and so expiation is never finished. Furthermore, expiation has nothing to do with the object-world, fixed by assignation, nor with the identifications with which the subject fixes that world. Nothing is ameliorated in that world by expiation. Yet without expiation the subject remains a novice vis a vis proximity and employs a dilettante's ear to listen for the heart word. The subject remains irresolute and divided.

In expiation, in exile, the paradoxical value of what is missing is felt with an upsurge of longing. Although surrounded with goods and preferences of its auto-erotic drives, the subject feels that the source of all valuation lies in absence. Longing does not diminish, moreover, when the subject is present to what is missing, but rather increases. For in longing is a knowledge that an ethics of presence—on which the whole Hellenic tradition is based—provides no adequate response to value, since value is in what is missing. The unsatisfiability of longing verifies that what is missing belongs to no present, was never present, and is therefore a particle of anarchaic time. Such a particle is incapable of representation but draws all forms of representation toward it in a fit of longing. The world is an ecstatic form of presence, though to be clear, that ecstasy expresses great sorrow, not joy. In being drawn out of itself, the rush of irritability follows a trajectory ever surpassing itself in a vain attempt to satisfy its aspiration and join with what is missing. That union, however, is not in the plot of subjectivity. However credible an ethics of presence makes the case for absorption into the one, God, Elohim, Brahman, or even Nothingness, subjectivity can never gain access to immemorial time. It can only be reminded of it and remembered by it, serving in relation to the other. If there is a one, it is not served by "becoming one" with it, since that one necessarily surpasses all becoming. *Becoming* means becoming present, coming into being or existence. But even human responsibility arises from a source that predates being as well as becoming. "Before you wert, *I am.*" An ethics of presence would convert the subject to unity and leave over nothing to weep longingly over the surpassing majesty of the heart's summons.

In the surpassing, the subject follows longing to beyond longing to the longing beyond longing, dissolving encrustations of the self in the salt of tears. Such is the potency of the surpassing, that bonds of identification, together with the superstructure of the automatism, are progressively melted in its ocean, and the subject set free to the somatic life within the skin. In an unsatisfiable longing that a subject's irritability knows lies a response that gives value to value, a value that lies in what is missing. Without the response, the value remains valuable but unvalued. One could say that the good, unpraised and without a congregation, weeps alone in its solitary kingdom and the countryside becomes a wasteland. Through the longing, a trajectory is traced which, if ever completed, would radiate directly toward that value. There is, however, no lamp to the longing. It follows a darkened way. One's sense of direction is more akin to a magnetic than an optical perception. Nonetheless, to trace the trajectory of surpassing is the responsibility of subjectivity, and there the grip of longing is an indispensable aid.

Unsatisfiability

The deep well of longing is fed by the spring of expiation. Because of the saline condition, the subject's thirst is never satisfied, perhaps is ever less ready to be satisfied. Chronically dissatisfied, with a belly swollen by dehydration, the subject nevertheless is summoned to say "*dyanu,*" "it is enough." Longing for what is missing, one is summoned to stop everything—even longing—and listen for the word of the heart, the sound at the well's bottom. The "word that surpasseth all understanding," the *I,* is in the hollow before expiation fills the cleft. Had the word been audible at the beginning, there would have been no need for atonement. Or rather, had the subject been attuned to the heart's word and gifted with knowledge of the heart's delay, there would be no day of atonement. Such is not the vocation of subjectivity. To long and the more so when the well overflows with the fruits of expiation and the word submerged by the swelling depths: this is subjectivity's saga. Difficulty alone brings the task to fruition, just as the fuller the well, the more intent the subject is on the task of listening.

In the face of its radical incompleteness, the triumph of expiation lies in saying, "it is enough." It is never enough but "it is enough": the formula is cognizant of the delay of the heart for it responds to the end of longing even though no end is in sight. The patience of the surpassing is thereby met by the patience of the subject, enigmatic mix of irritability, autoeroticism, and atonement that it is. The trajectory flung out in a direction of what is missing and its preeminent value is thereby met by an emanation from the source of value. The event is not one of union, as proposed by an ethics of presence, but of correspondence and relation. Unknowingly, the subject treads the allotted path, guided around pitfalls and traps by a magnetic sense of an interior movement of the soma. Under the patient, painstaking work of expiation, longing forms a more durable perception of what is missing, the source of value, and the surpassing itself. The matter out of which the perception is formed is, however, "never enough" to yield clarity and definition—which belong to assignation—but rather only an imperatival source of the summons. Yet the perception suffices to convey the heart-word.

It is never enough but "it is enough": is this not an exact expression of the surpassing? An infinitely expanding but bounded cosmos that physics speaks of is another rough equivalent. For the unbounded longing of subjectivity, that open wound, is itself an utterance, elongated over time, articulated a priori at the source of things, anterior to their being and becoming. It is the *arche*-word, sprung onto the tongue of creation and spoken by the surpassing for the surpassing of all things. Never fully articulated, fully articulate in each form, the *I* surpasses each articulation by being fully immanent in each. The entire cosmos is utterance. But just as any utterance once said, it too longs to retrace the trajectory to the very striking of the uttering, the initial alteration and expansion—when the force of speaking overcame an inertial muteness. The longing of subjectivity is an echo of this majestic surpassing. So is its expiation, which is atonement for the delay in hearing the initial utterance of the heart. But delay is no flaw unless necessity is. Delay is as inevitable as is longing. Indeed, longing is the emotional recognition of delay. In delay, the tears of the cosmos are borne through human ducts, and the eyes, wet with weeping, bear witness to the surpassing, which in its surpassing, tears itself moment after moment from what it caressingly speaks most dearly in order to repeat itself to new and yet unloved forms.

The endless repetition of the *I:* an inward prayer of the surpassing circulates in the circulation of the soma. Not of petition but praise and thanksgiving, the prayer is as audible as the pulse or the firing of the central nervous system. Yet because facility needs to train the ear on the source, one's hearing picks up signals already at some remove from their transmission. Thus to hear the prayer of the *I* is to feel need to atone for one's lateness, for does not an untended prayer give indication of a waywardness, a lack of compassion? To succeed in expiation, that is, to hear the prayer of the surpassing, is to feel need to go further in expiation. One could say that the subject's need to surpass echoes that of the surpassing itself in whose endless repetition of *I* is the labor of bringing each individual repetition back to the unutterable source. In the repetition is the effort. In the repetition is the prayer. In the prayer is the expiation.

The inevitability of delay is as inevitable as the interval between repetitions of the *I.* A drone is not a repetition but a sound continuously produced. The interval separating utterance from utterance is indicative of the deepening work of atonement since the greater the repetitions, the greater the degree of inclusiveness required to bear all in one memory. As the number grows, so does the work of remembering. The need to bear all repetitions in one memory is the essential need of integrity. The need to be remembered, on all levels and to all degrees, is borne by repetition of the *I,* the *arche*-word, whose very utterance simultaneously divides the cosmos and gives the formula for wholeness. Thus, the secret of delay, of the *mora,* pertains to the interval of repetition and how it relates to a life beyond dying, to a life beyond any single repetition of the *I.* The key to the secret is the work of expiation.

The "Birth" of Subjectivity

The exile of expiation plays a crucial role in providing for the surpassing quality of responsibility. Only responsibility surpasses responsibility, in breadth, width, depth, and height, since no sooner does the subject "remember itself" than the task of memory is superceded by a new summons. That is to say, utterance follows utterance, *I* follows *I,* but not by identity, like one heartbeat after another. The difference is in inclusiveness, that which repeatedly surpasses itself, and this difference also marks the difference between time that antedates all present time (immemorial time) and dated time. A need for expiation is born with the birth of presence. Until then, "all is one and shall be one," meaning that the state is already one of atonement. With responsibility, a little responsibility begets a little more responsibility, given the midwifery of expiation. Without the maieutic character, a response to proximity would perhaps never break the waters of labor, and the birth would be stillborn. Expiation effaces the automatism. Identification loosens, autoeroticism subsides, and a "magnetic" perception of the surpassing trajectory of value surges up. In effacement, there is never an exemption but the command to efface more contraction. If it does not cover the same ground, the Socratic project, in which Socrates makes repeated reference to the midwife's role in self-knowledge, parallels the edict of expiation.

There is, however, an important disanalogy with the trope of birthing. Given the surpassing quality of responsibility, at no time is the subject's responsibility "discharged." Having been born into the skin-cloth of responsibility, the subject has no way to terminate it, not even by death. Death in fact is a dereliction of responsibility, which does not mean that one is charged to live an immortal life, but rather that responsibility oversees the subject's life, not the converse. In the interminability of the subject's responsibility is a parallel with that of the surpassing itself. For to fail to respond to the summons to remember, in both cases, means closure, distance, and loss of the immemorial. Even the death of eternity, however, fails to absolve each of failure, a failure that adds a burden to the growing burden of atonement. The glory of the surpassing is in its relentlessness.

But is not subjectivity a matter of birth? Is there not a time when subjectivity fully measures up to its responsibility and "is born"? But does not the trope of birthing belong to an ethics of presence since birth is an unveiling? By contrast, a subject, summoned to the impossibility of remembering the immemorial, faces a measure that is at every point surpassing. That the measure invariably is surpassing is expressed in the fact of delay, a kind of nonappearance. The heart summons urgently, caressingly, but the subject responds tardily if at all. Although the subject never "catches up" with the summoner, the subject nonetheless is rewarded. The reward of tardiness is expiation, itself an attendance on birth. Surely, in the original sense, subjectivity—the peculiar irritability of being under commands foreign to its proclivities—is deeply involved in birth since both *birth* and *bear* share the same root, *bher-*. The subject bears the suffering of an expiate and thereby quickens its response to an impossible command. Does this mean that one is commanded to give birth to subjectivity and unless that event occurs, one has lived irresponsibly? Here, the trope of birthing is pushed beyond its limits, for if there is an "event," it is dissimilar to that of the infant who successfully descends the birth canal and is born. In its enigmatic, nonlinear numinosity, subjectivity's birth is more like a threshold crossed long before it is noticed. One is born because one has already been born. Or else, one can never be born.

In the heart's delay, in its surpassing quality, is contained the secret of death and of birth. In the schism it opens between memory and the immemorial, the automatism and proximity, and freedom and responsibility, delay tries me and finds me wanting in response. For this lack, I atone. Ever-deepening pulses of expiation fail to close the gap. Yet in the deepening insufficiency of subjectivity, I respond more fully to the need to be remembered. Even death, even birth, does not absolve me from responsiveness. Or if it does, I have ceased to be a servant of the other and instead have become a lackey. I have ceased to be tried and instead have been found to have failed. Henceforth, these words speak my wish to be tried.

Notes

Chapter 1. The Heart's Delay

1. *The Golden Epistle: A Letter to the Brethren at Mont Dieu,* tr. Theodore Berkeley. Spencer, MA: Cistercian Publications, 1971, from *the Works of William of St. Theirry, volume four,* p. 9.

2. "Memory . . . is of so great moment that, where it is wanting, all the rest of our faculties are in a great measure useless." *An Essay Concerning Human Understanding,* X, "Of Retention."

3. "Time is nothing but the form of inner sense, that is, of the intuition of ourselves and of our inner state. It cannot be a determination of our appearances; it has to do neither with shape nor position, but with the relation of representations in our inner state. And just because this inner intuition yields no shape, we endeavour to make up for the want by analogies." *Critique of Pure Reason,* tr. Normal Kemp Smith. London: Macmillan, 1950, A33=B49.

4. "Thus in each of these retentions is embodied a continuity of retentional modifications, and this continuity is itself again a point of actuality which retentionally shades off." *The Phenomenology of Internal Time-Consciousness,* ed. Martin Heidegger, tr. James S. Churchill. Bloomington: Indiana University Press, 1969, p. 51.

5. "Oblivion is not merely a *vis inertiae,* as is often claimed, but an active screening device, responsible for the fact that what we experience and digest psychologically does not, in the stage of digestion, emerge into consciousness any more than what we ingest physically does." *The Genealogy of Morals,* tr. Francis Golffing. New York, Doubleday, 1956, p. 189.

6. "If we abstract from *our* mode of inwardly intuiting ourselves—the mode of intuition in terms of which we likewise take up into our faculty of representation all outer intuitions—and so take objects as they may be in themselves, then time is nothing." *Critique of Pure Reason* A34=B51.

7. "Space is nothing but the form of all appearances of outer sense." Ibid. A26=B42. The crest of Kant's distinction, inward versus outward sense, evaporates in the loftiness of thought and turns out to be too vaporous to distinguish between objectifying and nonobjectifying experience.

8. "Anarchy is not a matter of disorder as opposed to order, just as the withdrawal from a theme is not a putative return to a diffuse 'field of consciousness' awaiting attention. Disorder is but another order, and the diffuse can possibly be thematized. Anarchy troubles being beyond these alternatives. It halts the ontological play, which, precisely as play, is consciousness in which being loses and rediscovers itself and is thereby lit up. Anachronistically *lagging* behind its present, incapable of recovering this lag and of thinking what touches it, the Ego is evinced in the ascendancy of the Other over the Same to the point of interruption, leaving it speechless: an-archic, obsession is persecution." Emmanuel Levinas, *Otherwise Than Being or Beyond Essence,* tr. Alphonso Lingis. The Hague: Martinus Nijhoff, 1981, p. 101.

9. "In brute experience, or shock, I have not only a clear indication, for my ulterior reflection, that I exist, but a most imperious summons at that very moment to *believe* in my existence." *Skepticism and Animal Faith.* New York: Dover, 1955, p. 141.

10. "By *intuition,* I mean, not the wavering assurance of the *senses* or the deceitful judgment of a misconstructing imagination, but a conception, formed by unclouded mental attention, so easy and distinct as to leave no room for doubt in regard to the thing we are understanding." *Rules for the Direction of the Mind,* Rule III.

Chapter 2. Memory

1. Op. Cit., 450b 17–19, in *The Basic Works of Aristotle,* ed. Richard McKeon. New York: Random House, 1941.

2. Ibid., 451a 3.

3. Ibid., 451a 18.

4. *The Confessions of St. Augustine,* tr. Edward B. Pusey. New York: Washington Square Press, 1951, pp. 154–155.

5. *Meditations on First Philosophy,* Second Meditation.

6. "The measure and boundary of each sort or species, whereby it is constituted that particular sort and distinguished from others, is that we call its *essence,* which is nothing but that abstract idea to which the name is annexed; so that everything contained in that idea is essential to that sort. This, though is be all the essence of natural substances that *we* know or by which we distinguish them into sorts, yet I call it be a peculiar name, the *nominal essence,* to distinguish it from the real constitution of substances . . ." Op. cit., "Of the names of substances," II.vi.

7. Op. cit., *Phaedrus* 275a.

Chapter 3. Embodiment

1. "At all events, in the whole phenomenological domain, . . . this remarkable duality and unity of *sensile* (*hyle*—matter) and *intentional* (*morphe*—form,

shape) plays a dominant part . . . so that over those sensile phases lies as it were an 'animating' *meaning-bestowing* stratum (or one with which the bestowal of meaning is essentially bound up), a stratum through whose agency, out of the *sensile-element, which contains in itself nothing intentional,* the concrete intentional experience takes form and shape." *Ideas* 85, tr. W. R. Boyce Gibson. New York: Macmillan, 1962, pp. 226–227.

2. "It belongs as a general feature to the essence of every actual *cogito* to be a consciousness *of* something. . . . All experiences which have these essential properties in common are also called *internal experiences . . . ;* in so far as they are a consciousness of something they are said to be '*intentionally related*' to this something." Op. cit., 36, p. 108.

3. "Further, there cannot be a special sense-organ for the common sensibles, either. . . . It is clearly impossible that there should be a special sense for any one of the common sensibles." Op. cit., 425a 15–25, in *The Basic Works of Aristotle,* ed. Richard McKeon.

4. "But only the *productive* synthesis of the imagination can take place *a priori;* the reproductive [memory] rests upon empirical conditions." *Critique of Pure Reason,* A 118.

5. "Experience is possible only through the representation of a necessary connection of perceptions." *Critique of Pure Reason* A176=B218.

Chapter 4. Initiation

1. Kant approaches the theme asymptotically, in discussing "Anticipations of Perception: Apprehension of means merely of sensation occupies only an instant [*Augenblinck*] . . . As sensation is that element in the appearance the apprehension of which does not involve a successive synthesis proceeding from parts to the whole representation, it has no extensive magnitude." *Critique of Pure Reason* A167=B209.

2. "Incarnation—the central 'give' of metaphysic. Incarnation is the situation of a being who appears to himself to be as it were *bound* to a body." Gabriel Marcel, *Being and Having,* tr. Katherine Farrer (New York: Harper, 1965) p. 11.

3. "The abiding and unchanging 'I' (pure apperception) forms the correlate of all our representations insofar as it is to be at all possible that we should become conscious of them." *Critique of Pure Reason,* A 123.

Chapter 5. Discrepancy

1. *The Confessions,* X, p. 219.

2. Inner speaking being the stream of words of "voluntary signs" that "in their primary or immmediate signification, stand for nothing but the *ideas in the mind of him that uses them.*" *Essay Concerning Human Understanding,* III.ii, "Of the signification of words."

3. *The Paris Lectures,* tr. Peter Koestenbaum. (The Hague: Martinus Nijhoff, 1975) p. 23.

4. The meaning of "phenomenology" is "to let that which shows itself be seen from itself in the very way in which it shows itself from itself." *Being and Time,* tr. John Macquarrie and Edward Robinson (New York: Harper, 1962) p. 58.

Chapter 6. Search

1. *The Confessions,* p. 220.

2. "An analogy of experience is, therefore, only a rule according to which a unity of experience may arise from perception. It does not tell us how mere perception or empirical intuition in general itself comes about. It is not a principle *constitutive* of the objects, that is, of the appearances, but only *regulative.*" *Critique of Pure Reason,* A180=B222.

Chapter 7. Schools

1. Hesiod, *Works and Days* and *Theogony,* tr. Stanley Lombardo. (Indianapolis: Hackett, 1993) 52–65, p. 62.

2. "The retentional 'content' is, in the primordial sense, no content at all. When a sound dies away, it is first sensed with particular fullness (intensity), and thereupon comes to an end in a sudden reduction of intensity. The sound is still there, is still sensed, but in mere reverberation." *The Phenomenology of Internal Time Consciousness,* section 12, p. 53.

3. "The passivity of wounds, the 'hemorrhage' of the for-the-other, is the tearing away of the mouthful of bread from the mouth that tastes in full enjoyment. . . . It is the openness, not only of one's pocketbook, but of the doors of one's home, a 'sharing of your bread with the famished,' a 'welcoming of the wretched into your house.'" [Isaiah 58] *Otherwise Than Being or Beyond Essence,* p. 74.

4. "Every kind of awareness is essentially awareness of something other than itself; so human living, driven in this way to dedicate itself, seems also essentially the living of something other than itself." Gabriel Marcel, *Mystery of Being,* volume 1, tr. G. S. Frazer. (South Bend, IN: Gateway, 1950) p. 171.

5. "In defiance of all the warnings of criticism, [the transcendental illusion] carries us altogether beyond the empirical employment of categories and puts us off with a merely deception extension of *pure understanding.*" *Critique of Pure Reason,* A295=B352.

6. "The mind's power of producing representations from itself, the *spontaneity* of knowledge, should be called the understanding." *Critique of Pure Reason* A51=B75.

Chapter 8. The Guide

1. *Critique of Pure Reason,* A509=B537, A616=B644.

2. Hesiod, Theogony, pp. 28–29.

Chapter 9. Resurrection of the Flesh

1. "The uneasiness a man finds in himself upon the absence of anything whose present enjoyment carries the idea of delight with it, is that we call *desire.*" *Essay,* "Of modes of pleasure and pain," p. 144.

2. For example, "There continually takes place, thereby, a shoving back into the past. The same complex continuously undergoes a modification until it disappears, for hand in hand with the modification goes a diminution which finally ends in imperceptibility." *The Phenomenology of Internal Time-Consciousness,* section 11, p. 52.

Chapter 10. Conscience

1. *De motu cordis,* 3:7.

2. Rainer Maria Rilke, *Duino Elegies,* tr. J. B. Leishman and Stephen Spender (London: Hogarth Press, 1963) p. 77.

3. *The Enneads,* tr. Stephen MacKenna (Burdett, NY: Larson, 1992) 6.4.7.32–38.

4. Arthur Schopenhauer, *The Will to Live: Selected Writings* (New York: Ungar, 1967), "Transcendent Considerations Concerning the Will as Thing in Itself," p. 35.

5. *Critique of Pure Reason* A426=B454.

6. *The Odes of Horace,* tr. David Ferry (New York: Farrar, Straus and Giroux, 1997) iii.30.

Chapter 11. Hope

1. William of St. Thierry, *On Contemplating God,* tr. Sister Penelope (Spencer, MA: Cistercian Publication, 1971) 12, p. 62.

2. *The Ethics,* tr. R. H. M. Elwes (New York: Dover, 1955), "On the origin and nature of the emotions," 3.XII. p. 176.

3. *The Philosophical Words of Descartes,* tr. Elizabeth S. Haldane and G. R. T. Ross (Cambridge: Cambridge University Press, 1969), vollume I, II.lvii, p. 359.

Bibliography

Aristotle. *Basic Works,* ed. Richard McKeon. New York: Random House, 1941.

Augustine. *The Confessions,* tr. Edward B. Pusey. New York: Washington Square Press, 1960.

Aurelius, Marcus. *The Meditations,* tr. G. M. A Grube. Indianapolis: Hackett, 1983.

Brentano, Franz. *Sensory and Noetic Consciousness,* ed. Oskar Kraus, tr. Margarete Schattle and Linda L. McAlister. London: Routledge and Kegan Paul, 1981.

Buber, Martin. *I and Thou,* tr. Walter Kaufmann. New York: Charles Scribner's Sons, 1970.

Cairns, Dorion, ed. *Conversations with Husserl and Fink.* The Husserl Archives, *Phaenomenologica* 50. The Hague: Martinus Hijhoff, 1973.

Epicetus. *The Handbook,* tr. Nicholas P. White. Indianapolis: Hackett, 1983.

Hesiod. *Works and Days, Theogony,* tr. Stanley Lombardo. Indianapolis: Hackett, 1963.

Husserl, Edmund. *The Paris Lectures,* tr. Peter Koestenbaum. The Hague: Martinus Nijhoff, 1975.

———. *The Phenomenology of Internal Time-Consciousness,* tr. James S. Churchill, ed. Martin Heidegger. Bloomington, IN: Indiana University Press, 1964.

———. *Ideas,* tr. W. R. Boyce Gibson. New York: Macmillan, 1962.

Kant, Immanuel. *Critique of Pure Reason,* tr. Norman Kemp Smith. London: Macmillan, 1950.

———. *Groundwork of the Metaphysic of Morals,* tr. H. J. Paton. London: Hutchinson University Library, 1948.

Kierkegaard, Sôren. *Concluding Unscientific Postscript,* tr. David F. Swenson and Walter Lowrie. Princeton: Princeton University Press, 1941.

Levinas, Emmanuel. *Totality and Infinity,* tr. Alphonso Lingis. Pittsburgh: Duquesne University Press, 1969.

———. *Otherwise Than Being or Beyond Essence,* tr. Alphonso Lingis. The Hague: Martinus Nijhoff, 1981.

———. *Basic Philosophical Writings,* ed. Adriaan T. Peperzak, Simon Critchley, and Robert Bernasconi. Bloomington: Indiana University Press, 1996.

Locke, John. *Essay Concerning Human Understanding,* ed. Maurice Cranston. New York: Macmillan, 1965.

Marcel, Gabriel, *Mystery of Being,* Volume I, tr. G. S. Fraser. South Bend, IN: Gateway, 1950.

———. *Being and Having,* tr. Katherine Farrer. New York: Harper, 1965.

Plotinus. *The Enneads,* tr. Stphen MacKenna. Burdett, NY: Larsen, 1992.

Schopenhauer, Arthur. *The Will to Live,* ed. Richard Taylor. New York: Ungar, 1962.

Spinoza. *On the Improvement of Human Understanding, The Ethics,* tr. R. H. M. Elwes. New York: Dover, 1955.

William of St. Thierry. *On Contemplating God,* tr. Sister Penelope. Spencer, MA: Cistercian Publications, 1971.

———. *The Golden Epistle,* tr. Theodore Berkeley. Spencer, MA: Cistercian Publications, 1971.

Index

A
Absolutism, 50
Accountability, 35
Accusative, 141–142
Achilles, 101
Action: automatic, 10; on basis of moral feeling, 83–84; of consciousness, 22; delay of, 9; of exchange, 84; of hermetic force, 94; homeopathic, 133; of hope, 134; of impressions, 33; possibility of, 103; of subject, 104; as submission, 103; unconditional imperative and, 83–84
Activism, 48
Acts: of intervention, xi, xii
Aesop, 80
Agency, 104
Aggression, 101
Agony, 104
Ambiguity, 24
Anarchy, 150*n8*
Anger, 101; fear and, 103; in inward divinity, 103; source of, 103
Annihilation, 47–48; of *cogito,* 21; of event, 125; of meaning, 125; of memory, 17; of signification, 67; substitution and, 48–50
Anxiety, 42, 50, 113; formula for, 42; moral, 94; provoking, 59; subjectivity and, 59
Apophasis, 118
Apperception: and the the *I,* 50–51
Approximation, 113–115
Aristotle, 17, 32, 35, 38, 41, 44, 72
Assignation, 107; as double movement, 24; equivocity and, 56–58; of identification, 129; as language, 61; of meaning, 24–25, 93; vocabulary constructed by, 25
Atonement, 137–147; death and, 137, 138; embittered cognition and, 140–141; need for, 137; subjectivity and, 145–147; unsatisfiability and, 144–145
Attainment, 11
Audibility: sensitivity and, 31–32
Audition: obedience and, xii
Augustine, 19, 53, 54, 55, 56, 65
Autoeroticism, 21, 22, 55–56, 63, 75, 85, 96, 98, 106; activation of, 98; discourse and, 23; hermetic force and, 93; intervention in, 102; limitation and, 79; power and, 104, 105; self-will and, 126; source of, 125; of thought, 6, 11, 55; waning of, 146
Autointoxication, 86
Automation, 10
Automatism, 21, 30, 64, 79, 107; ceasing, 59; of *cogito,* xii; deregulation of, 92; ethical work and, 39; functions of, 54; goal-productive activity of, 106; and the *I,* 73; interrogation and, 12; lack of intermediary in, 31; of mind, 66; proximity and, 101; self-willing, 33,

Automatism (*continued*)
104, 105; subjectivity and, 75; of thought, 18, 29, 30, 33, 38, 41, 57, 81
Autonomy, 21; ethics of self-realization and, 85; of tempo, 7–8; of thought, 7–8, 28
Awareness, 66; discursive, 33; hermetic, 94; inclusion and, 9; interior breathing and, 37; kinesthetic, 28; language and, 30; of other than self, 152*n4;* resistance and, 30; rhythm of thinking and, 3; somatic, 27–29, 32, 38, 45, 46, 50, 85, 87, 107, 138; subjective, 111; thought and, 18

B
Belief, 96, 97–98; false, 98
Boundary: blurring of, 24; disintegration of, 19; of the *I,* 23; of species, 150*n1;* world, 63
Breath, 71; awareness and, 37; interior, 37; speech and, 37–38

C
Calliope, 79
Caress, 105, 106, 107; of hope, 128; need to respond to, 111; nonassignation of, 108–110; of the Other, 111; subjectivity and, 109
Cause: formal, 88–89; intervening, 105; necessity of, 68
Choice, 59–61
Chronology, 45
Cicero, 17
Clio, 79
Cogito, 108; alteration of, 13; annihilation of, 21; automatism of, xii, 12; collapse of, 125; essence of, 151*n2;* imperishable life and, 29; interrogation and, 12; presumption of extension of, 34; retentive compulsion of, 70; as shadow of the exile, 141
Communis sensus, 35, 36, 38, 66, 151*n3*
Community: atonement and, 139–140; of consolation, 138, 139–140; memory and, 80–81
Compassion, 99
Conception, 96
Conscience, 113–123; approximation and, 113–115; dynamics of disclosure and, 115; inalterability and, 115–116; limit of, 116; longing and, 116–117; passivity and, 116–117; secrecy and, 120–121; speech of, 120; subjectivity and, 121–123
Consciousness: disclosing, 62; everyday, 22; exclusions from, 27; focal action of, 22; for-itself, 27, 30, 53, 61, 74, 86, 118; in-itself, 27, 37, 46, 54, 57, 66, 72, 74; intentional, 21, 22, 23, 24, 25, 30, 32, 36, 42, 53, 57, 58, 74; language of, 26; nonintentional, 37; obedience and, 24, 26; of object field, 24; opacity and, 27; positing, 63; secrecy of signs and, 24; somatic, 27–29; of "something," 151*n2;* of a state, 30; teleology of, 23; transformation of, 21; of vitality, 28
Consolation, 32, 138, 139–140
Continuity, 41; artifice of, 93

D
Daimonion, 117–119
Death, 103–105; atonement and, 137, 138; of death, 102; delimiting flesh, 102; as derivative cause, 137; of desire, 104; heart at, 122; inside death, 49; irritability and, 103; liberation from, 102; mortal, 49; mourning and, 102; resurrection of life and, 71; secret, 49; time as, 7; as weight, 122

Deceit, 95–97; discrepancy and, 96
Defiance, 22
Delay: of action, 9; amnestic, 79–80; approach of, 10, 11; as cause for restlessness, 2; existence of, 2; inevitability of, 145; as invention of need, 43; lag in, 23; mindfulness of, 15; mnemonic, 79–80; of one behind, 1, 2; persistence of, 2; as retardation, 6; sacred interval, 27; secret of, 48, 121, 122; separation and, 137; *soma* and, 28; of spoken word, 65; standpoints of, 1, 2; suffering and, 18; summons of, 6, 126; teleology and, 11–13; thinking and, 10; time and, 5, 10–11; voice of insufficiency and, 4
Delay of the heart, xii, 1–13, 36, 54, 55, 56, 58, 68; atonement and, 138; comprehension of, 15; deathlessness and, 102; inadequacy of memory and, 20–21; inclusion and, 8–10; knowledge of, 72; making communication known and, 23; memory of, 21, 88–89, 132, 139–140; moment and, 43; parable of, 92; search for understanding of, 67; secret of, 122; secret of death and birth in, 146–147; sensitivity and, 26; thought and, 28; upsurge of, 125
Descartes, René, xii, 12, 18, 22, 23, 29, 67, 109, 114, 134, 140
Desire, 23, 63, 85, 98; death of, 104; hermetic force and, 93; hopeless nature of, 134; irritability and, 101; privation of, 102; as restlessness, 101; suspended animation of, 103; thought and, 56; waning, 108
Dianoia, 33, 35
Difference, 53; as difference of non-congruence, 56; irremediable, 91; language of, 53, 54; penitence and, 55; unspeaking, 55
Discontinuity, 6
Discourse: autoeroticism and, 23; erotic choice and, 22; of objective reality, 22; of presence, 114; propositional, 6
Discrepancy, 53–64, 57, 73; as deposition, 63
Disruption, 54
Dissimulation, 69–71
Division, 119–120
Dostevsky, Fyodor, 12

E
Effacement, 72–74
Ego, 125, 150*n8*
Embodiment, 27–39; stages of, 107; of what is missing, 117
Engagement: stage of practice, xi
Equanimity, 53–55
Equivocity, 56–58; univocity and, 93
Erato, 79
Eroticism, 6, 21–23
Essence, 150*n1,* 151*n2*
Eternalism, 108
the Ethical: autonomic and, 20; capacity of sensing and, 38; connection with, 33; entering into, 41; losses to, 33; mainstream accounts of, 44; as meditation on life, 29; and memory, 16; as potency, 41–42; subjectivity and, 47; summons and, 41
Ethics: concern for, xii; initiatory, 16, 20; laws of, 30; of presence, 143; of responsibility, 130; of self-realization, 85
Eurydice, 4, 31, 44, 65, 91, 92, 93, 99, 100, 105, 122, 137
Euterpe, 79
Exchange, 81–83; groups and, 84, 85
Exclusion: time and, 9
Exile, 137–139; atonement and, 137–139; expiation and, 143; isolation of, 138; suffering of, 140; wandering thought and, 140
Expectation, 126
Experience: analogy of, 72, 152*n2;* commentary on, 55; continuation of, 92;

Experience (*continued*)
empirical, 36–37; extension of, 92; language and, 13; obedience and, 25; perception and, 151*n5;* possibility of, 74, 92; reduplication of, 25; schematic analogies of, 35; of self-concept, 74; sensory, 32, 33, 34, 35, 36; somatic, 32

Expiation, 142–143; need for, 145

F

Fear: wisdom and, 95

First-person, 50

Flesh: of the flesh, 105; irritability and, 101–103; resurrection of, 101–111

Forgiveness, 74–75

Formication, 101

Freedom: autonomous, 117; as compulsion, 56; illusion of, 56, 64

Fructification: stage of practice, xi; of thought, 27

G

the Gaze, 126

Grieving, 36

Groups, 84–86; formal cause and, 88–89; intersubjectivity and, 133; organization, 89–90

Guidance, 91–100; by the laggard, 91; middle voice of, 99–100; retardation of, 91–93; seeking, 99

H

Habit, 11, 12

Hades, 94, 107

Heart: anarchaic word of, 72; articulation and enunciation of, 77; audibility of words of, 6; communication of, 23, 27; at death, 122; interior intelligence of, 9; knowledge of, 125; rhythm of, 43; speaking from behind, 113, 114; speech from, 37, 38; summons from, 41; synchrony with thought, 4; temporality of, 122; utterances of, 53; words of, 75, 77, 94

Heidegger, Martin, 62, 117, 135

Heraclitus, 117

Hermes, 94, 95, 96, 97

Hesiod, 77, 78, 79, 97

Heteronomy, 132–133

Hope, 62, 125–135; absence of, 128; action of, 134; caress of, 128; constancy of, 128; deferment of, 128; deficiency of, 129; force of, 130; heteronomy and, 132–133; before hope, 129, 133; lamentation and, 125–127; language of, 133; localization and, 130–132; maturation of, 130, 131; origins of, 134; prostration and, 128–130; resonation and, 133–135; specificity and, 125; terms of, 104, 105; vertical column and, 127–128; vocalization and, 130–132

Horus, 1, 27, 122

Husserl, Edmund, 5, 11, 17, 22, 28, 32, 61, 62, 81, 108, 131

Hypertemporalization, 6–7

Hypnos, 82

Hypomnemata, xi, xii

I

the *I:* apperception and, 50–51; articulation of, 38; authentic voicing of, 131; automatism and, 73; boundaries of, 23; endless repetition of, 145; equals the *I,* 61; hope and, 133, 134; identity and, 73; intentionality and, 61–62; resonation of, 133; subjectivity of, 42

Identity: annihilation of, 60; assumed, 60; autonomous, 69; fractured, 19; and the *I,* 73; of identicals, 75, 93; illusory, 48; the missing and, 115; self, 6, 19,

62, 93; of speaker, 58; vulnerability of, 62
Imagination: hidden strategies of, 62; images utilized by, 33; inner sense and, 38; memory and, 33; *phantasia* and, 38; productive synthesis of, 151*n4*
Immortality, 49, 55
Impatience, 4; time and, 5
Impermanence, 49
Impossibility, 104, 105
Inalterability, 115–116; of the missing, 115
Incarnation, 151*n2*
Inclusion: awareness and, 9; direction of, 8–10; expansion of, 9; of opposites, 9; thought and, 9
Iniative, xi; thought construction and, 68
Initiation, 41–51; enigma of, 50; hope for, 47; the moment and, 42–43, 43; opening and, 42; as response, 41; responsibility to subjectivity and, 48; secret death and, 49; secret of, 49; as summons, 41
Initiative, 43, 44; as agreement, 45; change and, 45; derivation of, 44; inadequacy of, 47; as movement, 44; origin of, 46; practicability of, 46; summons and, 44; velocity of, 45
Initium, 43–45
Intentionality, 21–23, 53–55, 57, 66; being and, 61; correlate of, 61–62; decomposition of, 61; destruction of, 118; pretension and, 58; as representative of the *I,* 62
Interrogation: automism and, 12; derivation of, 59
Intersubjectivity, 86–87; hope as language of, 133
Intervention, 132; acts of, xi, xii; commandment to, xi; derivation of, 106; dynamism of, xii; intimacy and, xi; meaning of, 106; possibility of, 105; reality of, xi; requirement of, 104; transformation of subject and, 105; voluntary, 104; "welcoming the guest" and, 106
Intimacy, 108; intervention and, xi
Intuition, 8, 150*n10;* inner, 149*n6;* outer, 149*n6;* a priori forms, 72; of self, 149*n3*
Invisibility, 107
Irritability, 83–84, 101–103; connection with the divine, 101; death and, 103; desire and, 101; of existence, 142; motility of, 101; as passion for the holy, 106; response to, 105; root of, 101; source of, 102; as source of weeping, 116
Isis, 30

J

James, William, 22
Judgment, 36, 98; conviction and, 6; memory and, 21–23; summons and, 5; temporality of, 5; time of, 5
Justice, 41, 63, 83, 138; judgment and, 21–23; obligation and, 21; pure, 122
Justification, 62–64; thought and, 73

K

Kant, Immanuel, 3, 8, 16, 22, 33, 35, 44, 50, 62, 68, 72, 82, 83, 87, 92, 104, 108, 120, 125, 149*n7,* 151*n1*
Kierkegaard, Sôren, 84, 104, 115
Knowledge: of the heart, 125; of non-substitution, 49; objective, 24; of one's mortality, 78; optical errors in, 116; of the Other, 116; of the secret of death, 49; thought construction and, 68

L

Lamentation, 125–127
Language: anarchaic, 70; assignation as, 61; awareness and, 30; calm of, 54; of

Language (*continued*)
consciousness, 26; corruption of, 56; of difference, 53, 54; of discovery, 24; experience and, 13; of fragmentation, 95; of hope, 133; illusion of, 58; incomprehensibility of, 59; inner, 70; of justification, 62–63; levels of, 53, 54, 55, 56, 89; limits of, 54; loss of memory and, 25; as memory, 13; nominalism and, 6; ordinary, 53, 56, 57, 66; orphic, 66; of the Other, 56, 65; otherness of, 59; of proximity, 72; resistance and, 30; of return, 65–67, 66, 71; reverence for, 90; secret, 63; self-referential, 26; of sensation, 72; of sensitivity, 71; signs and, 24; speaking of itself, 25; of thought, 6, 54, 60, 65; totalitarian, 63; of totality, 94
Law of identicals, 53, 58–59, 118, 129, 132
Law of substitution, 113
Law of the excluded middle, 22, 95
Lethargy, 79, 80
Lethe, 79, 80, 89, 95, 96, 123; reciprocity with *Mnemosyne,* 80
Levinas, Emmanuel, 83
Life: body, 27–29; duality of, 75; earth as source of, 127; *mora* and, 78; obligation in, 104, 105; sensation of, 28; subjective, 101
Localization, 130–132
Locke, John, 2, 16, 25, 36, 55, 101
Logic: of exclusion, 9; objective reality and, 22; thought and, 6
Longing: fit of, 142–143; passivity and, 116–117
Loss, 36
Lumen naturale, 23
Lumen volens, 23

M

Marcel, Gabriel, 86, 121
Meaning, 12; absence of, 62; annihilation of, 125; of asking, 65; assignation of, 24–25; collapse of, 62; deviant, 57; discrepancy and, 57; enigma of, 16, 57; ethical, 33; of intervention, 106; of mortality, 122; paradox of, 106; quest for, 106; of respect, 114; source of, 89; substitution and, 53–54; of suffering, 84; univocal assignation of, 93; without variation, 57
Mediation, 7
Melpomene, 79
Memory, 15–26, 53, 149*n2;* annihilation of, 17; begetting memory, 30; collective, 79; community and, 80–81; cosmic, 78; daughters of, 79; delay of the heart and, 21; divine, 19; ethical and, 16; false, 98; forgetfulness and, 78; fugitive, 87; functional, 82; gaps in, 16, 18; group, 84–86; hollow of, 77–79; images utilized by, 33; imagination and, 33; of the immemorial, 16–18, 19, 20, 48, 49, 69, 72, 78, 86, 128, 132; interior of, 19; language and, 13, 25; lapses, 20; perception and, 17; persistence of, 16; personal, 50, 86; preservation of, 88, 90; primordial condition of, 78; of purpose, 12; remembering itself, 80, 81; reproductive, 151*n4;* of the response, 41; retentive, 2, 10, 17, 18, 36, 37, 55, 63, 66, 75, 78, 86, 95, 96; self-confirming, 20; sorrow of, 79, 80; specialized, 79; storage function, 81; subjectivity and, 17, 80, 88; tasks of, 15, 16, 18, 19, 33, 39, 42, 49, 69, 73, 79, 82, 85; thought and, 16, 18; unremembered, 17; unscripted, 86; unwanted, 17
Metanoia, 11
the Missing, 115; awareness of, 116
Mnemosyne, 15, 78, 89, 95, 98; delays in sorrow of, 79–80; derivation of, 80; groups and, 84, 85; reciprocity with *Lethe,* 80
the Moment, 42–43

Mora, 48; derivation of, 49; life and, 78; moral and, 94; waiting, 71
Mortality, 80; alliance with, 78; meaning of, 122; opaque, 71–72; tenuous, 71
Motility, 101
Mourning, 102, 116
Movement: circle and, 65; completed, 65; direction of, 67–68; initiative as, 44; intervention as, xi; itinerary, 68, 69, 70; neutral, 35; never ceasing, 29; origination of; out from, 65; as release from rest, 44; of sensitivity, 29; of subjectivity, 49; thought and
Muses, 15, 79, 95, 97, 98

N
Nietzsche, Friedrich, 6
Nihilism, 81
Nominalism, 6
Nondesire, 101–102
Nonsubstitution, 119–120

O
Obedience: audition and, xii; consciousness and, 24, 26; experience and, 25; negation of detachment and, 125; opacity of, 104; summons and, 5
Obligation, xii, 83; community, 21; justice and, 21; paradox of, 105; of subjectivity, 64, 84, 89
Oblivion, 149*n5*
Observance, 104
Organization, 89–90
Organon, 38–39
Orpheus, 16, 31, 44, 65, 91, 92, 93, 94, 99, 100, 105, 122, 137
Osiris, 30
the Other: approach to, 36; articulation of, 53; ascendancy over the Same, 150*n8;* caress of, 111; communication with, 32; in-the-one, 85; knowledge of, 116; language of, 56, 65; speech by, 34, 106; than-the-one, 60, 61, 86; touches by, 34; weakness in, 110
Other-in-Myself, 19–21

P
Paralysis, 110–111
Parousia, 37
Passivity, xii
Patience, 72
Penitence, 55
Perception: of absence, 114; anticipations of, 72; capacity for, 38; experience and, 151*n5;* memory and, 17; sense, 36; of time, 17
Perspective, 114
Phantasia, 32–34, 35, 36, 66, 133; embodiment of, 33; imagination and, 38; inner language and, 70; judgment and, 36; as potency, 32
Phantasm, 32; degeneration of, 33
Plato, 10, 25, 43, 96, 118, 119
Plotinus, 118
Polyhymnia, 79
Principles of Pure Understanding, 72
Production: breaks with, 82; continuity of, 68; of a state, 30; of thought, 3, 17, 57
Projection, 107; value of, 115
Proprioception, 36, 37
Prostration, 126, 127, 128–130; intersubjective dimension of, 129
Ptah, 1, 6, 27, 42

Q
Quietism, 47, 81

R
Rationality: reasonable, 30
Reality: contact with, 75; of intervention, xi; objective, 22; projective, 36; thought and, 12

Reason: antimony of, 120; inferential, 38; limits of, 29; practicality of, 104; pure, 104, 115; transcendental illusion of, 82, 87
Regulation, 74–75; concealed intent of, 92; speculative, 92
Release, 45
Reproduction, 3
Resonation, 133–135
Respect, 114
Responsibility, xi, 34, 98; actualization of, 77; begetting responsibility, 145, 146; credulity and, 98; demand for, 35; disclosure and, 12; encouraging, xii; enigma of, 128; ethics of, 130; initiation and, 41; need for, 93; object of, 130; pain of, 125; patience of, 126; possibility of, 34; potency of, 41; responsiveness and, 12; resurrection of, 72; seizing of, 109; skin of, 49; solitude of, 117; of subjectivity, 74, 90, 132, 133; subject of knowledge and, 121
Resurrection, 107–108
Reversal, 91

S

Santayana, George, 11
Schools, 77–90
Search, 65–75; derivation of, 65; dissimulation and, 69–71; effacement and, 72–74; forgiveness and, 74–75; intentional outcome of, 68; inward movement of, 67; mortality and, 71–72; regulation and, 74–75
Second nature, 36
Secrecy: mercy of, 120–121
Self-advancement, 3, 4
Self-concept, 62, 66, 71, 73, 74, 104, 130
Self-contradiction, 118
Self-creation, 36
Self-deception, 93
Self-determination, 82
Self-identity, 6, 19, 62, 93
Self-interrogation, 57
Self-justification, 63
Self-love, 85
Self-negation, 118
Self-obscurity, 6
Self-perception, 32, 36
Self-protection, 96
Self-realization, 85
Self-remembrance, 80, 81, 84, 89
Self-replication, 55, 58
Self-reproduction, 7
Self-sufficiency, 82
Self-will, 10, 29, 30, 63, 104, 105, 119, 126
Semele, 19
Sensation: acquiescence of, 31; inner, 31, 32, 33, 35, 37, 46, 69, 89; language of, 72; of life, 28; opacity of, 28; passivity of, 31; self-caused, 109
Sense(s), 32; distance and, 71; inner, 35, 38, 149*n3;* kinesthetic, 37; outer, 149*n7;* perception by, 36
Sensitivity, 66; audibility and, 31–32; delay of the heart and, 26; function of, 29; inner, 132; as keeper of the divine word, 27; language of, 71; misidentification of, 31; mobilization of, 66; movement of, 29; organic, 69; *phantasia* and, 38; proximate, 34; reinstatement of, 30; remembering, 29–31; as result of initiative, 46; return to, xii; *soma* and, 29; subjectivity and, 21; of sympathetic subject, 132; of thought, 4; touch and, 35; transcendental *I* and, 50
Separation: dread of, 50
Signification: annihilation of, 67
Signorelli, Luca, 107, 108, 109
Simonides, 17, 97
Socrates, 3, 118, 119
Soma: access to, 29; caress and, 107; delay and, 28; interior breath and, 37; ki-

nesthetic flow of, 45; marginalization of, 38; objectification of, 29; passivity of, 31, 32; sensitivity and, 29; signification of, 127; sympathy of, 31, 32; thought and, 27, 31; vitality of, 32
Speaking: of the speaker, 9
Specificity, 125
Speech, xii; articulation of origin in, 28; breath and, 37–38; of conscience, 120; daimonic, 118; Egyptian arrangement and, 8, 18; embodiment of presence and, 114; enigma of, 60; function of, 9; groups and, 84, 85; from the heart, 1, 37; illusion of freedom and, 56; inner, 35, 37, 55, 56; of kinesthesia, 30; of the Other, 106; points of reference for, 9; potency of, 37; proximal, 34–35; secret, 70; subject of, 57; thought-constructed, 54; thoughts behind, 8–9; transformation of, 9; unending, 55
Spinoza, Baruch, 29, 114, 127
Stoicism, xi
the Stop, 106
Subjectivity, 9; anxiety and, 59; atonement and, 145–147; automatism and, 75; being chosen for, 42; birth of, 145–147, 146; caress and, 109; conscience and, 121–123; destiny of, 121–123; entryway into, 67; fact of, 87; fragmentary, 39; growth of, 128; guides for, 67; of the *I*, 42; inattentiveness to, 57; individuality of, 133; induction into, 47; initiation into, xi, 12, 13, 48; internal cleavage in, 138; intersubjective character of, 87; memory and, 17, 80, 84, 87, 88; the missing and, 116; movement of, 49; objectivity and, 75; obligation of, 64, 84; passion of, 116; privilege of, 50; quest for, 86; remembering itself, 77, 78; as repetitive confinement, 101; requirements of, 99; responsibility of, 48, 74, 90, 132, 133; responsiveness to nondisclosure and, 121; risk of, 84; role in initiation, 43; secret, 48; self-willing, 105; sensitivity and, 21; as shared subject, 87; sorrow of memory and, 79, 80; as subject, 103; suffering and, 142; summoning of, 42; thinking and, 10; unfinished condition of, 111
Submission, 47; dynamics of, 104
Substitution, 45–46; annihilation and, 48–50; breakdown of, 93; of identicals, 58–59, 77, 79, 84; as logic of identification, 133; ordinary language and, 53; reliance of language on, 66; validity of, 58
Suffering, 7, 60; alleviation of, 117; amnestic, 83; cause of, 98; common, 117; delay and, 18; deletion of, 18; ethical meaning of, 84; of exile, 140; forms of, 33; greatness of, 117; holy, 142; joining another's, 75; knowledge of, 98; material deprivation and, 83; need to be remembered and, 83; of past life, 72; relief of, 142; sharing in, 117; subjectivity and, 142; suppressed, 82; of the unattended, 34
Summons: delay and, 126; derivation of, 42; in disruption's voice, 92; emanation from higher level, 107; the ethical and, 41; ethos of, 104, 105; from the heart, 41; initiative and, 44; issuance of, 4; judgment and, 5; necessities of, 4–5; obedience and, 5; paradoxical, 104, 105; receptivity to, 42; secret issuance, 42; as secret reminder, 4; to subjectivity, 42; thought and, 56
Susceptibility, 111
Sympathy, 31; power of, 132
Synonymy, 56, 60; rules of, 54

T
Tantalus, 22

Task delineation, 15–16
Teleology: of consciousness, 23
Terpsichore, 79
Thalia, 79
Theogony, 95
Thinking: about thinking, 3; anteriority to sensation, 32; delay and, 10; nonprescriptive, 34; origin and, 8; self-obscurity of, 3; tempo of, 3; vulnerability in, 10
Thomas Aquinas, 38, 113
Thoth, 1, 3, 6, 13, 19, 24, 94
Thought: in advance of itself, 2, 3; autoeroticism of, 6, 11, 55; automatism of, 7–8, 10, 18, 28, 29, 30, 33, 38, 41, 57, 81, 97; awareness and, 18; birth in the heart, 1; cessation of, 29; construction, 66, 67, 68; of death, 103; delay of the heart and, 28; desire and, 56; deviant, 73; dysfunctional ambivalence of, 3; fragmented, 10; fructification of, 27; function of, 36; gaps in, 34; habit of, 2, 3; hopeless nature of, 134–135; immortality of, 3; inclusion and, 9; insensitivity of, 4; intentionality and, 23; justification and, 73; language of, 6, 54, 65; lateness of, 28; logic and, 6; memory and, 16, 18; movement and; objectifying, 8; parthenogenetic, 3; perspective and, 114; production of, 3, 17, 121; propositional syntax and, 6; reality and, 12; as record of retention, 2–3; regulative principle of, 92; reproduction of, 17; retentive, 2, 32, 82; retrieving past conditions and, 2; rising to the mind, 1; self-identity of, 93; self-replication of, 57; *soma* and, 31; submission of, xii; summons and, 56; task of, 15; tempo of, 1–7, 4, 10, 63, 85, 92, 132; thought reproducing, 13; time as condition of, 8, 45
Time: anarchaic, 11, 15, 67, 91; autonomous, 8; as condition of thought, 8; constructed, 43; as death, 7; delay of, 5, 10–11; as derivative of thought, 108; exclusion and, 9; frangibility of, 11; high-velocity, 7; immemorial, 126, 143; impatience and, 5; infinite divisibility of, 11; as inner sense, 149*n3;* interruption of, 88; of judgment, 5; perception of, 17, 114; preoccupations of, 45; a priori, 15, 120; projection of, 10; reticence of, 48; shrinkage of, 7; of silence, 5; stretching, 63; thought-constructed, 48
Touch: noncognitive impression of, 35; origin of, 35; proximity of, 71; silent source of, 34; unadorned, 35–36
Transcendence, 28
Transformation: interior sensation and, 38; need for, 2; proprioception and, 37
Transparency: surrender of, 71
Truth, 95; assignation of meaning and, 93; availability of, 58; believable lies and, 97, 99; correspondence theory of, 95; imperative mood of, 58; speaking, 97; unpalatibility of, 83

U

Uniqueness, 59, 60
Univocity, 57, 58, 93, 95
Unsatisfiability, 144–145
Urania, 79

V

Vertical column, 127–128
Vocalization, 130–132
Voicing, 37–38
Vulnerability, 110–111

W

Watching, 74; awareness of language of

thought, 73; waiting and, 73; watchfulness of, 73
Weakness, 110
Will: contraction of, 132
William of St. Thierry, 1
Wisdom: fear and, 95

Y
Yearning, 115, 120

Z
Zeno, 45, 91
Zeus, 19